Pilgrims, Warriors, and Servants

Puritan Wisdom for Today's Church

St Antholin Lectures
1991-2000

Edited by Lee Gatiss

The Latimer Trust

Pilgrims, Warriors, and Servants: Puritan Wisdom for Today's Church edited by Lee Gatiss © The Latimer Trust and St Antholin's Lectureship Charity, October 2010

Hardback ISBN 978-0-946307-76-0

Paperback ISBN 978-0-946307-77-7

Published by The Latimer Trust, October 2010

Cover photograph: © Jeremy Wee - Fotolia.com

The Latimer Trust (formerly Latimer House, Oxford) is a conservative Evangelical research organisation within the Church of England, whose main aim is to promote the history and theology of Anglicanism as understood by those in the Reformed tradition. Interested readers are welcome to consult its website for further details of its many activities.

The Latimer Trust
PO Box 26685, London N14 4XQ UK
Registered Charity: 1084337
Company Number: 4104465
Web: www.latimertrust.org
E-mail: administrator@latimertrust.org

Views expressed in works published by The Latimer Trust are those of the authors and do not necessarily represent the official position of The Latimer Trust.

Contents

Acknowledgements 1

Introduction - To Satisfy the People's Hunger for the Word: St. Antholin's as the Prototype Puritan Lectureship *by Lee Gatiss* 3

A Man For All Ministries: Richard Baxter 1615-1691 *by J.I.Packer, 1991* 23

The Rediscovery and Renewal of the Local Church: The Puritan Vision *by Geoffrey Cox, 1992* 45

Evangelical Spirituality: Past Glories, Present Hopes, Future Possibilities *by Alister E McGrath, 1993* 63

'But We Preach Christ Crucified': The Cross of Christ in the Pastoral Theology of John Owen 1616 – 1683 *by Gavin J McGrath, 1994* 95

Using the Shield of Faith: Puritan Attitudes to Combat with Satan *by Peter Jensen, 1995* 125

An Anglican to Remember - William Perkins: Puritan Popularizer *by J. I. Packer, 1996* 141

Pilgrim's Progress and Contemporary Evangelical Piety *by Bruce Winter, 1997* 169

A Church 'Halfly Reformed': The Puritan Dilemma *by Peter Adam, 1998* 185

The Pilgrim's Principles: John Bunyan Revisited *by J.I.Packer, 1999* 217

Conversion to Communion: Thomas Cranmer on a Favourite Puritan Theme *by Ashley Null, 2000* 243

Index 264

St. Antholin's Lectureship Charity Lectures *1991-2010* .. 269

Pilgrims, Warriors, and Servants

Acknowledgements

A book such as this does not come together quickly or easily, and it is important to acknowledge and thank those who have played a part on the road to its appearance. First and foremost it is a delight to thank the St. Antholin's Lecturers themselves, not only for their original contributions and the great efforts that clearly went into their production, but for their kind permission to republish them now in this format. Their encouragements and advice along the way have also been most welcome, as is their continued personal example of faithfulness in following the path of godliness so beautifully illuminated for us by our puritan forebears.

The idea of publishing a compilation of the revived St. Antholin's Lectures was originally aired at meetings of the Latimer Trust Theological Workgroup. That the thought has experienced metamorphosis into reality is thanks to people who, over the years, have fought to keep this project on the growing agenda of that group. In particular, Matthew Mason, Andrew Atherstone, and the Latimer Trust office team all made significant contributions to the process whereby this book has finally come to see the light. Matthew was originally given an onerous and, finally, impossible commission in the early stages which he carried out with grace and fortitude. Andrew, on the other hand, gave an invaluable push at the very end which helped to deliver the final product safe and sound. Margaret Hobbs oversaw the laborious and meticulous work of design, typesetting, indexing and project management, and a succession of Administrators contributed to the initial task of establishing electronic versions of lectures from the original paper copies.

Finally, the vision and servant-heartedness of the Trustees who worked to revive the St. Antholin's Lectures in 1991 should not go unnoted. Bishop George Cassidy, then Archdeacon of London, chaired the original group of Trustees at that time, and helpfully encouraged the updating of the charity scheme. Dick Lucas, former Rector of St. Helen's, Bishopsgate no doubt contributed his characteristic clear-headedness to the discussions and decision-making. Sir Timothy Hoare, who managed to keep a great many plates spinning in the service of his Master with a joyful dignity and keen eye for detail would, I hope, be pleased to see this fruit of his quiet labour, if he were not already enjoying what Baxter called 'the Saints' everlasting rest.'

On behalf of the present Trustees of the St. Antholin's Lectureship Charity Trust (myself, Revd. Dr. Mark E. Burkill, and the Revd. William T. Taylor) it is my happy duty, then, to acknowledge and thank these pilgrims, warriors, and servants for making possible this inspiring and edifying volume.

Soli deo gloria!

Lee Gatiss

Cambridge

August 2010

Introduction

To Satisfy the People's Hunger for the Word: St. Antholin's as the Prototype Puritan Lectureship

Lee Gatiss

1. The Puritan Love of Preaching 5
2. St. Antholin's Church and Lectures 10
3. The Spread of Lectureships 17

LEE GATISS read Modern History at New College, Oxford before training for Anglican ministry at Oak Hill Theological College in London. He served a curacy in Northamptonshire before becoming Associate Minister of St. Helen's, Bishopsgate in the City of London in 2004. He holds a ThM in Historical and Systematic Theology from Westminster Theological Seminary in Philadelphia (USA) and his PhD at Cambridge University is on seventeenth century biblical interpretation. He is the Editor of *Theologian* (www.theologian.org.uk), Review Editor of *Churchman*, and Series Editor of the *Reformed Evangelical Anglican Library* as well as author of *The True Profession of the Gospel*.

1. The Puritan Love of Preaching

What does a third century Egyptian ascetic who spent much of his time alone in the desert have to do with a thriving Anglican church in the urban heart of Tudor London? St. Anthony, often known as 'the Father of Monasticism,' had little in common with the wealthy mercantile parishioners of the now demolished church on Watling Street to which his name (in corrupted English form) somehow came to be attached. The church, which became famous in the sixteenth century for its lectures, was founded at around the same time as another St. Anthony (of Padua, 1195-1231) was making a name for himself as a preacher and evangelist. He would seem perhaps a more appropriate patron for such a centre especially since, among the superstitious, he was considered the patron saint of 'lost things,' and the people of St. Antholin's, between what is now Bank and Mansion House tube stations, were certainly known for one thing above all: their zeal in seeking to recover and preach the 'lost word,' the Christian gospel as found in holy scripture.

Their enthusiasm for the word of God was not, of course, uncommon in those Reformation days. Some Archbishops, even, were known to favour and encourage preaching as the key to bringing spiritual enlightenment to the country. Before he was effectively removed from office by Queen Elizabeth I for his intransigence in this very matter, the Archbishop of Canterbury, Edmund Grindal (*d.* 1583) wrote to her to defend his support of evangelical preaching. At the heart of his defence was a theological definition of the importance of preaching:

> Public and continual preaching of God's word is the ordinary mean and instrument of the salvation of mankind. St. Paul calls it the ministry of reconciliation of man unto God. By preaching of God's word, the glory of God is enlarged, faith is nourished, and charity is increased. By it the ignorant is instructed, the negligent exhorted and incited, the stubborn rebuked, the weak

conscience comforted.¹

These may have been novel views for a prelate, but they were the very lifeblood of Puritanism. From Canterbury we travel to Cambridge, home to one of the outstanding Elizabethan preachers, William Perkins (1558-1602). In the preface to his classic and influential instruction manual, *The Art of Prophesying*, he wrote of preaching that, 'It is instrumental in gathering the church and bringing together all of the elect,' and also that 'It drives away the wolves from the folds of the Lord. Preaching is the *flexanima*, the allurer of the soul, by which our self-willed minds are subdued and changed from an ungodly and pagan lifestyle to a life of Christian faith and repentance.'²

A century after Grindal, John Owen (1616-1683), former Vice Chancellor of the other University, in Oxford, wrote in similar vein that preachers 'are used and employed in the work [of regenerating people's souls] itself by the Spirit of God, and are made instrumental for the effecting of this new birth and life.'³ Elsewhere he also reminds us that it is not just for the start of our Christian lives, but for our ongoing good: 'the preaching of the word is appointed of God,' he says, 'as food for our souls.'⁴ Hence the puritans, as people of the book who reverenced God's word written and sought to read, obey, and meditate on it daily, were also studious in attending the means of grace found in public expositions of the word. Since preaching is 'the application of the word of God unto our souls, by virtue of his command' as Owen puts it, 'there is the same reverence due to God in the word as preached, as in the word as written; and a peculiar advantage attends it beyond reading

---

[1] Grindal to Queen Elizabeth, 20th December 1576 from J. Strype, *The History of the Life and Acts of the Most Reverend Father in God, Edmund Grindal ... : To which is added an appendix of original mss* (Oxford: Clarendon Press, 1821), p 329.

[2] W. Perkins, *The Art of Prophesying; with, The Calling of the Ministry*, Rev. edn. (Edinburgh: Banner of Truth Trust, 1996), p 3. Text of the original modernised by Sinclair B. Ferguson.

[3] J. Owen, *Pneumatologia: or, A Discourse concerning the Holy Spirit* (London: Printed by J. Darby, for Nathaniel Ponder, at the Peacock in Chancery-Lane near Fleetstreet, 1674b), p 188.

[4] J. Owen, *Exercitations on the Epistle to the Hebrews, concerning the priesthood of Christ wherein the original, causes, nature, prefigurations, and discharge of that holy office, are explained and vindicated: with a continuation of the exposition on the third, fourth, and fifth chapters of said epistle to the Hebrews* (London: Printed by John Darby for Nathaniel Ponder, 1674a), p 396 (comment on Hebrews 5:11).

of the word, because God hath himself ordained it for our benefit.'[5]

This characteristic humility towards the Bible and to biblical preaching was obvious to any who observed the puritans in action. Sadly, however, 'it is scarcely imaginable,' observed Owen, 'with what rage and perversity of spirit, with what scornful expressions this whole work is traduced, and exposed to contempt.'[6] They were indeed mocked for their word-centred piety, which was epitomised by the parishioners of St. Antholin's church. 'When a zealous woman goes to St. Antholin's with her Bible under her arm,' said one wag, 'she looks like a goose with the gizzard thrust under her wing.'[7] Less crudely, but no less pointedly, Sir John Harington (1560-1612), whose epigrams satirizing the puritans circulated widely in the seventeenth century, wrote about a certain man he called 'Precise Taylor,'

> He bought a Bible of the best translation,
> and in his life, he showed great reformation:
> He walked mannerly, and talked meekly;
> he heard three Lectures, and two Sermons weekly.[8]

At the time, the one church known to have two sermons on Sunday (by no means as regular an occurrence then as it might be in churches today) as well as three lecturers speaking throughout the week was St. Antholin's. It is fascinating to hear this sardonic (albeit perhaps fictionalised) description of one of its members. The signs of 'great reformation' in a person's life, according to the puritans and clearly observed by their opponents, were investing in personal Bible study, a

---

[5] *Ibid.*, p 398.
[6] Owen, *Pneumatologia*, p 189.
[7] G. T., *Roger the Canterburian that cannot say grace for his meat, with a low-crowned hat before his face, or, The Character of a Prelatical Man Affecting Heighths* (London: Printed for William Larmar, 1642), p 3.
[8] J. Chalkhill & J. Clapham (eds.), *Alcilia Philoparthens loving folly. To which is added Pigmalions image. With the love of Amos and Laura. And also epigrammes by Sir J.H. and others* (London : Printed [by Thomas Snodham and Thomas Creede] for Richard Hawkins, dwelling in Chancery-Lane, neare Sarjeants-Inne, 1613). The 'best translation' would no doubt have been considered the 1560 Geneva Bible, which included Reformed study notes in the margins and was later banned by Archbishop Laud. However, N. E. McClure (ed.) *The Letters and Epigrams of Sir John Harington, together with The Prayse of Private Life* (London: Oxford University Press, 1930), p 156 has here 'new translation', following a 1618 reprint of Harington's poem, which made it refer to the 1611 Authorised or King James Version of the Bible.

changed and godly life, and a serious attention to the public teaching of the word whether in sermons or 'lectures.'

John Owen's contemporary, Dr. Thomas Horton, fellow of that puritan stronghold Emmanuel College, Cambridge and later President of Queens' and Vice Chancellor, was intimately involved in training a generation of young puritan ministers. His last appointment was as Rector of St. Helen's, Bishopsgate in the City, a post he took up just a few months before the Great Fire of London in 1666. His sermons from St. Helen's were published in the 1670s and one such, on 1 Corinthians 1:21 ('*it pleased God by the foolishness of preaching to save them that believe,*' KJV) gives a good sense of his views on the value of preaching. He also addresses those who consider this distinctly puritan concern to be 'foolishness', those who mock and undervalue preaching or who under-prepare for it. It is worth quoting at length to hear something of the puritan passion for preaching:

> 'As many men order the business, it is the foolishness of preaching indeed. There are some kind of persons in the world which have a great deal to answer to God for the offence which they give in this respect, and the scandal and ill report which they bring upon God's own ordinance by their unworthy managing of it. There are two extremes which in this case men run into: the one is of too much neglect and presumption on the one hand; and the other is of too much niceness and affectation on the other.
>
> First, there are some which are here grossly neglectful, care not what comes from them in their performances, though it be never so raw and undigested; they vent their own foolish fancies and conceits as if they were the word of God, and that also in expressions answerable to those conceits. These are one kind of persons which make it thought the foolishness of preaching, because they are so fond and foolish in the handling of it by their neglect and presumption.
>
> But then again, secondly, there's an occasion given to think preaching foolishness from too much niceness and affectation. The 'wisdom of words', as it is here mentioned in this chapter, and as follows afterwards in the text. *[Some]* make preaching a mere business of wit and a thing to tickle the fancy, an airy and empty discourse, carried with some high-flown language, but never touching nor coming near the heart, nor uttering

> anything which may be profitable to the soul... Thus a great many men in the world take a great deal of pains to do no good.'⁹

As Horton went on to say, preaching is 'not merely to speak somewhat of religion, to take a text and only descant and flourish upon it, and there's an end; to make a rambling and roving discourse and nothing to the purpose. But preaching is a ministerial and authoritative improvement [application] of the truths and doctrines of the Scriptures, to the good and benefit of men's souls, and the procurement of their eternal salvation.'¹⁰ We note again here the very high view expressed of the potential effects of good preaching. For Dr. Horton this had two great applications, one for preachers and the other for hearers. First, for preachers this eternally efficacious view of pulpit ministry should, in contrast to the disparagement of preaching amongst the worldly,

> quicken and encourage us in our work, and the conscionable discharge of it without fainting and giving out. For see what a work it is, and what a blessed and happy end it tends to – even no less than to bring men to heaven, and to make them heirs of eternal life. Who would not think himself honoured in such a noble employment as this, and accordingly go through it with a great deal of cheerfulness and alacrity in the midst of all discouragements whatsoever? Our very work itself is a reward though there were nothing else; and to save a soul is more than to gain a kingdom.¹¹

With such words many fine young men who heard Dr. Horton would have been encouraged to consider giving their lives to the high and noble employment of preaching. Second, the seriousness of the occasion ought to instil in all hearers a sober-minded attitude as they heard those 'three lectures and two sermons weekly':

---

⁹ T. Horton, *One Hundred Select Sermons upon several texts: fifty upon the Old Testament, and fifty on the new* (London: Printed for Thomas Parkhurst, 1679), p 260.
¹⁰ *Ibid.*, p 261.
¹¹ *Ibid.*, p 262. The phrase 'to bring men to heaven' by preaching echoes John Donne (1572-1631) in G. R. Potter & E. M. Simpson (eds.), *The Sermons of John Donne* (Berkeley & Los Angeles: University of California Press, 1953-62), VII: pp 300-301. See the 2006 St. Antholin's Lecture by P. Adam, "*To bring men to heaven by preaching*" : *John Donne's Evangelistic Sermons* (London: Latimer Trust, 2006).

let this teach us with what affections to come to the Ordinances, the preaching and hearing of the Word, namely as those which expect and desire salvation from it as the end whereunto it is intended. Let us not come to a sermon as to a prize, or a mere trial of wits, to see who can do best, only to spend our verdict on the preacher, or out of mere fashion and custom, only because others come before us. But let us come to it with meekness, and humility, and fear and expectation, as that whereby we must be judged, and whereby we must be saved (James 1:21).[12]

Despite ill-educated modern preconceptions, Puritanism was far from merely a negative, 'puritanical' movement. Rather, as Professor Packer puts it below in this volume, it was characterised by 'a total view of Christianity, Bible-based, church-centred, God-honouring, literate, orthodox, pastoral, and Reformational, that saw personal, domestic, professional, political, churchly, and economic existence as aspects of a single whole, and that called on everybody to order every department and every relationship of their life according to the Word of God, so that all would be sanctified and become "holiness to the Lord."' The powerful instrument by which this great reformation was to be brought about was the careful (they would say 'painful', as in painstaking) and prayerful exposition of God's word in sermons and 'lectures.' This was the thinking throughout the era of the puritans (from Perkins to Owen) and in every place where they had sway (from Canterbury under Grindal, to Oxford, Cambridge, London, and beyond).

2.   St. Antholin's Church and Lectures

After a whistle-stop tour of the major centres of Puritanism and a brief look at some key preachers in the sixteenth and seventeenth centuries, we can now zero in on one particularly significant pulpit. We come to rest between Watling Street and Budge Row in the City of London, where today there is a reconstruction of the remains of a Roman temple of Mithras but from the twelfth century until the nineteenth century there stood the parish church of St. Antholin.

---

[12] Horton, *One Hundred Select Sermons*, p 262.

St. Antholin's church building underwent several renovations, particularly in 1399 and 1513, benefiting from the patronage and wealth of the Lord Mayors of the time. It was extensively "repaired and beautified" in 1616 at a cost of more than £900 (a princely sum in those days) gaining a favourable mention in John Stowe's survey of London in 1633.[13] Sadly, it was entirely destroyed in the Great Fire of 1666 and Sir Christopher Wren took several years to rebuild it at the huge cost of £5702. With the changing demographics of London in the nineteenth century, the decision was eventually taken to amalgamate St. Antholin's with St. Mary, Aldermary, and the building was demolished (after no small resistance and with great regret) in 1874-1875.[14] The remains of Wren's church can be found in various places, notably in St. Mary, Aldermary and the eponymous St. Anthony's in Nunhead Lane, Peckham. The octagonal spire was sold privately for £5 to printer Robert Harrild in 1829 and part of it can still be seen on his property amidst a cul-de-sac of modern town houses in the suburb of Sydenham in South East London!

St. Antholin's gained a reformist reputation early on in the sixteenth century. In 1531, the Rector, Edward Crome D.D., was in trouble for preaching against purgatory and the veneration of saints.[15] A friend of the reformer Hugh Latimer, he had attended the famous discussions of Luther's theology in Cambridge at the White Horse Inn, and had been helped in his early search for an incumbency by Anne Boleyn.[16] He has been described as 'one of the most vigorous protagonists of the Reformation.'[17] As a respected and accomplished theologian, he often served on commissions for the examination of heretical books and the trial of heretics, particularly Anabaptists, which is ironic given that his successor at St. Antholin's was charged with

---

[13] J. Stow, *The Survey of London containing the original, increase, modern estate and government of that city* (London: Printed for Nicholas Bourn, and are to be sold at his shop at the south entrance of the Royal-Exchange, 1633), p 827.

[14] See G. Huelin, *Vanished Churches of the City of London* (London: Guildhall Library, 1996), p 35.

[15] F. J. Bremer & T. Webster, *Puritans and Puritanism in Europe and America: A Comprehensive Encyclopedia* (Santa Barbara, Calif. ; Oxford: ABC-CLIO, 2006), p 529.

[16] J. Venn (ed.) *Biographical History of Gonville and Caius College, 1349-1897. Volume 1. 1349-1713* (Cambridge, 1897), p 17 (entry for 1506).

[17] I. Morgan, *The Godly Preachers of the Elizabethan Church* (London: Epworth Press, 1965), pp 48-49.

holding some Anabaptist beliefs a decade later.[18] He was not the last clergyman associated with St. Antholin's to be somewhat at odds with the establishment as we shall see.

Many historians date the beginning of the midweek lectures at St. Antholin's to some point in Edward VI's reign (1547-1553),[19] and there certainly were such lectures at one or two London churches around that time.[20] The label 'lecture' may be a little misleading to modern ears. Today, the word conjures up, perhaps, the image of a somewhat dull and formal educational affair usually reserved for university departments, and a sermon is all too often merely a light and supposedly entertaining interlude in the midst of many other exciting elements of a 'worship service.' For the puritans, however, the sermon was a serious, passionate, hortatory, and urgent hour or more which dominated their gatherings on the Lord's day; lectures, on the other hand, were in some ways less formal than the sermon (though hardly jocular), and often took the form of a continuous commentary on a passage of scripture, 'making it clear and giving the meaning so that the people could understand what was being read,' as Nehemiah 8:8 puts it. At other times the lectures might focus on a doctrinal or practical topic: Thomas Bedford, Lecturer in the 1640s and later Rector of the nearby church of St. Martin, Outwich, published a book called *An Examination of the Chief Points of Antinomianism* in 1647, which was taken from his lectures at St. Antholin's.[21] Other published works from the original

---

[18] G. L. Hennessy, *Novum Repertorium Ecclesiasticum Parochiale Londinense; or, London diocesan clergy succession from the earliest time to the year 1898, with copious notes* (London: S. Sonnenschein, 1898), p 302 calls him William Colwyn, and also mentions a public recantation at St. Paul's Cross is 1541. Bremer & Webster, *Puritans and Puritanism*, p 529 gives his name as William Tolwyn.

[19] H. G. Owen 'The London Parish Clergy in the Reign of Elizabeth I.' Unpublished PhD diss. thesis, University of London, London (1957), pp 370-371; P. Collinson, *The Elizabethan Puritan Movement* (Oxford: Clarendon Press, 1990), p 50; Morgan, *The Godly Preachers of the Elizabethan Church*, p 49; Bremer & Webster, *Puritans and Puritanism*, p 529.

[20] P. S. Seaver, *The Puritan Lectureships: The Politics of Religious Dissent, 1560-1662* (Stanford: Stanford University Press, 1970), p 80.

[21] T. Bedford, An Examination of the Chief Points of Antinomianism, collected out of some lectures lately preached in the church of Antholines parish, London (London: Printed by John Field for Philemon Stephens, and are to be sold at his shop at the sign of the gilded Lyon in Pauls Church-yard, 1647). See Joel R. Beeke, 'Bedford, Thomas (d. 1653)', Oxford Dictionary of National Biography, Oxford University Press, Sept 2004 [http://www.oxforddnb.com/view/article/1932, accessed 30 August 2010].

St. Antholin's Lecturers also indicate an interest in practical divinity, and later in catechism instruction.[22]

The English word 'lecture' derives from the Latin *lectura* which can have the meaning simply of reading out loud, reciting a text. In that sense lecturers might be thought of as somewhat akin to lay readers, who were originally appointed to lead worship (that is *read* the service book — something not everyone was actually able to do in previous centuries) and preach or read homilies in parishes which had no regular incumbent or minister. Puritan lecturers were usually ordained clergy, however, often with scruples against reading the set forms of *The Book of Common Prayer* in the way prescribed. They both preached on Sundays, when invited, and lectured during the week (or on Sunday afternoons) in a position funded by the lay people of the parish, but did not necessarily have any further pastoral or leadership responsibilities. As Peter Adam says below in his presentation of puritan tactics for changing a church 'but halfly reformed', 'Lectureships were often founded in parishes where the Rector or Curate had little ability in preaching the Bible, and where the rising educational standards and expectations of the people led to a demand for good preaching. The Lecture was a teaching sermon, and the people expressed their eagerness by paying for and attending the lectures.' In some places this led to great tension between the officially-sanctioned non-preaching (or even non-resident) incumbent, living off tithes and fees, and the lecturer who was funded by voluntary parish contributions.

Things were not usually so tense at St. Antholin's, where the lectures were a way of multiplying and expanding ministry throughout the week, rather than supplying the deficiencies of the incumbent. We know for certain that the lectures here resumed after the Marian

---

[22] See R. Gray, *An Alarm to England Sounding the Most Fearful and Terrible Example of God's Vengeance* (London: Printed by S. S[tafford] for John Budge, and are to be sold at his shop, at the great South door of S. Paul's Church, 1609); S. Willoughby, *A Scourge to the Rebellious, or, A Sermon Preached at the Parish Church of St. Antholin, in the City of London, June the 28th, 1685* (London: Printed by D. Mallet, for the author, 1685); W. E. L. Faulkner, *Sermons by the Late Rev. William Elisha Faulkner* (London: Printed by Bye and Law, 1799); H. Draper, *Lectures on the Church Catechism, etc* (London, 1799); H. Draper, *Lectures on the Liturgy; delivered in the Parish Church of St. Antholin, Watling Street* (London, 1806); H. Draper, *Lectures on the Collects which are appointed to be read in the service of the Church of England* (London, 1813).

persecution, or began for the first time, in 1559 under Rector William Colwyn.[23] They are mentioned by contemporary diarist Henry Machyn who wrote in his journal that on 21st September, 'began the new morning prayer at Saint Antholin's in Budge Row, after Geneva fashion.'[24] The church's bells began to ring at five o'clock each morning, he tells us, and an earnest congregation gathered at that early hour to sing Psalms until the lecture itself began at six. St. Antholin's was unique in the City for having three lecturers who preached six mornings like this during the week. The Genevan aspect of the meeting to which Machyn referred was, of course, the congregational singing. 'Men and women all do sing,' he wrote, 'and boys.' In all probability this was done using the 1549 metrical translation of the Psalter made by one of the first St. Antholin's Lecturers, Robert Crowley (1517-1588).[25]

Crowley had written a preface to the 1547 reprint of William Tyndale's book, *The Supper of the Lord* and was well known in puritan circles. He was much admired for 'combining firm Protestantism with compassion for the oppressed' and his conviction was that 'the poor needed not only relief from rapacious landlords, but also a new preaching clergy to divert them from adherence to superstitious ceremonies.'[26] He was for a time Archdeacon of Hereford and Prebendary of Mora in St. Paul's Cathedral, but the controversy over vestments in 1566 saw him lose all his preferments in the Church of England. He responded, after consulting many of the other clergy in London who were opposed to surplices and such apparel, with a tract against 'Popish garments,' which Patrick Collinson calls 'the earliest puritan manifesto.'[27] In that year there were nine clergymen known to be employed in the City as lecturers, and three of them – Crowley, John

---

[23] Hennessy, *Novum Repertorium Ecclesiasticum Parochiale Londinense*, p 302.

[24] J. G. Nichols (ed.) *The Diary of Henry Machyn: Citizen and Merchant-Taylor of London, from A.D. 1550 to A.D. 1563* (London: Printed for The Camden Society by J. B. Nichols and Son, 1848), p 212.

[25] R. Crowley, *The Psalter of David Newly Translated into English Metre in such sort that it may be the more decently, and with more delight of the mind, be read and sung of all men. Whereunto is added a note of four parts* (London, 1549).

[26] Basil Morgan, 'Crowley, Robert (1517x19–1588),' *Oxford Dictionary of National Biography*, Oxford University Press, Sept 2004; online edn, Jan 2008 [http://www.oxforddnb.com/view/article/6831, accessed 30 August 2010].

[27] R. Crowley, *A Brief Discourse against the Outward Apparel and Ministering Garments of the Popish Church* (Emden: Printed by Egidius van der Erve, 1566). Collinson, *The Elizabethan Puritan Movement*, p 77.

Gough, and John Philpot – were at St. Antholin's. All three had lost benefices elsewhere in the City because of arguments over the wearing of vestments.[28]

This indicates that lecturers could be part of the disaffected and more radical section of the puritan movement. Independents, Presbyterians, and even some Anti-paedobaptists such as John Tombes were chosen by the people as lecturers in various places, when it would have been very difficult indeed for them to be appointed as incumbents.[29] Yet this was not always the case, and Crowley himself became wary of some of the younger, more hot-headed Presbyterian types who were a new feature on the Elizabethan landscape. As Irvonwy Morgan puts it, Crowley eventually 'made his peace with the church authorities since the reformed Church of England gave him sufficient liberty to preach the conversion of men's souls and their calling to holiness. This liberty he felt was adequate and he had little sympathy with the younger Godly Preachers who wanted to shape the Church into what they thought would be a more effective instrument for reform.'[30] By 1576 he had been appointed vicar at St. Lawrence, Jewry and in 1578 of St. Giles, Cripplegate. Though often strong opponents of ceremonialism, later Lecturers at St. Antholin's would be able to hold down benefices within the established church alongside their lectureship; John Oliver, for example, was one of the lecturers at St. Antholin's in 1590-1593 while also being Rector of St. Helen's (1590-1600).[31]

St. Antholin's had always been a very well-connected and well-heeled church. Evidence from the first half of the seventeenth century indicates that there were around fifty-five families resident in the parish, many of whom were poor but some of which were extremely prominent within the City, and extremely wealthy.[32] Thomas Tymme was Rector of St. Antholin's between 1566 and 1592. He was a prolific writer and translator of theological and historical books, notably producing in 1577-

---

[28] See Owen, 'The London Parish Clergy in the Reign of Elizabeth I.' p 375.
[29] T. Liu, *Puritan London: A Study of Religion and Society in the City Parishes* (London: Associated University Presses, 1986), p 108.
[30] Morgan, *The Godly Preachers of the Elizabethan Church*, p 54.
[31] *Ibid.*, p 55. See also page 51 where Morgan mentions another St. Antholin's Lecturer who was simultaneously Vicar of St. Peter's, Cornhill.
[32] Liu, *Puritan London*, p 28.

1578 English translations of Calvin's commentaries on 1-2 Corinthians and Genesis. That he dedicated some of his works to men such as the earls of Sussex, Devonshire, and Warwick as well as Archbishop Grindal, shows that he had powerful friends and patrons.[33] He was followed as Rector by Nicholas Felton, who was also an able networker and figure at court. Felton left St. Antholin's to become bishop of Bristol in 1617 and was later translated to Ely. He moved in the circle of evangelically-minded bishops, had amongst his chaplains a well-known puritan preacher called George Walker, who was also a lecturer at St. Helen's, Bishopsgate, and managed to use his influence to secure a lectureship at Holy Trinity, Cambridge for the godly puritan divine, John Preston.[34]

All this meant that by the time James I ascended to the throne in 1603, St. Antholin's was at the heart of the puritan movement in the capital and 'in the early years of the seventeenth century it was not only the fashionable place for Puritan weddings and funerals but also the recognised centre for the training of Puritan Preachers.'[35] Despite this, 'the ambitions of the parish continually outran the available income,'[36] and, as is frequently the case with growing churches seeking to multiply ministry, the accounts were often in danger of falling into deficit. As H. G. Owen points out, 'It is worth noting that even the most heavily endowed of all Elizabethan lectureships was to some extent dependent on parochial benevolence.'[37] By all accounts that benevolence continued to be forthcoming as the traders, merchants, craftsmen, and nobles of the City continued to crave clear biblical teaching. Even more importantly, if pamphleteer and lawyer William Prynne is to be believed, God's benevolence and favour rested on St. Antholin's in a most concrete and practical way. It was his contention that where there is

---

[33] See T. P. J. Edlin, 'Tymme, Thomas (d. 1620)', *Oxford Dictionary of National Biography*, online edn, Oxford University Press, Sept 2004 [http://www.oxforddnb.com/view/article/27945, accessed 30 Aug 2010].

[34] Kenneth Fincham, 'Felton, Nicholas (1556–1626),' *Oxford Dictionary of National Biography*, Oxford University Press, Sept 2004; online edn, Jan 2008 [http://www.oxforddnb.com/view/article/9274, accessed 30 Aug 2010]; Seaver, *The Puritan Lectureships*, p 261.

[35] Morgan, *The Godly Preachers of the Elizabethan Church*, p 48.

[36] Seaver, *The Puritan Lectureships*, p 163.

[37] Owen, 'The London Parish Clergy in the Reign of Elizabeth I,' p 424 note 1.

> least knowledge and service of God, there is most danger of the plague, and experience proves it true for the most part, it ever raging more in the disorderly suburbs of London, where they have usually least and worst preaching, more than in the City, where is better government, life and preaching. Powerful preaching therefore being the chief means to turn men from their sins and evil lives, and win them unto God, and the suppression of it a means to continue and harden men in their evil ways; it must necessary follow, that frequent powerful preaching is an antidote and cure against it; and the suppression of it, the high way and means to bring it [the plague].[38]

If this powerful logic were not thought sufficient, said Prynne, experience should teach us the same lesson in the power of preaching. In places where the puritan lectures had been suppressed by the bishops, God had almost immediately ('the very selfsame week'!) sent the plague to that place. 'But in St. Antholin's Parish and some others, where the Lectures yet continue, (in the first every morning) no Pestilence (blessed be God) hath hitherto been heard off.' This is better propaganda than it is theology or logic, but it indicates something of the high esteem in which St. Antholin's and her lectures were held. Prynne's theory of public health aside, the puritan doctrine of the spiritual power of the preached word to save souls for eternity ensured that the tactic of employing lecturers to expand opportunities for gospel ministry – epitomised by St. Antholin's – would be imitated in other parishes.

3. The Spread of Lectureships

The historian H. G. Owen called St. Antholin's, 'the prototype of the Protestant lectureship.'[39] The pattern of parishioners banding together to fund Bible teaching in their churches, regardless of what the ecclesiastical establishment might think, was certainly replicated in

---

[38] W. Prynne, *The Unbishoping of Timothy and Titus. Or A Brief Elaborate Discourse, Proving Timothy to be No Bishop* (Amsterdam: Printed by J. F. Stam, 1636), p 156. I have updated the spelling here and in other quotations from early sources.

[39] Owen, 'The London Parish Clergy in the Reign of Elizabeth I,' p 415.

other parts of the capital, and in the rest of the country. By 1600, about half of London's parishes had hired lecturers, to satisfy the people's hunger for the word. Richard Sibbes, the moderate puritan and cautious reformer, exclaimed in one of his sermons, 'I think there is no place in the world where there is so much preaching!'[40] As Paul Seaver has shown in his detailed study of the puritan lectureships, 'In a city little more than a square mile in area and with a population of just under a quarter of a million, approximately one hundred sermons were preached each week by lecturers.' By the late 1620, he calculates, 90% of London parishes had records of hiring lecturers.[41]

Holding a lectureship became a customary part of a clerical career after 1560. Seaver estimates that 'between 1560 and 1662 at least 700 clergymen held lectureships at one time or another in London.'[42] An ordinary puritan ordinand might serve a title post or curacy somewhere first, move to a London lectureship in his early thirties, and then finally settle in a Rectory elsewhere. The lectureship, in that sense, was akin to our modern Associate Minister or Team Vicar posts, although Seaver claims that London vestries could be quite choosy and preferred 'men with at least a budding reputation' to lecture them![43] William Taylor, erstwhile lecturer at St. Peter's, Cornhill, went on to become Rector of one of the most staunchly puritan and radical parishes in the City, St. Stephen's, Coleman Street for example, and Simeon Ashe came from a village vicarage in the country to lecture at Cornhill and become one of the most significant preachers (and fervent Presbyterians) in the capital.[44]

Churches which were not puritan also employed lecturers, of course, but the majority seem to have been in those puritan strongholds. Many, including several from St. Antholin's, were firmly Presbyterian. That was certainly the case for three of the lecturers we know about from St. Helen's at this time: Richard Gardiner, lecturer at St. Helen's and graduate of Peterhouse during a period when it was a

---

[40] See M. Dever, *Richard Sibbes: Puritanism and Calvinism in Late Elizabethan and Early Stuart England* (Macon, Ga.: Mercer University Press, 2000), p 80.
[41] Seaver, *The Puritan Lectureships*, p 125.
[42] *Ibid.*, p 30.
[43] *Ibid.*, pp 190-191.
[44] See L. Gatiss, *The Tragedy of 1662: The Ejection and Persecution of the Puritans* (London: Latimer Trust, 2007), p 8 note 14, p 11 and Seaver, *The Puritan Lectureships*, p 272.

haven for Calvinists under the Mastership of Robert Some, played a part in the London Presbyterian movement; Thomas Barbor was also a Presbyterian lecturer at St. Helen's, and was associated with the big names of Presbyterianism at that time, Cartwright and Field; and George Walker was at Bishopsgate from 1639 but his 'budding reputation' saw him become the leader of the first London classis or presbytery (a grouping of elders and pastors) upon its foundation in 1645.[45]

The Presbyterian leanings of many lecturers had an effect on how the role of lecturer was perceived and how it developed. For many people, it was perhaps only a temporary expedient, to be used for a time until a properly trained preaching pastor could be installed in every church. For others, it appeared to be a way of introducing the Presbyterian understanding of the four orders of ministry: deacon, elder, pastor, and 'doctor' (or teacher). Presbyterians saw the office of pastor as distinct from that of the doctor: the former was called to pray, and administer the sacraments, and preach for exhortation while the latter gave himself more to the interpretation of scripture and the preaching of sound doctrine. For these, the institution of lectureships was a means of restoring true order to the church, and they were to have a permanent place in it.[46]

Whatever the theory, hunger for the word does not appear to have been abated by an increase in competent clergy. The educational credentials of London incumbents rose dramatically during the puritan era: the proportion who trained at university rose from 47% in 1560 to 75% in 1601, and the number licensed to preach (that is, actually capable of writing their own sermons rather than simply reading out the set homilies) doubled from 44% in 1560 to 88% in 1601.[47] In this same period, however, lectureships in the capital also rose dramatically from 3 in 1560 to 40 in 1601, and over 100 from the mid-1620s.[48] Far from a better educated clergy doing away with the demand for lecturers, it

---

[45] Seaver, *The Puritan Lectureships*, pp 185, 209, 236 and David R. Como, 'Walker, George (bap. 1582?, d. 1651),' *Oxford Dictionary of National Biography*, Oxford University Press, Sept 2004; online edn, Jan 2008 [http://www.oxforddnb.com/view/article/28478, accessed 30 Aug 2010].
[46] See Collinson, *The Elizabethan Puritan Movement*, p 343; Seaver, *The Puritan Lectureships*, pp 23-24.
[47] Seaver, *The Puritan Lectureships*, p 130.
[48] *Ibid.*, pp 203, 245, 275.

seemed only to fuel the people's appetite for good preaching.

Some commentators, more critical of the institution as a whole, saw the lecturers as very much like the medieval friars. Both were more interested in preaching than in the sacraments, and both were more popular with the people than with the ecclesiastical and secular hierarchies, who were often the target of their rhetoric. What's more, 'Lecturers do in a Parish Church what the Fryers did heretofore,' complained lawyer and linguist John Selden (1584-1654), they 'get away not only the Affections, but the Bounty, that should be bestowed upon the Minister.'[49] Patrick Collinson thinks they were 'the natural successors to the preaching friars, and many of them observed an old tradition in their disregard of episcopal discipline.' Certainly he is correct to point out that a lecturer's more tenuous connection to the institutional Church meant that (early on at least) 'he could afford the extremism which his relatively irresponsible situation encouraged.'[50] Lectures may well have filled a spiritual vacuum left by the preaching friars when the religious orders disappeared after the Reformation, but they were different animals. Friars were itinerant and did not rely on preaching for a living, whereas the lecturers were trained and ordained to preach, and to do it in a fixed location to a settled congregation, often provided for by a significant endowment.[51]

Lectureships inevitably sprang up outside London, in a variety of different guises. In some places there were 'lectures in combination', where country ministers would take it in turn to give market day sermons in a local town. During the puritan period, eighty-five places in twenty-six counties are known to have had such arrangements to provide the word of God to people where they were working and trading during the week.[52] The people of Lawshall in Suffolk sought relief from 'a decrepit and immoral vicar' by raising £10 a year to support their own

---

[49] J. Selden, *Table-talk, Being the Discourses of John Selden* (London: Printed for E. Smith, 1689), p 31.
[50] Collinson, *The Elizabethan Puritan Movement*, p 85.
[51] See Seaver, *The Puritan Lectureships*, pp 73-74.
[52] See J. Spurr, *English Puritanism 1603-1689* (Basingstoke: Macmillan, 1998), p 53. On the combination lectures generally, see P. Collinson, J. Craig & B. Usher, *Conferences and Combination Lectures in the Elizabethan church: Dedham and Bury St Edmunds, 1582-1590*, Church of England Record Society (Woodbridge: Boydell Press, 2003).

lecturer.[53] Such things often happened 'spontaneously' at a local level, but there were also more concerted efforts to increase the number of preachers and lectureships in the country as a whole. Space precludes a look at the story of that development in the seventeenth century here, but suffice to say lectures were not imposed on local churches. More often than not they were greatly desired by an educated laity who longed to be as intellectually engaged with their faith as they were in other areas of their lives. As Seaver nicely sums it up, 'The Reformed faith created a need for an educated and preaching clergy, and when the public authorities failed to satisfy that need, free enterprise and voluntary associations stepped in to meet the demand.'[54]

Archbishop Laud would later complain in a rather condescending way that the lecturers as a class were 'the people's creatures.' The hierarchical structure of the Church of England with its complex relationships for command and subordination must have been bewildering, distant, and ridiculously formal to many laypeople. The immediate reality though was 'the presence of an educated and confident laity who followed the thought of the preacher critically, who expected substantial emotional and intellectual fare from the pulpit,' notes Seaver, 'and who were not much interested in preserving the niceties of traditional relationships in order to get it.'[55] Men and women from every class of society willingly gave to support the lectures,[56] which seemed to provide them with what they wanted in a way that the *status quo* of the Established Church often dismally failed to do.

There was the danger that concentrating solely on preaching would shrink religion into an entirely cerebral matter for many people. Potentially, it could separate word and sacrament in an unhelpful way, as critics of the puritans noted, and encourage an extremism in those preachers who did not have the enlarged vision and responsibilities of community leadership in a more traditional beneficed ministry. It may

---

[53] Collinson, *The Elizabethan Puritan Movement*, p 343.
[54] Seaver, *The Puritan Lectureships*, p 264.
[55] *Ibid.*, p 292.
[56] Two notable women benefactors were Lady Elizabeth Martin in 1581, and Lady Mary Weld in 1623 who left £120 to St. Antholin's for the lectures. See Owen, 'The London Parish Clergy in the Reign of Elizabeth I,' 423 and Ian W. Archer, 'Weld , Mary, Lady Weld (*bap.* 1560?, *d.* 1623),' *Oxford Dictionary of National Biography*, Oxford University Press, Oct 2005; online edn, Jan 2008 [http://www.oxforddnb.com/view/article/66941 , accessed 30 August 2010].

also, ironically, have made many preachers more remote from the people; employing a person just to teach and weigh doctrine, and not explicitly to pray and pastor, implicitly severs the link between the word and its application in real lives. In such a situation, the nature of preaching itself is altered, and it can become merely an exegetical performance without engaging with actual people in the intimacy of their messy everyday struggles to believe or to be holy. The puritans were of course aware of all these dangers, but they were impatient and entrepreneurial folk who were thirsty for the pure spiritual milk of God's word and tried to find the best ways and means of quenching that thirst. Lectureships, like those at St. Antholin's in London, were one of the most important ways in which they sought to accomplish that godly goal.

****

In the introduction to the next volume of these modern St. Antholin's Lectures, we will continue the story of St. Antholin's into the seventeenth century. There we will look in more detail at some of the struggles faced by the lecturers and the strategic importance of St. Antholin's as a centre for the puritan movement, as well as meeting some of the influential figures who were associated with the church in the seventeenth to nineteenth centuries.

In the following pages, we have collected the first ten of the modern St. Antholin's Lectures which were begun again in 1991. Some are biographical and explore the lives and ministries of significant puritan individuals such as Richard Baxter, William Perkins, and John Bunyan. Others expound particular themes which were important in puritan theology and preaching, such as spiritual warfare, conversion, and the cross of Christ. The contributors, all Anglicans in the puritan mould and with great sympathy and love for their subjects, cast their expert eyes over the past glories of this tradition, with their minds always on its contemporary relevance and application. I hope you will enjoy meeting, and be greatly edified by, these pilgrims, warriors, and servants.

A Man For All Ministries: Richard Baxter 1615-1691

J.I. Packer

1. Baxter in context 25
2. Background 27
3. Motivation 30
4. Ministry 35
5. Conclusion 41
For Further Reading 42

JAMES I. PACKER began his ministry as Curate of St. John the Baptist, Harborne Heath in Birmingham. After several years in England as Principal of Tyndale Hall, Bristol and Warden of Latimer House, Oxford he moved in 1979 to Regent College, Vancouver (Canada). He is arguably the most significant and influential Reformed Evangelical Anglican writer of the last 100 years, and has played a key role in the revival of interest in Reformed and Puritan theology over the last six decades. His 1955 DPhil from Oxford was on redemption in the thought of Richard Baxter. He has since published a large number of books including the classic *Knowing God* and *Among God's Giants: The Puritan Vision of the Christian Life*. He is also General Editor of the English Standard Version.

1. Baxter in context

The seventy six years of Richard Baxter's life spanned an era in English history that was tragic, heroic, and pathetic by turns to an extraordinary degree. It was a time of revolution and counter-revolution in church and state; of brutal religious persecution, of fierce controversy in print about almost everything; of disruptive socio-economic shifts which nobody at the time understood; of widespread bad health, growing towns innocent of hygiene, and nightmarishly primitive medicine; in short, it was a time of hardship for just about everyone. And at the head of the list of factors that led to the tragedies, the heroisms, and the miseries, stood rival understandings of Christianity. That is a sad thing to have to say, but it is true.

Had you been a Christian of consistent principles, whatever they were, living through those 76 years, you too would have had a rough ride. If you had been a Roman Catholic, you would have been an object of general distaste in the community all the time, constantly suspected of being a political subversive. Had you been a High Anglican, wedded to the Prayer Book, the ministry of bishops, and the royal supremacy in church and state, you would have watched your side lose the Civil War in the 1640's, you would have wept over the (to you) traitorous act of executing the king for treason against his people, you would have seen Prayer Book and episcopacy at one stage outlawed by Parliament, and if you had been a clergyman you would have lost your living for the best part of 20 years before the Restoration (1660). And if, like Baxter, you had been a Puritan, practising and propagating the religion of St Augustine on the basis of the theology of John Calvin, you would have had to endure the Arminianizing of Anglican leadership for two decades before the Civil War, the ejecting of almost 2,000 Puritan-type clergy from English parishes at the Restoration, the consequent Anglican slide away from the gospel, and the great persecution of Protestant nonconformists that put tens of thousands in gaol for not using the Prayer Book in their worship of God during the quarter-century before toleration came in 1689. Whatever your principles, you would have experienced much unhappiness during those years.

A moment ago I called Richard Baxter a Puritan; and since that word still carries prejudicial overtones for many, as it did throughout

Baxter's own life, I had better say at once that my reason for using it is simply that it was as a Puritan that Baxter saw himself. Noting in 1680 that two of his opponents in print had called him (in Latin) a dyed-in-the-wool Puritan and one who oozed the whole of Puritanism from every pore, he responded by commenting: "Alas I am not so good and happy". Though he was, as we would say, ecumenically oriented, sympathetically alert to all the main Christian traditions and happy to learn from them all, he constantly equated the Puritan ideal with Christianity – "mere Christianity" to use his own phrase, which C S Lewis later borrowed from him – and all his writings display him as the classic mainstream Puritan that he ever sought to be.

What, then, was Puritanism? Matthew Sylvester, the not-too-competent editor of Baxter's posthumous narrative of his life and times (published as *Reiquiae Baxterianae*, 800 folio pages, 1696) notes in his preface that in matters of history, as in everything else, Baxter had: "an Eagle's Eye, an honest Heart, a thoughtful Soul, a searching and considerate (i.e. reflective) Spirit, and a concerned frame of mind to let the present and succeeding generations duly know the real and true state and issues" of things[1]: what description of Puritanism, then, would Baxter have acknowledged as fair and true? The question is not too hard to answer. Puritanism, as Baxter understood it and as modern scholarship, correcting centuries of caricature, now depicts it, was a total view of Christianity, Bible-based, church-centred, God-honouring, literate, orthodox, pastoral, and Reformational, that saw personal, domestic, professional, political, churchly, and economic existence as aspects of a single whole, and that called on everybody to order every department and every relationship of their life according to the Word of God, so that all would be sanctified and become "holiness to the Lord". Puritanism's spearhead activity was pastoral evangelism and nurture through preaching, catechizing, and counselling (which the Puritans themselves called casuistry), and Puritan teaching harped constantly on the themes of self-knowledge, self-humbling, and repentance; faith in, and love for, Jesus Christ the Saviour; the necessity of regeneration, and of sanctification (holy living, by God's power) as proof of it; the need of conscientious conformity to all God's law, and for a disciplined use of the means of grace; and the blessedness of the assurance and joy from the Holy Spirit that all faithful believers under ordinary circumstances

---

[1] Preface to *Reliquiae Baxterianae (RB)*, sec 2, p 2.

may know. Puritans saw themselves as God's pilgrims, travelling home, God's warriors, battling against the world, the flesh, and the devil, and God's servants, under orders to do all the good they could as they went along. This was the Christianity with which Baxter identified, and of which he was a shining example throughout the vicissitudes of his own long life.

2. Background

Let us get a little closer to Baxter. Here are the key personal facts. Summarized in *Who's Who* fashion, with a few intrusions as we move through them, they are as follows:

"Baxter, Richard, gentleman" (for his father owned a small estate); "born 12 November 1615, at Rowton, Salop; educated at Donnington Free School, Wroxeter, and privately" (Baxter never went to a university); "ordained deacon by Bishop of Worcester, 1638; curate of Bridgnorth, 1639-40; lecturer" – that is, salaried preacher – "of Kidderminster, 1641-42; with the Parliamentary army, 1642-47; vicar of Kidderminster, 1647-61" – a ministry during which he just about converted the whole town – "at Savoy Conference, 1661" (this was the abortive consultation between Puritan and Anglican leaders for the improving of the Prayer Book for the restored Church of England); "lived privately in or near London, 1662-91; married Margaret Charlton (1636-81), 1662; imprisoned for one week in Clerkenwell gaol, 1669, for 21 months in Southwark gaol, 1685-86; died 8 December, 1691; author of "*The Saints' Everlasting Rest* (1650)" – an all-time devotional classic on how thoughts of God and heaven can renew the heart for service here below, an 800 page volume that sold an edition a year for the first decade of its life; "*The Reformed Pastor* (1656)" – another all-time classic, admonishing, motivating, and instructing the clergy, "*A Call to the Unconverted* (1658)" – the first evangelistic pocket-book in English, which in its year of publication sold 20,000 copies, and brought an unending stream of readers to faith during Baxter's lifetime; "*A Christian Directory* (1673)" – a unique million-word compendium of Puritan teaching about Christian life and conduct; "and over 130 other books; special interests, pastoral care, Christian unity; hobbies, medicine, science, history." Such was the man the tercentenary of whose death we are now commemorating.

Is it important for later generations to remember Baxter? In 1875 in Kidderminster they thought it was, and a fine statue of him preaching was erected in the town centre, with the following inscription:

BETWEEN THE YEARS 1641 AND 1660

THIS TOWN WAS THE SCENE OF THE LABOURS OF

RICHARD BAXTER

RENOWNED EQUALLY FOR HIS CHRISTIAN LEARNING

AND PASTORAL FIDELITY.

IN A STORMY AND DIVIDED AGE

HE ADVOCATED UNITY AND COMPREHENSION

POINTING THE WAY TO THE EVERLASTING REST.

CHURCHMEN AND NONCONFORMISTS

UNITED TO RAISE THE MEMORIAL, A.D. 1875.

The phrases used show what it was about Baxter that was thought worth remembering in 1875. "Christian learning", for instance, points to the fact that he was in fact an omnivorous polymath, always studying, reading quickly and remembering well what he had read, and consistently thoughtful and discerning in the opinions he expressed on what the books set before him. Once he complained that the loss of time for study due to his many illnesses (for he was a sick man all his life) was the greatest burden he had to bear; anyone, however, who observes his mastery of biblical material, of the entire Christian tradition, and of the dozens of positions that he controverts, will marvel at the amount of studying that he actually accomplished. He was in fact the most voluminous English theologian of all time, and in addition to the approximately four million words of pastoral, apologetic, devotional and homiletic writing that are reprinted in his *Practical Works* he produced about six million more on aspects of the doctrine of grace and salvation, church unity and nonconformity, the sacraments, Roman Catholicism, antinomianism, millenarianism, Quakerism, politics and history, not to mention a systematic theology in Latin; and in all of these writings, whether or not one finally agrees with Baxter's positions, one finds oneself confronted with the mature judgment of a clear, sharp, well-stocked, wise mind, as distinguished for intellectual integrity as for spiritual alertness. I do not think Baxter was always right, but I see him, as did the memorialists of 1875, as one of the most impressive of Christian thinkers, and I urge that there is just as much reason to honour him as such today as there was 116 years ago.

Then, again, the 1875 inscription celebrates Baxter's constant pleas, uttered both *viva voce* and in print over more than 40 years, for "unity and comprehension". In his own day, Baxter's pleading on these topics went unheeded, partly because of the sharpness of the rhetoric in which much of it was couched, but mainly because it was an age in which party spirit and dog-eat-dog wrangling were taken as proper signs of Christian seriousness. By 1875, however, the basic right-mindedness of what Baxter was saying had become apparent, and it ought to be even more apparent today. Baxter's call to unity depended on distinguishing tolerable from intolerable differences among professing Christians and churches; his plea was, first, that love, peace, and communion should be maximized on the basis that in reality all Christian essentials are already held by those who accept the Apostles' Creed, the Ten Commandments, and the Lord's Prayer, as fixing the shape of their Christianity, and, second, that all would henceforth observe the maxim, unity in necessary things, liberty in non-necessary things, charity in all things. Baxter's call for comprehension depended on his view of the Church of England as being what its first Reformers saw it as – namely, a federation of congregations standing for "mere Christianity", that is, a Christianity defined in terms of the essentials and no more, and committed together to the task of evangelizing and discipling the English. Here, his plea was for a relaxation of the restored Anglican uniformity of 1662 that would allow Presbyterian, Independent, and Baptist groups a place within the federation, for the furtherance of the common calling. His reasoning was noble and cogent in itself, and more than timely during those years in which all nonconformists (120,000 or so, according to one estimate) faced fines and imprisonment if they were caught worshipping in company in their own way. Baxter's pitch was queered by Anglican hatred and suspicion of nonconformists as being all revolutionaries at heart, by the prevalence among Anglicans of High Church theology which saw non-episcopal churches as no churches and their ministers as no ministers, and non-conformist bitterness and contempt for the persecuting Church of England, and unwillingness ever to associate with it again, so that in the event his argumentation was ignored throughout his lifetime. But we can see why in 1875, before hurricanes of unbelief laid waste great sections of both the Free Church and the Anglican worlds and permanently changed the shape of the comprehension issue, the memorialists wished to celebrate the witness Baxter had borne.

And what, now, of ourselves? Are Baxter's theological attainments, and pastoral strengths, and arguments for unity and comprehension, and testimonies to the supreme importance of fixing one's hopes on the saints' everlasting rest, worth our remembrance today? I maintain not only that they are worth remembering in themselves as inspiring examples of vision, vitality, and wisdom in Christ, but that Baxter has more to say, and to give, to those who remember him in 1991 than was the case with the men and women of 1875, just because we have drifted further from that vision, vitality, and wisdom than they had. The title of this lecture is "A Man for All Ministries". I propose to spend the rest of my time looking more closely at Baxter the man and at the serving roles that he fulfilled, and my suggestion at each point will be that we today need to learn from him in the way that small, superficial, shallow people always need to learn from the giants. To this agenda I now turn.

3. Motivation

Often described as seraphic, because of the way that his rhetoric soars when he is dilating on the grace of God and the blessings of the gospel, Baxter appears throughout his ministry as the very epitome of single-minded ardour in seeking the glory of God through the salvation of souls and the sanctification of the church. To contemplate the independence, integrity, and zeal with which the public Baxter fulfilled his ministry is fascinating and inspiring; but even more fascinating and inspiring, to my mind at any rate, is contemplation of the private Baxter, the man behind the ministry, who in an elaborate self-analysis, written it seems about 1665, when he was 50, and published posthumously as part of his *Reliquiae*, opens his heart about the changes he sees in himself since his younger years in Christian service. In general, what he delineates is a progress from raw zeal to ripe simplicity, and from a passionate narrowness that was somewhat self-absorbed and majored in minors to a calm concentration on God and the big things, and a profound capacity to see those big things steadily and whole. I subjoin some extracts from this gem of humble, honest witness to the transforming work of God in a human life so that you may get the flavour of Baxter directly, and judge for yourself whether I exaggerate in what I have just said.[2]

> "I have perceived that nothing so much hindereth the reception of the truth as urging it on men with too harsh importunity, and falling too heavily on their errors."

> "In my youth I was quickly past my fundamentals and was running up into a multitude of controversies ... But the elder I grew the smaller the stress I laid upon those controversies and curiosities (though still my intellect abhorreth confusion) ... And now it is the fundamental doctrines of the Catechism which I highliest value and daily think of, and find most useful to myself and others. The Creed, the Lord's Prayer and the Ten Commandments do find me now the most acceptable and plentiful matter for all my meditations. They are to me as my daily bread and drink ... I value all things according to their use and ends, and I find in the daily practice and experience of my soul that the knowledge God and Christ, and the Holy Spirit, and the truth of Scripture, and the life to come, and of a holy life, is of more use to me than all the most curious speculations. That is the best doctrine and study which maketh men better and tendeth to make them happy ..."

> "Heretofore I placed much of my religion in tenderness of heart, and grieving for sin, and penitential tears ... but my conscience now looketh at love and delight in God, and praising him, as the top of all my religious duties ..."

> "My judgment is much more for frequent and serious meditation on the heavenly blessedness than it was heretofore in my younger days ... now I had rather read, hear or meditate on God and heaven than on any other subject ... I was once wont to meditate on my own heart ... poring either on my sins or wants, or examining my sincerity; but now, though I am greatly convinced of the need of heart-aquaintance ... I see more need of

---

[2] Quotations are from *The Autobiography of Richard Baxter*, ed J M Lloyd Thomas, (London: J M Dent, 1931), pp 106, 107f, 112, 115, 117, 118f, 125, 130f.

> a higher work, and that I should look often upon Christ, and God, and heaven, (rather) than upon my own heart."

> "I now see more good and more evil in all men than heretofore I did ... I less admire gifts of utterance and bare profession of religion than I once did ... I once thought that almost all that could pray movingly and fluently, and talk well of religion, had been saints. But experience hath opened to me what odious crimes may consist with high profession ..."

> "I was wont to look but little further than England in my prayers, as not considering the state of the rest of the world ... But now, as I better understand the case of the world and the method of the Lord's Prayer ... no part of my prayers are so deeply serious as that for the conversion of the infidel and ungodly world ..."

(He goes on to express admiration for the missionary pioneer John Eliot, "the apostle of the Indians in New England", whose work he helped to support financially, and to voice the wish that all 2,000 Puritan clergy ejected in 1662 could have become overseas missionaries.)

> "I am deeplier afflicted for the disagreements of Christians than I was when I was a younger Christian. Except the case of the infidel world, nothing is so sad and grievous to my thoughts as the case of the divided churches. And therefore I am more deeply sensible of the sinfulness of those prelates and pastors of the churches who are the principal cause of these divisions. The contentions between the Greek Church and the Roman, the Papists and the Protestants, the Lutherans and the Calvinists, have woefully hindered the kingdom of Christ."

> "Though my works were never such as could be any temptation to me to dream of obliging God by proper merit in commutative justice, yet one of the most ready, constant, undoubted evidences of my ... interest in his covenant is the consciousness of my living as devoted to him. And I the easier believe the pardon of my failings through my Redeemer while I know that I serve no other master, and that I know no other end, or trade, or business, but that I am imployed *(sic)* in his work, and make it the business of my life, and live to him in the world, notwithstanding my infirmities. And this bent and business of

my life, with my longing desires after perfection in the knowledge and belief and love of God, and in a holy and heavenly mind and life, are the two standing, constant, discernible evidences which most put me out of doubt of my sincerity." (He means, of his being truly regenerate and born again.)

"And though I before told of the change of my judgment against provoking writings, I have had more will than skill since to avoid such. I must mention it by way of penitent confession, that I am too much inclined to such words in controversial writings which are too keen, and apt to provoke the person whom I write against ... And therefore I repent of it, and wish all over-sharp passages were expunged from my writings, and desire forgiveness of God and man."

It is surely apparent that these are the words of a great and holy man, naturally gifted and supernaturally sanctified beyond most, humble, patient, realistic, and frank to a very unusual degree. The quiet peace and joy that shine through these almost clinical observations on himself are truly impressive; here is an endlessly active man whose soul is at rest in God all the time as he labours in prayer Godward and in persuasion manward. And the poise of his spirit is the more impressive when we recall that of all the great Puritan sufferers – and the Puritans as a body were great sufferers – none had a heavier load of pain and provocation to endure than did he. He suffered throughout his adult life from a multitude of bodily ailments (a tubercular cough; frequent nosebleeds and bleeding from his finger-ends; migraine headaches; inflamed eyes; all kinds of digestive disorders; kidney stones and gallstones; and more), so that from the age of 21 he was, as he says, 'seldom an hour free from pain", and expected death constantly through the next 55 years of partial disablement before his release finally came. Then, after 1662, he suffered a great deal of hatred and harassment because he was a prominent nonconformist leader: this led to several arrests for preaching, some spells in prison, the distraining (confiscation) of his goods to pay fines, including on one occasion the very bed on which he was lying sick, and finally a trial, if it can be called that, before the appalling Judge Jeffreys, Lord Chief Justice of England (answerable therefore to no one) and James II's human whip for flaying rebels. This was the lowest point of public degradation that Baxter was ever reduced to, and it is worth pausing to get a glimpse of it.[3]

The charge was sedition: a ridiculous, trumped-up accusation based on expository words in his *Paraphrase of the New Testament* about the Pharisees and Jewish authorities, into which was read an attack on England's rulers in church and state. (Baxter later commented that by the same logic he could have been indicted for uttering the words, "Deliver us from evil," in the Lord's Prayer.) Jeffreys would not let Baxter and his six legal representatives say anything coherent at any stage, and the disputed passages in the *Paraphrase* were never discussed; Jeffreys simply ranted on against the 70-year-old Puritan veteran as (these are the words of an eye-witness) "a conceited, stubborn, fanatical dog, that did not conform when he might have been preferred (that is, been a bishop: Baxter was offered the see of Hereford at the Restoration); hang him! This one old fellow hath cast more reproach upon the constitution and excellent discipline of our Church than will be wiped out this hundred years ... by God! he deserves to be whipped through the city." When he had finished haranguing the jury, Baxter said: "Does your lordship think any jury will pretend to pass a verdict on me upon such a trial?" "I'll warrant you, Mr Baxter," replied Jeffreys; "don't you trouble yourself about that." And the jury promptly found him guilty without retiring. The result for Baxter was eighteen months in gaol.

It should be added, however, that after Baxter was dead at 76, and Jeffreys had drunk himself into the grave at the age of 40, and it was known that Matthew Sylvester was to be Baxter's biographer, Tillotson, the Archbishop of Canterbury, wrote Sylvester a letter of encouragement containing the following sentences about the trial:

> "Nothing more honorable than when the Rev Baxter stood at bay, berogued (slandered), abused, despised; and never more great than then. Draw this well ... This is the noblest part of his life, and not that he might have been a bishop. The Apostle (2 Corinthians 11) when he would glory, mentions his labours and strifes and bonds and imprisonments; his troubles, weariness, dangers, reproaches; not his riches and coaches and advantages.

---

[3] The details are from an eye-witness account reproduced in *Autobiography*, pp 258-264.

God lead us into this spirit and free us from the worldly one which we are apt to run into."[4]

One can only say: Amen to that.

4. Ministry

We have seen something of Baxter the man; let us now look at some of the ministering roles he fulfilled. First, I focus on Baxter as an evangelistic and pastoral communicator – preacher, teacher, and writer.

The best curtain-raiser for this section is Baxter's own account of the fruitfulness of his Kidderminster ministry. He found the town's 2,000 adults "an ignorant, rude, and revelling people, for the most part ... they had hardly ever had any lively serious preaching among them". Soon, however, things began to happen. Wrote Baxter:

> "When I first entered upon my Labours in the Ministry I took special notice of everyone that was humbled, reformed or converted; but when I had laboured long, it pleased God that the Converts were so many, that I could not afford time for such particular Observations ... Families and considerable Numbers at once ... came in and grew up I scarce knew how ...
>
> "The Congregation was usually full, so that we were fain to build five Galleries after my coming thither ... The Church would have held about a thousand without the galleries. Our private Meetings (small groups, as we would nowadays call them) were also full. On the Lord's Day (which had been sports days before Baxter arrived) there was no disorder to be seen in the streets, but you might hear an hundred Families singing Psalms and repeating Sermons, as you passed through the Streets. In a word, when I came thither first, there was about one Family in a Street that worshipped God and called on His Name, and when I came away there were some streets where there was not past one Family in the side of a Street that did not so; and that did not by professing serious Godliness, give us hopes of their

---

[4] Quoted from *Autobiography*, p 298.

sincerity ... When I set upon Personal Conference and Catechising them, there were very few families in all the Town that refused to come (Baxter asked them to call on him at home, since his bad health constantly disabled him from visiting their homes). And few families went from me without some tears, or seemingly serious promises of a Godly Life."[5]

What was the secret of Baxter's success (so far, at least, as this can be analysed in terms of means to ends)? He notes, as significant factors in the situation, that his people had not been gospel-hardened; that he had good helpers, both assistant clergy and members of the flock; that his converts' holy living was winsome while the town's black sheep made sin appear most repulsive; that Kidderminster was free of rival congregations and sectarian bickerings; that most of the families were at home most of the time, working as weavers, so that they had "time enough to read or talk of holy Things ... as they stand in their Loom they can set a Book before them or edify one another;"[6] also, it was helpful (Baxter continues) that he fulfilled a long ministry; that he practised church discipline; that, being unmarried, he could concentrate on serving his people; that he gave out Bibles and books (he received every fifteenth copy of each of his own books in lieu of royalties for free distribution); that he gave money to the needy; and that he fulfilled for a time the role of amateur physician – effectively, it seems, and without charge – until he could persuade a qualified doctor to move to the town. He held that all these factors helped the gospel forward, and no doubt he was right. But the key element in his success, humanly speaking, was undoubtedly the clarity, force, and skill with which he communicated the gospel itself.

The content of Baxter's gospel was not in any way distinctive. It was the historic Puritan, evangelical, New Testament message of ruin, redemption, and regeneration. Baxter called for conversion from the life of thoughtless self-centredness and sin to Jesus Christ, the crucified Saviour and risen Lord, and he spelt out in great detail what this must mean in terms of repentance, faith, and new obedience. He saw the unconverted as on the road to hell, and as spiritually asleep in the sense of not recognizing their danger, so he set himself both in the pulpit and

---

[5] *RB*, part 1, pp 21, 84f.
[6] *Ibid*, p 89.

in his annual personal conversation ("catechising", as he called it) with each family of the parish, to wake them up and persuade them to thoroughgoing Christian commitment before it was too late. What he said, and how he said it, may be learned from his classic writings on conversion, among them *A Treatise of Conversion, Directions and Persuasions to a Sound Conversion*, and *A Call to the Unconverted* (full title: *A Call to the Unconverted to Turn and Live, and Accept of Mercy while Mercy may be Had, as ever they would find Mercy in the Day of their Extremity: from the Living God*): all of these were originally sermons preached in series to Baxter's Kidderminster congregation.

We should not suppose that conversion was Baxter's only theme in his Kidderminster ministry. He himself tells us that he ranged much wider:

> "The thing which I daily opened to them, and with the greatest importunity laboured to imprint upon their minds, was the great Fundamental Principles of Christianity contained in their Baptismal Covenant, even a right knowledge, and belief of, and subjection and love to, God the Father, the Son, and the Holy Ghost; and Love to all Men, and Concord with the Church and one another: I did so daily inculcate the Knowledge of God our Creator, Redeemer, and Sanctifier, and Love and Obedience to God, and Unity with the Church Catholick, and Love to Men, and Hope of Life Eternal, that these were the matter of their daily Cogitations and Discourses, and indeed their Religion."[7]

But Baxter was an evangelist, and he constantly led his hearers back to the life-and-death question: will you, or will you not, turn and live? Will you now take seriously the things you say you believe about sin, and Christ, and heaven, and hell?

Here is a sample of Baxter's evangelistic rhetoric as he applies a message on Hebrews 11:1, "Faith is the substance of things hoped for, the evidence of things not seen." He has made the point that faith treats as real the realities of which Scripture speaks: God, Christ, Satan; the final judgment, heaven, and hell. He has pressed the question: "Are you in good earnest, when you say, you believe in a heaven and hell? And do you think, and speak, and pray, and live, as those that do indeed believe

---

[7] *Ibid*, p 93f.

it? ... Deal truly ... if you would know where you must live for ever, know how, and for what, and upon what it is that you live here." He has invited his hearers to think what difference it would make to them if they could actually see, with their physical eyes, Christ, their own forthcoming death, judgment day, with Satan accusing, and the condition of those already experiencing heaven and hell. Now he pins the congregation to the wall:[8]

" ... Answer these following questions, upon the foregoing suppositions.

"1. If you saw but what you say you do believe, would you not be convinced that the most pleasant, gainful sin is worse than madness? And would you not spit at the very name of it?

"2. What would you think of the most serious, holy life, if you had seen the things you say you do believe? Would you ever again reproach it as preciseness [a long-standing contemptuous label for the Puritan lifestyle], or count it more ado than needs, and think your time were better spent in playing than in praying; in drinking, and sports, and filthy lusts, than in the holy services of the Lord?

"3. If you saw but what you say you do believe, would you ever again be offended with the ministers of Christ for the plainest reproofs, and closest exhortations, and strictest precepts and discipline ...? Then you would understand what moved ministers to be so importunate with you for conversion; and whether trifling or serious preaching was the best.

"4. I durst then ask the worst that heareth me, Dare you now be drunk, or gluttonous, or worldly? Dare you be voluptuous, proud, or fornicators any more? Dare you go home, and make a jest at piety, and neglect your souls, as you have done? ...

"5. And oh how such a sight would advance the Redeemer, and his grace, and promises, and word, and ordinances in your esteem! It would quicken your desires, and make you fly to Christ for life, as a drowning man to that which may support him. How sweetly then would you relish the name, the word,

---

[8] *Practical Works* (Ligonier PA: Soli Deo Gloria, 1991) III p 585f.

the ways of Christ, which now seem dry and common things!"

That is vintage Baxter, arousing the complacent. It remains only to add that he was preaching before King Charles II, England's merry monarch, and his merry court, and that the sermon was in fact published by royal command, though not, it seems, heeded by the royal conscience. The quality that the 1875 inscription calls "pastoral fidelity" made Baxter willing to say "boo" to any goose, even a royal one. That was the kind of preacher he was.

The second sphere of Baxter's ministry at which we glance is the field of ecclesiastic statesmanship, where Baxter, the advocate of a comprehensive national church, as we saw, was in constant action after 1662 negotiating for agreement with the Independents and a rapprochement with the Church of England, and writing documents and publishing books to that end. Not much need be said about this, because it was an area in which he did not shine at all. His provocative manner in discussion and debate totally thwarted his unitive purpose. His schoolmasterly strictures upon the cherished beliefs of others only made enemies. As the sermon just quoted would suggest, he was too blunt and oracular in style to be a bridge-builder. The position from which he reached out in all these discussions, however, was a non-sectarian, noble one, which when applying for a license to preach under the royal Indulgence of 1672 he formulated as follows:[9]

> "My religion is meerly Christian; but as rejecting the Papal Monarchy and its attendant evils, I am a Protestant.
>
> "The rule of my faith and doctrine is the law of God in Nature and Scripture.
>
> "The Church which I am a member of is the Universality of Christians, in conjunction with all particular churches of Christians in England or elsewhere in the world, whose communion according to my capacity I desire."

Sometimes he called this position "Catholicism against all sects". In his day it was thought eccentric; in ours, it might appear as prophetic, marking the path whereby the exclusiveness of denominationalism comes to be transcended. It was never correct to call Baxter a

---

[9] *Autobiography*, p 293.

Presbyterian, as was often done, nor after 1662 could one call him an Anglican; he was a "mere nonconformist" in relation to the Anglican settlement, and that, denominationally speaking, was all. In an ecumenical age it is worth reflecting on the significance of Baxter's non-denominational stance.

A further sphere of ministry in which Baxter moved was the delineating of Christian social justice, and here he shows great skill in reforming medieval formulae and bringing them up to date for seventeenth-century Protestant use. Part IV of the *Christian Directory*, comprising about 200,000 words, deals in detail with rulers and subjects, lawyers, physicians, schoolmasters, soldiers, murder and suicide, scandal, theft, contracts, borrowing, buying and selling, the charging of interest (i.e. usury), wages, landlords and tenants, lawsuits, distilling out practical guidance for serving and pleasing God in all these relationships, by managing them as expressions of neighbour-love and cooperative service, and avoiding any form of callous or careless exploitation. One must not try, he says, "to get another's goods or labour for less than it is worth," nor must one make profit out of the customer's ignorance or necessity: "it is a false rule of them that think a commodity is worth so much as anyone will give" for it. "To wish to buy cheap and sell dear is common (as St Augustine observes), but it is a common vice."[10] And landlords must not squeeze rents so that tenants cannot live decently, or have leisure to care for their souls. This point Baxter made again, later, in a separate tract, *The Poor Husbandman's Advocate to Rich Racking Landlords*, which he finished only six weeks before his death (it was his last writing), and which did not in fact see the light of day till this century.[11]

I wish that time allowed me to explore the idyll of Baxter's marriage, a 19-year partnership with a brilliant woman, 21 years younger than himself, whom he memorialized in an account of her life written "under the power of melting Grief" a few weeks after her death in 1681. The account was well and lovingly edited by J T Wilkinson in 1928 under the title *Richard Baxter and Margaret Charlton : A Puritan Love-Story*; it deserves to be reprinted. "When we were married," writes Baxter, "her sadness and melancholy vanished: counsel did something

---

[10] *Puritanism and Richard Baxter*, Hugh Martin, (London: SCM Press, 1954) p 173.
[11] Published as *The Reverend Richard Baxter's Last Treatise*, ed F J Powicke, (Manchester: John Rylands Library, 1926).

to it, and contentment something; and being taken up with our household affairs did somewhat. And we lived in inviolated love and mutual complacency sensible of the benefit of mutual help." Baxter's account of his wife's ministry to him has in it many such hints of his ministry as a husband to her, and it is evident that in this he did well, although he writes of himself, with that devastating perfectionist honesty that we saw in him before: "My dear wife did look for more good in me than she found, especially lately in my weakness and decay. We are all like pictures that must not be looked on too near. They that come near us find more faults and badness in us than others at a distance know".[12] Well, maybe so; yet if one picks up all the hints in the narrative, Baxter's marital ministry appears as something to be very much admired, and in days like ours to be viewed as something of a model. But that theme cannot be explored now.

5. Conclusion

It was usual to end Puritan funeral sermons with a reference to the dead person's final hours; for it was an age in which people died at home, in company, without pain-killing drugs, and often in full consciousness to the very end, and it was taken for granted that their dying behaviour and their last words, spoken from the edge of eternity, would have special significance for those whom they left behind. This is not a funeral sermon, but a celebratory speech; nonetheless it is, I think, fitting to end it in this Puritan way. So let it be said that on the day before he died, as on every day of his life, it seems, for the previous forty and more years, Baxter was meditating on heaven, focusing on the description of the heavenly Jerusalem in Hebrews 12:22-24, a passage which, so he told two of his visitors, "deserves a thousand thousand thoughts"; and that he told those same visitors, "I have peace; I have peace"; and that he brushed aside praise for his books with words of almost arrogant humility, "I was a pen in God's hand; what praise is due to a pen?"; and that his last words, spoken through pain, to Matthew Sylvester, whose pastoral assistant he had been for the

---

[12] *Richard Baxter and Margaret Chariton*, ed J T Wilkinson (London: George Allen and Unwin, 1928) pp 110, 152.

previous four years, were: "Oh I thank him, I thank him. The Lord teach you to die." And let it further be said that Sylvester himself, preaching Baxter's memorial sermon on Elisha's words, "Where is the Lord God of Elijah?", was constrained to end by looking ahead to resurrection day, (which, of course, for God's people will be reunion day also), and to ask aloud:

> "What must I do to meet with our Elijah and his God in peace? Must not my eye be inward, upward, forward, backward, round about? Must I not endeavour to know my errand, warrant, difficulties, duties and encouragements? Must I not ... tell what I believe? ... practice what I preach? and promote the Christian interest with all wisdom, diligence, and faithfulness; as my predecessor did before me?"[13]

Baxter's brand of spiritual straightforwardness in the service of the triune God regularly affects Christians as it affected Sylvester; it makes one seek to be energetic and businesslike in one's discipleship and service, just as he was, and gives one a conscience about aimlessness, and casualness, and spiritual drift. For this reason alone it is good for us to remember Baxter, and I have counted it a privilege to be able to introduce you to him in this all-too-sketchy way. From my own acquaintance with him, which now goes back 45 years, I say to you all – clergy, layfolk, young Christians, senior Christians – get to know Baxter, and stay with Baxter. He will always do you good.

For Further Reading

Baxter's *Practical Works*, in four vast volumes, are available by mail order from Soli Deo Gloria, 213 West Vincent, Ligonier, PA 15658, USA. Volume 1 contains *A Christian Director*; volume 2 Baxter's treatises on conversion; volume 3 *The Saints' Everlasting Rest* and other writings on discipleship and fellowship with God; volume 4 (1991) includes *The Reformed Pastor*.

---

[13] Matthew Sylvester, *Elisha's Cry After Elijah's God*, appended to *RB*, p 18.

The Reformed Pastor is in print separately (Edinburgh: Banner of Truth, 1974).

The Autobiography of Richard Baxter, ed J M Lloyd Thomas (1925) and re-edited by N H Keeble (London: J M Dent, Everyman's Library, 1974) is a drastic abridgement of *Reliquiae Baxterianae*, concentrating on Baxter himself.

The standard *Lives* of Baxter by F J Powicke (2 vols, 1924, 1927) and G F Nuttall (1965) are unhappily out of print, as is *Richard Baxter and Margaret Charlton: A Puritan Love-Story* (= *The Life of Margaret Baxter, by Richard Baxter*), ed J T Wilkinson, 1928.

Hugh Martin, *Puritanism and Richard Baxter* (1954) and N H Keeble, *Richard Baxter: Puritan Man of Letters* (1982), are good general introductions.

The Rediscovery and Renewal of the Local Church: The Puritan Vision

Geoffrey Cox

1. The Puritan Vision 47
2. Difficulties of Definition 49
3. Lessons from History.. 52
4. Three Areas of Debate 53
5. Conclusion 61
Bibliography 62

GEOFFREY S. R. COX is a graduate of Merton College, Oxford and was a student of Dr. Packer's at Tyndale Hall, Bristol in preparation for his ordination in 1958. After curacies at St Barnabas Cray and Christ Church Bromley, he served as Incumbent of churches in Gorsley (1964-1979) and Hucclecote (1979-1989) in the Diocese of Gloucester, and of Wollaston and Strixton in the Diocese of Peterborough until his retirement in 1996. He was a contributor to and Secretary of the original Puritan Conference at Westminster Chapel (1960-1968).

1. The Puritan Vision

Visions are both living and life-giving, and as a friend said, "Visions may be hard to quantify, but, boy, don't they motivate!" The Puritans were men with a vision, a vision very relevant to our aim and desire in this conference. What motivated them? Let me try to show you.

"The thought of *communion with God* takes us to the very heart of Puritan theology and religion,"[1] said Dr Packer, giver of last year's Lecture on Richard Baxter, but this was some thirty years earlier at a Puritan Conference. He showed us then how the Puritan concern with the many-sided problem of the nature of man came from their concern for man's *communion with God,* how Puritan concern for the Covenant of Grace – the hall-mark of Puritan theology in the same way as justification by faith is the hall-mark of Luther's theology – was because they saw that the great purpose of the Covenant of Grace was to bring man into *communion with God.* In the same way, the end and purpose of the mediation of Christ is made plain to us by John Owen, perhaps their greatest theologian, when he speaks of Christ's "great undertaking in his life, death, resurrection, ascension, being a mediator between God and us (is) … to bring us to an *enjoyment of God.*"[2] This is where I want us to start. The outstanding distinguishing mark of the Puritans, and the one thing above all that they would want to teach us is: *"to be concerned with God's glory for God's sake, and with communion with God for our own sake."* As they taught, and it has gone down in history, "Man's chief end is to glorify God and to enjoy him for ever."[3] This was their **purpose.**

But where is this God to be found? For Richard Baxter this is obvious. Why,

> the assemblies of his saints that worship him in holy communion are places where he is likelier to be found than in

---
[1] J I Packer, "The Puritan Idea of Communion with God" in *Press Toward the Mark,* Puritan Conference Paper, 1962, p 5.
[2] John Owen, *Works,* ed. Goold 11, p 78.
[3] Westminster Shorter Catechism answer to Question 1.

an alehouse or a playhouse ... Nowhere is God so near to man as in Jesus Christ; and nowhere is Christ so familiarly represented to us as in this holy sacrament. Here we are called to sit with him at his table as his invited welcome guests ... we are entertained by God as friends. If ever a believer may on earth expect his kindest entertainment, and near access, and humble intimacy with his Lord, it is in the participation of this sacrifice feast which is called The Communion, because it is appointed as well for our special communion with Christ as with one another. It is here that we have the fullest intimation, expression, and communication of the wondrous love of God.[4]

The Puritans had a vision of the *local church* as the place where God was glorified, particularly as he met with his people in worship. This was their **vision**.

They had a **purpose**. They had a **vision**. They also had what I may call a **quarry**, both for their foundation stone, Christ, and for the building blocks of their lives, and that was the Bible. (Space is too limited and candidates for quotation too numerous to say other than as has been well said, "the Puritan was committed to the Word of the Lord because he was committed to the Lord of the Word.")

Men with a vision. But who were these men and what were they like? Let me quote from last year's description concerning those around Baxter.

> Puritanism, as Baxter understood it and as modern scholarship, correcting centuries of caricature, now depicts it, was a total view of Christianity, Bible-based, church-centred, God-honouring, literate, orthodox, pastoral, and Reformational, that saw personal, domestic, professional, political, churchly, and economic existence as aspects of a single whole, and that called on everybody to order every department and every relationship of their life according to the Word of God, so that all would be sanctified and become 'holiness to the Lord.' Puritanism's spearhead activity was pastoral evangelism and nurture through preaching, catechising, and counselling (which the Puritans themselves called casuistry) ... Puritans saw themselves as God's

---

[4] R Baxter, *Works*, 1983 ed, III, p 816.

pilgrims, travelling home, God's warriors, battling against the world, the flesh, and the devil, and God's servants, under orders to do all the good they could as they went along.[5]

They were people obedient to the Word of God, committed to extend the worship of God through the local church because, enjoying communion with God, they carried the responsibility of believing that they had been given to understand what God had called them to. They recognised God's call to holiness at whatever cost, both in individual and in church life, and for them this was non-negotiable, because it came from Scripture and the Holy Spirit had written it there.

The Puritans were thoroughly practical people. Every sermon had to have a 'use,' their technical term for a practical application, and a sermon that had no 'use' was no use! Let us follow this example and apply what we have gathered so far in our own answers to three questions:

Question 1.   Do I truly want to obey God the Holy Spirit as he speaks in his Word?

Question 2.   Do I have a vision to make my local church a place where God is glorified and enjoyed?

Question 3.   Is my chief purpose to glorify God and to enjoy Him for ever?

We shall look first at the difficulties in examining the matter, then a brief history, a survey of the three main areas of dispute, leading into a consideration of the basic division, with an attempt finally to apply all this to our own situation.

2. Difficulties of Definition

A first difficulty is that we have to use the word Puritan to describe both Anglican and Presbyterian Puritans. One writer says that the only true Puritans were those Anglicans who conformed, another that the only

---

[5] J I Packer, *A Man for All Ministries,* St Antholin Lecture, 1991, pp 28-32 above.

true Puritans were those who did not conform.[6] We shall use Puritan for both, and Anglican for conformist, Presbyterian for non-conformist. Similarly with the idea of division. There was division between Elizabeth and the Establishment on the one hand and the Puritans on the other. There was also division between the Anglican and Presbyterian Puritans. We face some difficulties in telling this story because it has been viewed and written up for over four hundred years from different points of view reflecting the *a priori* of the writers. Since there is such a mass of evidence – "the materials for sixteenth century history are so vast that no-one can hope to master them in the allotted span of human life"[7] wrote someone ninety years ago! – the selection, quotation and interpretation of the evidence can be open to question. When one writer can assert that the deprived Puritans ('deprived' being a technical term for losing their positions) lost their pastoral contacts and therefore suffered badly by being confined to 'lecturing,' while another claims that the deprived Puritans were freed from other pastoral intrusions so that they were free to concentrate on preaching which they loved most and did best,[8] what can one say? We need to be aware that we shall find equally godly and sincere Christians differing honestly from one another, sometimes through differences of interpretation or approach which may or may not be spiritually based, sometimes through differences of personality or character or temperament which are merely natural – and sometimes even sinful.

Another obstacle to our understanding of the period and people lies in the purely physical differences. For example the population of England in Tudor times was approximately three million. Travel was not easy as the roads were appalling. When we talk of London we can mean only what is now the old City of London with its hundred parish churches and clergy, with every other town and village comparatively smaller. We readily assume that most people were illiterate, yet the many ex-chantry Edwardian Grammar Schools must have had a startling effect since Baxter could mention in his spiritual autobiography[9] how, twice in his youth, godly literature had come to

---

[6] Basil Hall, *Cambridge Modern History*, and M Lloyd-Jones, *The Puritans, their Origins and Successors*, (Edinburgh: Banner of Truth, 1987).
[7] A F Pollard, *Thomas Cranmer*, (Eugene, Oreg.: Wipf & Stock Publishers., 2004).
[8] M Lloyd-Jones, *op cit*, and Peter Toon, *Puritans and Calvinism* (Svengel Pa.:Reiner Publications, 1973).
[9] R Baxter, *Reliquiae Baxterianae*, 1696, p 3f.

him through the hands of travelling pedlars, and these would not waste valuable porterage space on printed materials for which there was no demand.

But the most important and weighty difficulty is how to enter another age and atmosphere. Let a famous biographer speak of someone within our period, Thomas Cranmer.

> Cranmer has been termed the most mysterious figure in the English Reformation. The obscurity is not in his character but in the atmosphere which he breathed, and atmosphere is the most difficult of all things to recreate. As a rule there are no materials; for the people who live in it, a political or religious atmosphere is a familiar thing which needs no explanation and therefore is not recorded in documents. Then the atmosphere changes, and can only be recalled to posterity by an observation compared with which the mere ascertainment of facts is easy.[10]

We who have lived – and are living – through the changes of atmosphere in this country since the Second World War can well understand such a statement. Let me sketch a couple of differences briefly. Certain matters were taken for granted – the authority of Scripture, the authority under God of the sovereign, and the magistrate, and the state. Again, there was no thought of toleration for those who differed from you. One could go on. We shall have to listen hard to these people who are speaking our language, which was theirs first, (remembering how it was said of the British and Americans that they were one race divided by the same language), and taking their intended meanings without trying to smuggle in or superimpose our own critical judgements on their concepts. I have mentioned some of the difficulties we face because I want you to be aware that there are many unanswered and unanswerable questions, and areas where we cannot be sure, even varying with which part of the country we are looking at. All generalisations should be treated with caution – including my own.

---

[10] A F Pollard, *op cit.*

3. Lessons from History

For historical background, English Puritanism can find its immediate *roots* in Wycliffe and the Lollards, and its *stock* in Tyndale and the early English Reformers, both Hooper and Cranmer, although the first recorded use of the *word* Puritan comes in 1567. You will not need reminding of the Continental Reformation, with Luther influencing Tyndale and Cambridge in the days of Barnes and Bilney and Cranmer and Latimer, nor of Zwingli in Zurich and the second generation Reformers like Calvin in Geneva, and Bucer and Peter Martyr at Strasbourg. You will also be familiar enough with the English Reformation, largely political under Henry VIII, more spiritual under Edward VI, sealed with the blood of the martyrs and thus firmly cemented into the common life under Mary, and then restored, politically by Elizabeth, and spiritually, so they hoped, by the returning exiles. (These, you will remember, had sought safety on the Continent from the fires of Smithfield, and had discovered the glories of Geneva and the freedom of Frankfurt, where, after the 'Troubles,' even such as my namesake actually saw no value in the surplice and did without!)

Three things particularly make this event relevant to us today. First, English Puritanism came out of a time of revolution, comparable to the series of revolts which have just toppled the Soviet empire in Eastern Europe, individuals attacking the 'system' and suddenly finding themselves with sufficient support; monarchs and scholars backing protest to such an extent that the big Roman stick could not be used as it had before, in kingdom after kingdom.

Secondly, we must understand that the Elizabethan Settlement was first and foremost an attempt to establish peace and order in a disrupted community. Elizabeth was doing what Boris Yeltsin is trying to do today – and history may show that Elizabeth did a better job than Yeltsin. Elizabethan Puritanism had to grow within a situation where Elizabeth was steering for stability, and sectional interests were anathema because they were potentially politically divisive.

Third, the story of the Elizabethan Puritans revolved round the local church. Just as today many evangelicals are motivated by a vision of revival, the Puritans were motivated by the vision of a reformed church, where the confession of faith was right, all the worship forms were right, the congregation godly and well-taught, who having praised God together, would go out into the world and make it holy. Their imaginations were stirred by the vision of a national church that was a federation of local churches, of which each was right in godliness and worship and impact. This was an important and fresh part of the vision. For the mediaevals, as for Hooker, the local church was not primary. For those who had gained it from Scripture and Geneva, the local church was the centre. When Edward Dering is criticising Elizabeth, he says, "I will lead you to your *benefices!*"[11] and Elizabeth, like Gallio before her, is not at all interested. *They* wanted the local church to be a centre for God, where people grew by prayer and study and conference. Elizabeth, on the other hand, viewed these gatherings very differently since she dreaded dissension, and so was remarkably uncooperative. (It should be said in her defence that she faced very serious dangers on her accession, an undefined but threatening Catholic opposition, Protestant exiles returning to exercise a profound influence in Parliament, all set within a nation so externally weak that it might easily be swallowed up by the surrounding unfriendly powers.) In spite of her religious views, Elizabeth proved an exceptionally successful monarch in so protecting and developing the third – the nation – and suppressing the first – the Catholics – that she could at least partially confine the second with whom we are concerned. She nevertheless supported and encouraged Protestants in the Netherlands and Scotland throughout her reign. One tragedy of the Puritan conflict was that Elizabeth was right politically and in terms of good government, while the Puritans were right in their vision of godliness in the local church.

4. Three Areas of Debate

The debate covered three areas. The first dispute, over order in public worship, began with clothes. The Act of Uniformity of 1559 retained all the Ornaments of the second year of Edward VI 'until further order' – to prevent further misappropriation, it was said. (The 'further order' was to be found in the 'Advertisements' of 1566, including 'a comely surplice with sleeves.') The protesters said, "These things are *indifferent* and should not be insisted on!" The authorities said, "These things are *indifferent* and should be worn for decencies' sake." Neither would

---

[11] Edward Dering, *Works*, 1597, p 27.

yield, the former because their case was grounded on conscience, the latter because uniformity was important to maintain law and order. The Continental Reformers when appealed to, advised temporary conformity so that the preaching of the gospel should not be hindered and Calvin, for one, expressed reasonable content with an episcopacy that was trying to reform itself and be biblical. (Calvin actually said that what is right in the New Testament could not be wrong for us, and that the best way to increase godliness would be to go back to the New Testament, but that God would not require this as an absolute. That was left to Beza. Interestingly enough, in a comparable context, Luther more than once advised correspondents to ignore the outward trappings and concentrate on the preaching of the gospel which God would honour in his own time.) Nevertheless the protesters increased their agitation over details like the use of organs, the sign of the cross in baptism, kneeling at communion and so on, and these complaints were presented to Convocation and discussed in 1563. The strength of Puritan feeling was shown by the narrowness of their defeat – one vote! Agitation continued for it was a time of considerable disorder and variation. For example, in some churches the Holy Table was in the centre, in others altarwise a yard from the east wall; some celebrated in a surplice, others without; some used wafers, others bread; some baptised in a font, others in a basin. Elizabeth told her Archbishop to establish order, and while the bishops sympathetic to reform regarded this as a temporary measure – indeed all those who conformed only regarded these as temporary measures with a hope of better things to come – and enforced her instructions leniently, the action still had the effect of dividing the Puritans into two groups, those who conformed because they thought it right in the circumstances, and those who regarded it as such a serious matter of conscience that they had rather be deprived than conform. (While in London 37 clergy were suspended, in the end no more than nine were permanently removed.)

The second debate can be focused in the work of the theoretical Presbyterian, Thomas Cartwright. Immensely popular preacher and lecturer at Cambridge, his basic principles were simple: God has revealed his will in Scripture. Scripture has laid down the rule of church government. That rule is not episcopacy as set up by Elizabeth in the English Church, but presbyterianism as conceived by Thomas Cartwright after the model of Calvin's Geneva. (He was deprived of his professorship in 1570.) Since proposals for minor reforms had been rejected at the beginning of 1571, an "Admonition to Parliament" appeared in June declaring that,

> we in the Church of England are so farre off from having a church rightly reformed according to the prescrypt of God's Word, that as yet we have not come to the outward face of the same.

A Second Admonition detailing the 'popish abuses yet remaining in the Church of England,' earned imprisonment for both authors, though also considerable sales. Most of the older Puritans withdrew their support from these extremists. Thomas Norton, who translated Calvin's Institutes, "misliked much these men's course and fancies and matters contained in their book," and even Beza in Geneva disapproved of it. The Queen's rejection in the same year of a Bill for the Reform of the Prayer Book, as an attack on her prerogative, sealed the division, driving the radicals to despair of reforming the church and convincing them of the need to work for a new church polity.

The third area of debate concerned the whole area of pastoral competence, or as the Puritans would have thought of it, holiness in both pastor and congregation. As to individual pastors, we can note the activities of Richard Greenham, the archetypal Puritan pastor, who left Dry Drayton after twenty years in which he felt, "I perceive no good wrought by my ministry on any but one family"[12] because of "the untractableness and unteachableness of the people." Even so, during that time he prepared and trained many students in the patterns of pastoral care that he was himself developing. He never published what he learnt, but taught it to a new generation of pastors who went out and established the Puritan ideals. Richard Rogers of Dedham and William Perkins at Cambridge, both carried out and exemplified to those who emulated them rich, converting, and nurturing ministries of great distinction. All this time at the grass roots the Puritan movement was developing a fruitful programme of regular meetings known as 'exercises for prophesyings.'

Meetings of preachers of an area, gathering at a local centre such as the market town, were very popular and attended by large public audiences, including local dignitaries, and the increasingly belligerent Parliaments showed the spread of Puritan sympathies among the gentry

---

[12] Samuel Clarke, *Lives of 32 English Divines*, 1677, p 12f.

as well as among the clergy. As Bishop, and then Archbishop, Grindal had fully encouraged these meetings, as did the Privy Council, and when he politely refused to suppress them he was suspended until his death in 1583. Those who had been denied the opportunity to reform the national church but still conformed, devoted all their energies to their congregations, teaching them the Christian faith in its Puritan expression, and training them in the Puritan way of life, usually most simply described as "the walk with God," particularly the importance of family religion and the practical application of holiness to every part of their existence. How widespread and successful this proved can be shown some years into the next century from John Bunyan's experience before his conversion. When walking through Bedford, he overheard three or four poor women sitting at a door in the sun.

> Their talk was about a new birth, the work of God in their hearts, also how they were convinced of their miserable state by nature; they talked how God had visited their souls with his love in the Lord Jesus, and with what words and promises they had been refreshed, comforted and supported against the temptations of the devil. Moreover they reasoned of the suggestions and temptations of Satan in particular; and told to each other by which they had been afflicted and how they were borne up under his assaults ... and me thought they spake as if joy made them speak.[13]

How grateful we would be if even our more mature saints would concern themselves with such subjects. But then Puritanism was essentially a religion of 'heart-work,' a sustained practice of seeing the face of God in a way which our own brand of Christianity too often is not. (The practical application is obvious: what are we teaching and what effect does it have on the lives and godliness of those to whom we minister?)

We come now to the outward divisions between the Puritans and the authorities, for one of our concerns is to see how we, who seek to be obedient to the Word of God, can rightly cope with authorities within church and state who have departed from the Word of God and may require us to do the same. We start with church government. There were, as we have seen, two opposing views, both held by godly men. The

---

[13] John Bunyan, "Grace Abounding," *Works,* ed Offor, I, p 10.

first said, "Scripture lays down a definite and final form of church government." The second said, "Not so!" The argument could have been quickly settled from Scripture, if the premise had been correct. That it was not so can be shown in two ways. First, we see the inability of good men to agree, in this period when both sides, as perhaps at no other time in English history, were concerned to obey the Holy Spirit in his written Word. Second, when we turn to Scripture itself, we find that every proffered doctrine of the church includes certain parts supplied 'by necessary deduction.' Puritan ecclesiology abounds in this concept in various verbal forms, and it ignores the possibility that what is a 'necessary deduction' to you may well be a *non-sequitur* to me! What had happened was that the apparent simplicity, freedom and freshness of the 'greener grass' of Geneva, so attractive compared with the unreformed structure within which they lived, led people to be willing to accept as 'logical conclusions' what were not necessarily so. (Remember that we too are sometimes encouraged in certain ways of thought by our temperament as well as by more 'spiritual' motives.) Hooker's words, "He that goeth about to convince a multitude that they be not as well governed as they might be shall never lack hearers,"[14] have some relevance here. That various gatherings of believers in the New Testament are referred to as churches or congregations and that elders are mentioned with various activities, ruling, teaching and so on, does not bind us to deduce a fixed number of each in a set pattern, nor call some 'offices' of perpetual obligation, any more than does 1 Peter 3:20, "only a few, that is eight," limit us forever to define 'a few' as 'eight'! Underlying this question was an outwardly less important, but actually more substantial matter, the rituals and ceremonies usually called 'adiaphora,' the Greek word for 'things indifferent.'

It started from, but is distinct from, the principle that tainted ceremonies, which hide the truth from the worshipper and buttress superstitious error, should be dropped as both dishonouring to God and impeding edification. On this latter *principle* all the English Reformers were agreed from the start, as the 1549 Prayer Book Preface on Ceremonies shows. That they did not agree on its *application* was why Hooper in 1550 clashed with the authorities over episcopal vesture, and why in the 1560s the Puritans felt obliged to campaign against the Prayer Book requisites of surplice, ring in marriage, sign of the cross in

---

[14] R Hooker, *Laws of Ecclesiastical Polity*, Introduction.

baptism, and kneeling at communion. As controversy increased and the lines of battle hardened, this developed into a *new principle,* that direct biblical warrant in the form of precept or precedent is required to sanction every item of consequence in the public worship of God. (The word 'consequence' is my own, to distinguish between things of no matter for which no warrant was required – always the criterion in such cases was the appeal to reason or logic, 'necessary deduction' again – and things that they did regard as important. This attempt led to some curiosities of exposition, such as the 'proof' that two services were obligatory from Numbers 28:9 which prescribes two burnt offerings, or the 'proof' that the minister should stand in one place throughout the service from Acts 1:15, where Peter 'stood up in the midst of the disciples.') It is sometimes said that whereas Luther's rule in ordering public worship was to allow traditions which were not contrary to Scripture, Calvin's was to admit nothing not specifically prescribed therein, and that Cranmer followed Luther via Osiander. While superficially true, at least of Beza if not of Calvin, it is misleading since it gives the impression that Luther and Cranmer did not regard Scripture as fully authoritative. All the Reformers regarded Scripture as of final authority. The question was how this authority was to be applied.

Two basic principles were held by the non-conformist Puritans: first, that everything introduced into the church without scriptural sanction is unlawful, and second, that the form of the visible church in the New Testament is perpetually binding upon all generations of Christians.[15] William Perkins had put it succinctly: "God is not worshiped of us but where it is his will to accept our worship, and it is not his will to accept our worship but when it is according to his will."[16] To listen to the debate is to remember Sidney Smith's comment on seeing two women hurling invective at each other across a street.

"Those two will never agree," he said.

"Why not?"

"Because they are arguing from different premises!"

---

[15] Iain Murray, "Scripture and Things Indifferent" in *Diversity in Unity,* Puritan Conference Paper 1963, p 16.
[16] W Perkins, *A Golden Chain,* 1608.

In reply Whitgift and Hooker maintained that the Puritans had misconceived the intention of Scripture; while the Bible was binding in all matters relating to salvation, it did allow liberty to the church to introduce things indifferent. They denied that the pattern of the New Testament church was permanently obligatory on the grounds that the information that the Scriptures give us is *not* sufficient, but incomplete and indecisive, suggesting that Christ did not intend any one form of church government to be of divine authority.

As you will have noticed, we have now passed from what I would want to describe as the 'presenting symptoms' of 'adiaphora' and church government to the central matter of the approach to Scripture, what the Puritans called the Regulative Principle. What does this say, how did they deduce it, and is it actually scriptural? We take the second question first.

The Puritans were facing attack throughout this period, and regrettably when involved in polemic one can easily be drawn into overstatement to provide a watertight case, even in default of evidence. Follow the Puritan line of thought with me. They came to the Old Testament and found it full of direct commands and instructions from a God who demanded complete and detailed obedience. They found a coherent set of laws suitable for a people settled in a geographical area, very explicitly set out so that by the time of Jesus the rabbis had established some 613 of them. Clearly some were of special and limited relevance to people who lived in a warm climate. Some were particularly apt for the Tabernacle and priesthood and sacrificial system of the Old Covenant. Some such as the Ten Commandments were obviously of permanent value. (Did you notice the words 'clearly' and' obviously? We are now back in the realm of 'necessary deduction,' and some have made the 'necessary deduction' that the Old Covenant Law needs to be divided for our purposes into three codes, the civil, the ceremonial and the moral, in spite of the very definite biblical statement that the Law is one and indivisible.) The little matter that before the Passover and Sinai there was no such detailed instruction, if indeed any at all, concerning priesthood or sacrifice or sabbath was glossed over.

The Puritans came to the New Testament, and being of tidy minds, and walking with a consistent and reliable God, they looked for the same conditions here. (Being asked once, "Why are you so precise?" for they were also nicknamed Precisians, one replied, "Because I serve a precise God"!) They found in the words of Jesus in the Great

Commission, Matthew 28:20, "teaching them to *obey everything I have commanded you*" the Regulative Principle that they were seeking, with support from Paul in, for example, 1 Corinthians 7:17, "This *is the rule I lay down for all the churches.*" While it is possible to find clear instructions – which is what the Regulative Principle needs – in Paul, it is not so easy to do so with Jesus. There are probably four clear universal commands: Repent and believe the gospel; Love one another as I have loved you; Do this in memory of me; Go and make disciples, baptising and teaching. Apart from these it would be difficult to make a collection of commandments of universal application after the completion of Jesus' atoning work. When we go further into the New Testament, we find the first possibly general commands from the Council of Jerusalem, with the prohibition of blood as one that has been totally ignored. As we read the writings of the apostles we have to pick and choose from the instructions as to which have been taken up by different groups in the history of the church, and which, for one reason or another, have been left on one side. As someone wisely said, "If a man appeals to Caesar, to Caesar he must go." If we claim that the New Testament is *Regulative,* that is, made up of collections of permanently obligatory *rules,* then those rules must be obeyed without exception. While the Old Testament can rightly be called Regulative, the New Testament cannot! The New Testament can only be called Normative; that is governed by the application of *principles.* Since as one Puritan said, "The plainest words are the profitablest oratory in the weightiest matters," let me say bluntly, the so-called Regulative Principle is both a contradiction in terms which cannot hold both ideas logically within the same phrase, and also is not accurate biblically. It should be challenged as a product of Puritan scholasticism and discarded. (It is worth pointing out that in at least three areas where the Reformation took root, the second or third generation of Reformers turned 'scholastic,' and developed highly logical but legalistic systems of thought, either subtly departing from or wresting or even forcing Scripture in certain matters: the successors of Melanchthon and Luther in Germany, Theodore Beza after Calvin in Geneva, and the Puritans in England. In support I offer the doctrine of predestination as Beza developed it in Geneva, and the Covenant of Grace as the Puritans worked it out with a 'necessary' but not so clearly scriptural Covenant of Works as its counterpart.)

5. Conclusion

To sum up and conclude. What can we learn for the rediscovery of the local church in our day from the Puritan vision? Had we started from the Thirty-Nine Articles, a thoroughly reformed confession of faith, we would have found in Article 19 that we have got it right: "The church of Christ is a *congregation of faithful ...,*" that is, the basic church is the local church. All the other superstructures of deaneries and dioceses, of archdeacons and bishops, are only valuable as they serve the gospel and godliness. As with the Puritans, it may be difficult to persuade others of these truths, but we can live by them – and if necessary, call the bluff of some of the empire-building ecclesiastical politicians who often afflict the church of God. Moving further practically in this area, we should see that the government of the local church must be in accordance with the principles in the New Testament, and that it is quite possible for any of us with biblical teaching to establish a polity that fits closer to those of the early churches than most do at the moment.

What can we learn from those we have studied? They were concerned to serve the will of God in their own generation, in what ever situation opened to them. Laurence Chaderton as Master of Emmanuel College, Cambridge, did for his generation exactly what Charles Simeon did for his. Many, many others did what they could in the places where God had put them. Like the Reformers before them, they believed in working where they could until they were evicted. Until the 'Regulative Principle' allowed people to pick and choose what Scriptures they wanted (for that was a by-product of the principle) secession was never a biblical possibility. Apart from a misapplication of Paul's exhortation to holy separation in Corinth, the one place where the Lord Jesus could so easily have encouraged the theory and practice of secession from an apostate church, in his letters to the churches of Asia Minor, he did not, in fact, do so.

These are men from whom we can learn much, for their situation has many similarities to ours, and the same resources are available to us. Their *quarry* was the Word of God. They were concerned to obey the Holy Spirit in his Word. They would have followed that model bishop, Hugh Latimer, who said, "I dare go no further than the text doth, as it were, lead me by the hand." Their *vision* was of God active and glorified in the local church – "where the rubber meets the road" – *and* where God delights to meet his people. This, admittedly, sometimes overwhelmed them. "Truly for sinners to have fellowship with God, the infinitely holy God, is an astonishing dispensation,"[17] said John Owen and he was typical. Their *purpose* was slightly more fully developed in the Larger Catechism: "Man's chiefest and highest end is to glorify God and fully to enjoy him for ever." And 'for ever' started now and their purpose was also their joy and their delight.

For the rediscovery and renewal of the local church in our age, let me point you to these men of God.

Bibliography

P Collinson	*The Elizabethan Puritan Movement*, Cape 1967
A G Dickens	*The English Reformation*, Collins/Fontana 1967
W Haller	*The Rise of Puritanism*, University of Pennsylvania 1938
L F Lupton	*The Geneva Bible*, especially Vol 23 Up to Hampton Court
J I Packer	*Among God's Giants*, Kingsway 1991
Peter Toon	*Puritanism and Calvinism*, Reiner 1973

---

[17] John Owen, *op cit*, p 7.

Evangelical Spirituality: Past Glories, Present Hopes, Future Possibilities

Alister E McGrath

Introduction		65
1.	Evangelicalism and the Call to Personal Faith	67
2.	Spirituality, Evangelicalism, and Spiritual Growth	69
3.	Clarifying Terms: 'Spirituality'	72
4.	Clarifying Terms: 'Evangelical'	73
5.	Evangelical Spirituality: Problems and Proposals	79
	5.1 Ignorance of the heritage of the past	*80*
	5.2 Things have changed!	*82*
	5.3 The Evangelical Neglect of the Human Factor	*83*
	5.4 A Lack of Evangelical Role Models	*86*
	5.5 Spirituality is still not a Core Element in Evangelical Theological Training and Education	*87*
6.	Rediscovering the Sacraments	87
7.	Role Models for Evangelical Spirituality	89
8.	Conclusion	93
For Futher Reading		93

ALISTER E. MCGRATH trained for ordination at Westcott House in Cambridge but after a curacy in Wollaton in Nottingham has spent the bulk of his ministry serving in Oxford, as Chaplain to St. Hilda's College, Tutor and Principal of Wycliffe Hall, and then Director of the Oxford Centre for Christian Apologetics. He is currently Professor of Theology, Ministry and Education at King's College, London and Head of the Centre for Theology, Religion and Culture there. A prolific author, he has the enviable ability to write at both an academic and popular level, particularly focusing on religion and science, Reformation history, doctrine, and spirituality.

Introduction

'Spirituality' is one of the most rapidly developing fields of Christian thought and practice. It has caught hold of the imaginations of many people, especially in the United States. The New Age movement is seen by many observers as a reaction against the spiritual aridity and barrenness of modern culture. There is a real thirst for the 'spiritual' element in life. Evangelicalism has not been immune from this development. Despite its many strengths, some sense that the movement can too easily become dry and cerebral, lacking any real spiritual vitality. The question of whether there are distinctively evangelical approaches to spirituality, which might enable us to consolidate still further the appeal and hold of the gospel proclamation, is clearly of some considerable importance.

For reasons that I shall explore presently, there is a real need to develop evangelical forms of spirituality that are faithful to the gospel on the one hand, and to the pressures of modern life on the other. The powerful thrust of the Decade of Evangelism runs the risk of being dissipated unless those who come to faith are kept in faith by every proper means of spiritual nourishment, encouragement and guidance. Some come to faith because of the power of an evangelistic sermon, delivered by a preacher skilled in the art of delivery and a master of the oratorical arts. Yet the content of that sermon may live on only in the presence and personality of the preacher. The sense of immediacy, of personal dynamism and excitement, is lost once the preacher moves on. The resulting believer is left on his or her own, to discover the full implications of that important decision to begin the Christian life and adjust accordingly. It is here that Christian spirituality has a vital role to play.

At the height of the Great Awakening in eighteenth-century Massachusetts, a young woman convert wrote a letter to Jonathan Edwards. She had come to faith; now she needed guidance, as she put it, as to 'the best manner of maintaining a religious life'. In that letter may be seen an anticipation of the modern realization of the need for follow-up in relation to evangelism. One of the most significant aspects of the Springboard initiative within the Church of England, headed up by Michael Green and Michael Marshall, has been the realization of the vital role of spirituality in a considered and realistic approach to evangelism. Michael Green has stressed the importance of apologetics prior to evangelism, and spirituality subsequent to it. Apologetics is seen as leading naturally into evangelism, which in turn naturally leads on to spirituality, as a means of keeping converts, and enabling them to grow in faith. An earlier emphasis upon evangelistic techniques has been supplemented with a recognition of the need for the long-term spiritual care of those who come to faith. Evangelism makes Christians; spirituality keeps them.

On December 11, 1989, James I. Packer was installed as the first Sangwoo Youtong Chee Professor of Theology at Regent College Vancouver. The title he chose for his inaugural lecture, as much as its content, is telling: 'An Introduction to Systematic Spirituality'. In that lecture, Packer spelled out the importance of spirituality to all concerned with the preaching and ministry of the gospel:

> We cannot function well as counsellors, spiritual directors, and guides to birth, growth and maturity in Christ, unless we are clear as to what constitutes spiritual well-being as opposed to spiritual lassitude or exhaustion, and to stunted and deformed spiritual development. It thus appears that the study of spirituality is just as necessary for us who hope to minister in the gospel as is the study of physiology for the medical trainee. It is something that we cannot really manage without.[1]

My concern is that evangelicals have not paid anything like the necessary attention to this major theme of Christian life and thought. As a result, evangelicalism has become impoverished, where it ought to be rich; it has depended upon the insights of others, where it ought to be contributing to the life of the church. I wish to suggest that the time has come to throw off the cult of dependency, and move towards the development and rediscovery of spiritualities which will complement and nourish the great evangelical emphases upon the sufficiency of Scripture, the centrality of the death of Christ, the need for personal conversion, and the evangelistic imperative. Evangelism gets us started in the Christian life; but spirituality keeps us going, and refreshes us along the way.

---

[1] James I. Packer, 'An Introduction to Systematic Spirituality', *Crux* 26 No. 1 (March 1990), pp 2-8; quote at p 3.

1. Evangelicalism and the Call to Personal Faith

Evangelicalism is without question the powerhouse of the modern Christian church, in England and elsewhere. Time and time again, people put their discovery of the vitality and excitement of the gospel down to the witness of evangelicalism. Richard Holloway, Bishop of Edinburgh and Primus of the Scottish Episcopal Church, is but one of many recent writers from outside evangelicalism to pay tribute to its commitment and success in evangelization.[2]

In an increasingly secular age, evangelism is of decisive importance in reaching out beyond the bounds of the church, and bringing men and women the good news of Jesus Christ. There is a growing realization, even within the depths of a frequently rather complacent British church establishment, that the future existence and wellbeing of the churches depends upon a determined and principled effort to proclaim the gospel. The embargo on evangelism is over.

Let me illustrate this point with reference to events in the United States, some forty years ago. In the first quarter of 1954, the evangelist Billy Graham was invited to speak at Union Theological Seminary in New York. By that time, Graham had attracted considerable attention.[3] The success of the 1949 Los Angeles Crusade had been widely reported in the secular press, giving Graham a high profile. Union Theological Seminary, a bastion of mainline Protestantism, would hardly be expected to receive him warmly. In the event, Graham spoke for forty-five minutes in the seminary chapel, and answered questions afterwards for another thirty minutes. When he had finished, he was greeted with one of the longest and most enthusiastic ovations that institution had known.[4] It seemed to many that evangelicalism had suddenly become respectable.

But not everyone at Union Theological Seminary was pleased

---

[2] Richard Holloway, 'Evangelicalism: An Outsider's Perspective', in R. T. France and A. E. McGrath (eds), *Evangelical Anglicans* (London: SPCK, 1993), p 175.
[3] For the background, see Marshall Frady, *Billy Graham: A Parable of American Righteousness* (Boston: Little Brown, 1979); William G. McLoughlin, *Billy Graham: Revivalist in a Secular Age* (New York: Ronald Press, 1960).
[4] See John C. Bennett. 'Billy Graham at Union', *Union Seminary Quarterly Review* 9 (May 1954), pp 9-14.

with this development. The noted theologian Reinhold Niebuhr, who had joined the faculty of Union as professor of Christian ethics in 1927, was distinctly disgruntled about the growing enthusiasm for evangelicalism. He wrote scathingly of Graham's theological incompetence and naivete.[5]

> Billy Graham is a personable, modest and appealing young man who has wedded considerable dramatic and demagogic gifts with a rather obscurantist version of the Christian faith. His message is not completely irrelevant to the broader social issues of the day — but it approaches irrelevance. For what it may be worth, we can be assured that his approach is free of the vulgarities which characterized the message of Billy Sunday, who intrigued the nation about a quarter century ago. We are grateful for this much 'progress.'[6]

Niebuhr's peremptory dismissal of Graham was seen by many of his readers as little more than sour grapes on the part of an academic theologian, fearful of being marginalized by the new enthusiasm for evangelical Christianity. None other than the president of this same Union Theological Seminary, Henry P. van Dusen, weighed in with a devastating response.

> Dr Niebuhr prefers Billy Graham to Billy Sunday. There are many, of whom I am one, who are not ashamed to testify that they would probably have never come within the sound of Dr Niebuhr's voice or the influence of his mind if they had not been **first** touched by the message of the earlier Billy. Quite probably five or ten years hence there may appear in the classrooms and churches of Billy Graham's severest critics not a few who will be glad to give parallel testimony to his role in **starting** them in that direction.[7]

As if that was not enough, it was followed up by a spirited attack on Niebuhr by E. G. Homrighausen, dean of Princeton Theological Seminary. Writing in the leading liberal journal Christian Century,

---

[5] *Christianity and Crisis* 16 (March 5, 1956), p 18. On Niebuhr, see Richard Wightman Fox, *Reinhold Niebuhr: A Biography* (New York: Pantheon, 1985).
[6] James I. Packer, 'An Introduction to Systematic Spirituality', *Crux* 26 No. 1 (March 1990), pp 2-8; quote at p 3.
[7] *Christianity and Crisis* 16 (April 2, 1956), p 40.

Homrighausen, head of the National Council of Churches' Department of Evangelism, accused Niebuhr and his sympathizers of being 'hesitant and weak in calling persons to a positive faith'. Niebuhr could, he suggested, learn some useful lessons from Billy Graham. Why, he asked, was 'Niebuhrian neo-orthodoxy' so hesitant over calling people to conversion?

> I have, frankly, been disappointed in its inability to lead the way in the revival or rebirth or restoration of a relevant Protestantism in the local church. And if men like Graham have arisen, and are being heard by the thousands, it may be that what he is and says in sincerity ought to be said in a better way by the neo-orthodox with all their accumulation of intelligence about the Bible and history and personality in our times.[8]

The point being made was clear. Evangelicalism was calling people to faith in a way that nobody else was. The most fundamental criticism made of Niebuhr in this respect was that he was parasitic, feeding off the fruits of the work of earlier evangelists without 'calling persons to a positive faith' himself. Many people who would not now regard themselves as evangelicals owe their Christian beginnings to evangelicalism – and, in our English context, I think of people such as John Habgood, John Hick, David Jenkins, and Maurice F. Wiles in making this point.

2. Spirituality, Evangelicalism, and Spiritual Growth

But having won people for the gospel, can evangelicalism keep them? In this lecture I want to address a serious anxiety which I know is shared by many within evangelicalism. The perceived lack of a credible, coherent and distinctive spirituality is one of the greatest weaknesses facing evangelicalism today. I do not in any way wish to be alarmist, and suggest that we are confronted with a crisis arising from a total lack of

---

[8] *Christian Century* 73 (1956), pp 848-849. This response was provoked by an earlier article by Niebuhr in the same journal: *Christian Century* 73 (1956), pp 640-642.

evangelical interest in spirituality.⁹ My concern is simply to identify what seems to me to be a serious weakness at present – but a weakness which can, given commitment and concern, become a future strength.

As we have seen, many people begin their Christian lives as evangelicals. They have been attracted by the power of evangelical testimony, and the obvious difference that faith makes to the lives of their evangelical friends and neighbours. But what happens next? I have seen the same pattern happen too often for comfort in my own ministry at Wycliffe Hall. Many students begin their ministries as evangelicals, yet end up – often after a period of many years – committed to a form of catholicism. And what has attracted these people away from evangelicalism? They seem to gain the impression that it is of relatively little help to those who are trying to deepen their understanding of God, and develop approaches to prayer and meditation which will enrich their faith, and sustain them in the Christian life. In short: it fails to take the pressures and realities of Christian living in the modern period seriously enough to devise spiritual strategies to allow new and struggling Christians to cope with them.

A case study from the United States will illustrate the importance of this point. It is generally recognized that the only churches that are growing in the United States are evangelical in orientation; indeed, for many secular observers, 'evangelical' has become synonymous with 'active and growing'. But some – admittedly, very few – churches of a much more liberal orientation are also expanding. An example is All Saints Episcopal Church, Pasadena,¹⁰ which has received widespread media attention because it bucks the trend: it is one of the very few growing liberal congregations within the mainline denominations in the United States. Its liberalism is not in doubt; it is strongly pro-choice in its attitude to abortion, and it made

---

⁹ There is a useful survey in Gordon James, *Evangelical Spirituality* (London: SPCK, 1991). Although the volume includes much interesting material, the only writers to be dealt with in the period subsequent to the Second World War are Martin Lloyd-Jones and John Stott. A more perceptive analysis, drawing upon developments in the last two decades, may be found in David Parker, 'Evangelical Spirituality Reviewed', *Evangelical Quarterly* 63 (1991), pp 123-148, and James Houston, 'Spirituality', in W. A. Elwell (ed), *Evangelical Dictionary of Theology* (Grand Rapids: Baker, 1984), p 1046.

¹⁰ Material here is taken from the *Los Angeles Times*, dated 12 December 1989, part B, p 1.

international headlines in November 1990 when its rector announced that he would begin performing blessings in church of 'same-sex' couples.

So why is this church growing, when it is not evangelical? Just about every other church with such liberal social commitments is losing members in droves. Because the phenomenon is so unusual, it has been studied with particular care. Donald E. Miller, professor of religion at University of Southern California's school of religion, puts his finger on the point at issue: although the church is liberal in its politics, 'it is also deeply conservative in its recognition of the importance of worship, pastoral care, and personal spiritual disciplines.'[11] Attention to the personal spiritual needs and concerns of its individual members seems to have been the key in this situation. People need help with prayer, devotion and personal discipline – and if evangelicalism is not providing it, is it really surprising that they may turn elsewhere?

Evangelicals are often told by their catholic colleagues that they have no spirituality worth talking about. It is perhaps inevitable that this becomes a self-fulfilling prophecy, in that it brings about a sense of inferiority within evangelical circles. Many evangelicals, convinced that they have nothing to offer in this area, promptly draw on the resources of other traditions. It is little surprise to note that many who begin their Christian life as evangelicals end up on the more catholic wing of the church, on account of the perceived superiority of its spirituality.

I write as one who is deeply appreciative of the catholic tradition, especially within my own Church of England. I have no hesitation in declaring that I have learned much from my more catholic colleagues, especially concerning the need for personal discipline and the importance of community for spiritual development. I expect to learn more so in the future, when I finish my study of the great French spiritual writers of the late seventeenth century, such as Bossuet and Fénelon. My concern is clearly not to criticize catholicism, in any of its forms. It is simply to note that, for some evangelicals, catholic forms of spirituality can be the thin end of a wedge. For some, catholic

---

[11] Donald E. Miller, 'Bucking a Powerful Trend', in *All Saints Church Every Member Canvas '90* (Pasadena, 1990). See also his paper 'Liberal Church Growth: A Case Study', delivered at the Society for the Scientific Study of Religion, Salt Lake City, Utah, 27-29 October 1989.

spirituality leads to more catholic forms of theology. And why? Because there is something wrong with evangelical theology? No. It is, quite simply, that evangelicalism is seen to lack a spirituality to give its theology staying power in the modem period.

3. Clarifying Terms: 'Spirituality'

Spirituality has become one of the buzz words of our time. It has been taken up with enthusiasm by many evangelicals. It is, however, a word with highly questionable associations, and a dubious historical pedigree. Let me indicate the anxieties which I have in mind. In a careful study, Owen Chadwick, until recently professor of modern history at the University of Cambridge, points out how the origins of the modern term 'spirituality' and many other related terms (such as 'the inner life' or 'the interior life') lie in the French spiritual writings of the seventeenth century.[12] From its beginnings, the term has strong associations with 'a striving after the purely material'. Seventeenth-century French writers, deploring the development of negative attitudes towards the material order, were prone to lay the blame firmly upon la nouvelle spiritualité de Madam Guyon.[13]

The word 'spirituality' thus appears to have been associated initially with a radical division between the spiritual and the physical, between the soul and the body, between contemplation and everyday life. It implies that its subject is primarily the interior nurture of the soul, undertaken in withdrawal from the distractions of ordinary life. The older vocabulary of the Protestant tradition reflects more faithfully a central aspect of its spirituality – the total integration of faith and

---

[12] Owen Chadwick, 'Indifference and Morality', in P. N. Brooks (ed.), *Christian Spirituality: Essays in Honour of Gordon Rupp* (London: SCM Press, 1975), pp 203-230.

[13] Jeanne Marie Bouvier de la Mothe, generally known as Madam Guyon (1648-1717), was a vigorous defender of the 'Quietist' doctrines of total indifference to everything, including the hope of salvation, and the practice of non-cognitive meditation, in which the believer refuses to focus on definite ideas, such as the nature of God or the life of Christ. Her concept of spirituality, especially as it is found in her *Moyen court et trés facile de faire oraison* (1685), brings out the radically introverted associations of the term at this time.

everyday life.[14]

We can begin to neutralize this difficulty if we are more attentive to the Pauline idea, so faithfully echoed by Luther, of the 'spiritual' as life in the world orientated towards God, and move away from the unhelpful association of the term with the idea of 'life undertaken in withdrawal from the world'. In its fundamental sense, spirituality is concerned with the shaping, empowering and maturing of the 'spiritual person (*pneumatikos anthrōpos*)' (1 Corinthians 2:14-15) – that is, the person who is alive to and responsive to God in the world, as opposed to the person who merely exists within and responds to the world. As Luther reminded us, the reference is to *totus homo* – the 'entire person', and not just the mind.[15] Robert Banks expresses this holistic view of spirituality well when he speaks of it as 'the character and quality of our life with God, among fellow-Christians and in the world'. Banks deliberately avoids two inadequate approaches to spirituality – a purely intellectual or cerebral approach, which engages the mind and nothing else, and a purely interiorized approach, which bears no relation to the realities of everyday life. Spirituality concerns our 'spirit' – yet, as Banks forcefully reminds us, 'not only our spirit – also our minds, wills, imaginations, feelings and bodies.'[16] There is no difficulty in reclaiming this authentic sense of the term within the evangelical tradition, with its vital concern – shaped and nourished both by Scripture and the Reformers – to map out the contours of responsible Christian living in the world.

4. Clarifying Terms: 'Evangelical'

It may be helpful to pause at this point, and explore the contours of that elusive term 'evangelical'. The term 'evangelical' dates from the sixteenth century, and is used to refer to catholic writers wishing to revert to more biblical beliefs and practices than those associated with

---

[14] Thus there is no entry on 'spirituality' in D. McKim (ed.), *Encyclopaedia of the Reformed Faith* (Louisville, KY: Westminster/John Knox Press, 1992); the material relating to this theme is to be found under the entry 'piety' (pp 278-279).

[15] Gerhard Ebeling, Lutherstudien II: Disputatio de homine, Text und Hintergrund (Tubingen: Mohr, 1977), pp 31-43.

[16] Robert M. Banks, 'Home Churches and Spirituality', *Interchange* 40 (1986), p 15.

the late medieval church. It is used especially in the 1520s, when the terms *'evangelique'* and *'evangelisch'* come to feature prominently in polemical writings of the early Reformation. In the 1530s, the term 'Protestant' came to become more significant. However, this term was imposed upon evangelicals by their opponents, and was not one of their own choosing. 'Evangelical' is the term chosen by evangelicals to refer to themselves.

Evangelicalism began to emerge as a movement of major public importance in the United States in the period after the Second World War. Billy Graham, perhaps the most publicly visible representative of this new evangelical style, became a well-known figure in English society, and a role model for a younger generation of evangelical ordinands in England. His three-month crusade at Harringay during 1954 proved to have a major impact upon British Christianity. The public recognition in America of the new importance and public visibility of evangelicalism dates from the early 1970s. The crisis of confidence within American liberal Christianity in the 1960s was widely interpreted to signal the need for the emergence of a new and more publicly credible form of Christian belief.[17] In 1976, America woke up to find itself living in what Newsweek magazine designated the 'Year of the Evangelical', with a born-again Christian (Jimmy Carter) as its President, and an unprecedented media interest in evangelicalism.[18]

These developments could not pass unnoticed and unheeded in England. The result has been a changing attitude towards evangelicalism, with even the British quality press discovering that there is more to evangelicalism than the mere playing of guitars in church. The older stereotypes have died. In 1955, Canon H. K. Luce of Durham complained that Billy Graham was being allowed to lead a mission to the University of Cambridge. Universities, he argued, existed for the advancement of learning; so why was Billy Graham being allowed to speak at Cambridge?

---

[17] Leonard E. Sweet, 'The 1960s: The Crises of Liberal Christianity and the Public Emergence of Evangelicalism', in Marsden, *Evangelicalism and Modern America*, pp 29-45.

[18] There is a massive literature: see, for example, Robert C. Liebman and Robert Wuthnow, *The New Christian Right: Mobilization and Legitimation* (New York: Aldine Publishing, 1983); Richard Quebedeaux, *The Young Evangelicals* (New York: Harper & Row, 1974); Judith L. Blumhofer and Joel A. Carpenter, *Twentieth Century Evangelicalism: A Guide to the Sources* (New York: Garland Publishing, 1990).

Is it not time that our religious leaders made it plain that while they respect, or even admire, Dr Graham's sincerity and personal power, they cannot regard fundamentalism as likely to issue in anything but disillusionment and disaster for educated men and women in this twentieth-century world?[19]

Luce's prophecy of doom and gloom was unfounded, despite the widespread support it gained from older Anglicans, threatened by this new development. A single episode will illustrate the changing mood within the Church of England within my lifetime. (I was born in 1953, the year before the Harringay crusade.) In 1957, John Stott led a student mission at the University of Durham. This provoked a hostile and ill-tempered attack from Michael Ramsay, then bishop of Durham, who wrote scathingly of 'our English Fundamentalism' – referring to the views associated with John Stott.[20] Just over thirty years later, it became clear that such wooden stereotypes now firmly belonged to the past; Robert Runcie, towards the end of his period as Primate, described this same John Stott as the greatest Anglican since William Temple.

It is still, sadly, true that some recent writers of an older generation still use the term 'fundamentalist' and 'evangelical' interchangeably, to mean little more than 'someone committed to the authority of Scripture'. As Clark Pinnock observes, the word 'fundamentalist' is 'more often than not a word of contempt, a theological swear-word'. This is certainly the case with James Barr's abusive and polemical book *Fundamentalism* (1977).[21] As Pinnock observes, 'the people Barr is sharply and vehemently criticizing, the British evangelicals, do not like the term being applied to them because they are not, in fact, fundamentalists'.[22]

In order to understand the essential differences between 'evangelicalism' and 'fundamentalism', it is necessary to turn to the North American situation, and the careful analysis of the relation between fundamentalism and evangelicalism presented by leading

---

[19] Letter to *The Times*, dated 15 August, 1955.
[20] See his earlier letter to *The Times*, dated 20 August 1955, in which he spoke of the 'crudity' of he doctrines of evangelicalism, and its 'stifling of the mind'.
[21] James Barr, *Fundamentalism* (London: SCM Press, 1977).
[22] Clark Pinnock, 'Defining American Fundamentalism: A Response', in N. J. Cohen (ed.), *The Fundamentalist Phenomenon* (Grand Rapids: Eerdmans, 1990), pp 38-55; quotes at pp 40-41.

(non-evangelical) historians of American religion; most notably George Marsden (Duke University) and Martin E. Marty (University of Chicago). Fundamentalism arose as a religious reaction within American culture to the rise of a secular culture.[23] It was from its outset, and has remained, a counter-cultural movement, using central doctrinal affirmations as a means of defining cultural boundaries. Certain central doctrines (most notably, the absolute literal authority of Scripture and the premillenial return of Christ) were treated as barriers, intended as much to alienate secular culture as to give fundamentalists a sense of identity and purpose. A siege mentality became characteristic of the movement; fundamentalist counter-communities viewed themselves as walled cities, or (to evoke the pioneer spirit) circles of wagons, defending their distinctives against an unbelieving culture.[24]

The emphasis upon the premillenial return of Christ is of especial significance. This view has a long history; it never attained any especial degree of significance prior to the nineteenth century. However, fundamentalism appears to have discerned in the idea an important weapon against the liberal Christian idea of a kingdom of God upon earth, to be achieved through social action. 'Dispensationalism', especially of a premillenarian type, became an integral element of fundamentalism. Such dispensationalist views, it must be stressed, have had minimal impact within English evangelicalism of any shape during the twentieth century.

Evangelicalism centres upon a cluster of four assumptions. These are not 'doctrinal', if this term is understood to refer purely to a set of objectively-valid beliefs; they are 'existential', in that they affirm the manner in which the believer is caught up in a redemptive and experiential encounter with the living Christ.

1. The authority and sufficiency of Scripture.

2. The uniqueness of redemption through the death of Christ upon the cross.

3. The need for personal conversion.

---

[23] The definitive study remains George Marsden, *Fundamentalism and American Culture: The Shaping of Twentieth Century Evangelicalism 1870-1925* (New York: Oxford University Press, 1980).

[24] Martin E. Marty, 'Fundamentalism as a Social Phenomenon', in *Evangelicalism and Modern America*, ed. George Marsden (Grand Rapids: Eerdmans, 1984), pp 56-70.

4. The necessity, propriety and urgency of evangelism.

All other matters have tended to be regarded as 'matters of indifference', upon which a substantial degree of pluralism may be accepted.

I have stressed that evangelicalism is not characterised purely by a set of doctrines. If anything, it is more of an ethos, an approach to Christian thinking and living which centres upon a number of guiding principles, rather than specific doctrinal formulations. Scripture is treated as far more than a theological source; it is the basis of Christian living and devotion, personal and corporate. Evangelicalism has always refused to treat 'knowledge of God' as something abstract; instead, it recognizes it to be strongly experiential and personal, capable of transforming both the heart and the mind. There is a sense in which evangelicalism is better defined as a devotional ethos than as a theological system. There is a creative intermingling here of the Reformed and the Pietist – an emphasis upon right doctrine, linked with a real concern for a 'living faith' – that is, a personally appropriated and assimilated faith, expressed in such terms as 'a personal relationship with Christ'.

The devotional use of Scripture is thus of central importance to evangelicals. It must be appreciated that this approach involves reading Scripture in a certain manner – not as the basis of a theological system, nor merely for intellectual stimulation, but for the spiritual nourishment of the reader. The 'knowledge' of God which is aimed at is at least as experiential as it is cognitive, with its concern for a 'deeply based consciousness'[25] of the Lord.

Again, evangelicalism is not committed to a specific theological theory of conversion, but to a recognition of the need for personal conversion.[26] Kern Robert Trembath, in a perceptive analysis of evangelicalism's emphasis upon the experiential aspects of faith, comments that:

> In defining as 'evangelical' members of a great range of denominations, evangelicalism discloses a greater implicit emphasis upon the experience of salvation in Jesus than upon

---
[25] Houston, 'Spirituality', p 1046.
[26] Note the emphasis placed on the idea by Max Warren, *What is an Evangelical?* (London: Church Book Room Press, 1944), p 23.

cognitive, dogmatic and historical articulations of this experience. Such articulations are not valueless altogether, but are simply of less value than they are to a non-evangelical or 'denominational' mindset. Thus, considered ecclesiologically, evangelicalism is Protestantism's clearest attempt to recapture the pluralist nature of the early church.[27]

An evangelical spirituality will thus be Bible-centred, and concerned more with the facilitation and enhancement of the personal redemptive encounter of the believer with Christ than with precise theological formulation, or with an emphasis upon the merits of one particular denominational approach to the matter. 'The test of Christian spirituality is conformity of heart and life to the confession and character of Jesus as Lord'.[28] Evangelical approaches to spirituality thus aim to resonate with these central concerns, while opening the way to serious engagement with personal discipline, spiritual formation, and the various difficulties that anyone trying to deepen the quality of their spiritual life routinely encounters.

Yet where evangelicalism ought to be devoting its enormous creativity and theological strengths to the forging of patterns of spirituality suited to the evangelical ethos, it appears instead to have been crippled by some form of lethargy in this vital area. This is a feature of evangelicalism worldwide, not simply in England. Australian evangelical John Waterhouse contributed a significant article to the April 1992 number of the leading Australian Christian magazine *On Being*, with the provocative title 'The Crisis of Evangelicalism.'

> Ten years ago, I felt we were on the edge of an evangelical renaissance in Australia, a flowering of biblical scholarship that would touch secular society at its point of need and lead Australians to a new awareness of their creator. It even had a name: 'a theology of everyday life' or 'incarnational theology'. We got out some books that seemed to do the job ... but then

---

[27] Kern Robert Trembath, *Evangelical Theories of Biblical Inspiration* (New York: Oxford University Press, 1987), p 4.

[28] T. R. Albin, 'Spirituality', in S. Ferguson and D. F. Wright (eds), *New Dictionary of Theology* (Leicester: Inter-Varsity Press, 1988), pp 656-8; quote at p 657.

they stopped.[29]

Waterhouse, the founder and publishing director of the New South Wales publishing house Albatross Books, did much to encourage this new spirituality.[30] But it dried up. For Waterhouse, part of the 'crisis' is that evangelicalism has suffered 'a loss of spiritual energy, originality and creativity'. In short: evangelicalism has become spiritually derivative. Instead of falling back on its own distinctive approach to spirituality, evangelicalism has become lazy. It has borrowed other people's.

In failing to give full attention to this network of issues centring upon spirituality, evangelicals fail the modern church. Evangelicalism owes that church the duty of ensuring that its distinctive approaches to spirituality remain alive, credible and available. It is shocking that evangelicalism should be so parasitic in this manner, exploiting the spiritual riches of other traditions, yet failing to make its own distinctive contributions available to the church at large. Evangelicalism has too often become blind to its own heritage, unable to discern this heritage itself, let alone share it with others. As a result, the modern church is being denied access to a resource which ought to be there – a spirituality which is radically and consistently grounded in Scripture, and orientated towards the cross. Modern evangelicalism has a duty to ensure that this kind of spirituality remains a viable option in today's church. But how? In the remainder of this lecture, I want to identify the difficulties, and make some suggestions concerning the way ahead.

5. Evangelical Spirituality: Problems and Proposals

In the past, evangelicalism has been associated with certain quite definite approaches to the spiritual life, especially the personal 'Quiet Time'. However, these approaches to spirituality, which have worked well in the past and have a distinguished history of use behind them, do

---

[29] John Waterhouse, 'The Crisis of Evangelicalism', *On Being* 18 No. 2 (April, 1992), pp 4-8. Quote at p 4.

[30] An example of the works that Waterhouse has in mind would presumably be Robert M. Banks, *All the Business of Life: Bringing Theology Down to Earth* (Sutherland, NSW: Albatross, 1987).

not seem to work as well as we might like today. Why not? I would like to suggest several reasons which allow us to understand the problem we are faced with today, and allow us to be realistic in planning for the future.

5.1   Ignorance of the heritage of the past

Evangelicals are often inattentive to or confused about their own spiritual heritage. In part, this difficulty arises from the circumstances of their conversion. Many evangelicals are 'born-again' Christians, who have come to faith from a secular context, sometimes at later stages in their lives. They have not been nurtured in the evangelical tradition from birth. It is something that they have to discover in later life, as part of the total package of reorientation which accompanies their conversion. Few have the time to become acquainted with the evangelical spiritual heritage of the past, when they have other matters which require to be given higher priority.

A colleague of mine, having just read a work on prayer by the well-known evangelical writer, Joyce Huggett, put the book down with intense irritation.[31] 'Doesn't she know anything about evangelical spirituality?' he asked in utter exasperation. The medieval catholic spiritual tradition seemed to be well represented. But what of evangelicalism? What of the great Puritan writers, whose writings on prayer remain among the classics of Christendom?[32] This lectureship is intended to celebrate the achievements of the 'Puritan School of Divinity'; in pointing to that past spiritual greatness, I find myself embarrassed to turn back to the present, both in its state of spiritual impoverishment and its ignorance concerning the past. There is a powerful challenge to us here from the past. The Reformers and the Puritans – to name only two groups of people – have enormous spiritual resources to offer the modern church. Yet the Reformation work ethic – which is not the same as the secularized Protestant work ethic – seems

---

[31] The work in question was Joyce Huggett, *Listening to God* (London: Hodder & Stoughton, 1986).

[32] For an excellent introduction, see James I. Packer, *Among God's Giants: Aspects of Puritan Christianity* (Eastbourne: Kingsway, 1991). The potential of Puritan spirituality to the situation of the modern church is further explored in Packer's 1991 St Antholin lecture, 'A Man for All Ministries: Richard Baxter, 1615-1691.' See pages 25-45 above.

to have had virtually no impact in modern evangelicalism.

In his recent survey of the outlooks of younger American evangelicals, James Davison Hunter pointed out that they had no real idea of the spiritual relevance of work.[33] It had become something ordinary and humdrum. Something has been lost here. Yet this case is cited, not because it is of vital importance in itself, but because it points to a seriously worrying trend: evangelicals are unaware of their own roots, and the riches that these have to offer the modern church.[34]

One of the reasons for the considerable success of evangelicalism in recent years has been its willingness to relate to the issues of the day, rather than indulge in the luxury of nostalgia for the past. This has, however, often led to a devaluation of our heritage. The publication of the Library of the Fathers and Library of Anglo-Catholic Theology gave the nineteenth-century catholic wing of the Church of England a solid intellectual and spiritual foundation upon which it could build. We can learn from that example.

Some are learning already. Many younger evangelicals, especially in the United States, are rediscovering classic evangelical spiritualities, and are working towards refashioning them to meet the needs of our own day and age.[35] Jim Packer's *Among God's Giants* is an excellent example of a work by an older evangelical leader which conveys the relevance of this tradition to the needs of the modern church; others can be instanced without difficulty. The Puritans emerge as individuals with real insights for the spiritual difficulties and dilemmas which confront Christians in the modern period. But much more needs to be done. We need, as a matter of some urgency, to make past forms of spirituality – such as those linked with the Puritans – intelligible and accessible, as a duty both to evangelicalism and to the wider church at large. Current neglect of our heritage in no way precludes its rediscovery, along with other new approaches awaiting to be found and used. Just as the woman rejoiced at finding her missing

---

[33] James Davison Hunter, *Evangelicalism: The Coming Generation* (Chicago: University of Chicago Press, 1987).

[34] I explored this point with particular reference to the neglect of the spirituality of the sixteenth-century Reformation in *Roots that Refresh: A Celebration of Reformation Spirituality* (London: Hodder & Stoughton, 1992).

[35] An example is provided by Timothy Keller, 'Puritan Resources for Biblical Counselling', *The Journal of Pastoral Practice* 9 No. 3 (1988), pp 11-44.

coin (Luke 15:8-9), so we can share the joy of rediscovering spiritualities that our forebears knew, and which have since been lost. Yet there are surely other Christ-centred and Scripture-nourished ways of living the Christian life, waiting to be uncovered and developed! Our task is not simply to rediscover the past; it is to construct the future.

5.2   Things have changed!

Many of the classical evangelical approaches to the spiritual life were developed in the seventeenth and eighteenth centuries. They reflect the periods of their origin. Often, they presupposed degrees of leisure and an absence of personal pressure which are totally unrealistic in the midst of the stress and tensions of modern western life. Whatever their past greatness, they have often proved unworkable in the modern era. For example, the classic 'Quiet Time' is a virtual impossibility for many of my colleagues in the highly stressed worlds of business and medicine, where personal space is a rare and cherished luxury. Echoing the received wisdom of the past, Billy Graham counselled new Christians to read their Bibles daily; without this 'daily spiritual nourishment', they could expect to starve and lose their spiritual vitality.[36] That advice, given forty years ago, has become increasingly problematic, with changes in the pace of living and modern lifestyles leading to many new Christians finding themselves being presented with demands which prove to be quite unrealistic. Their faith comes to be made dependent upon something which cannot be sustained in the long term.

Yet evangelicalism has traditionally – and, it must be said, with considerable wisdom – reacted against any tendencies which could lead to the reification or the invalid objectification of spiritual practices, so that these become seen as an end in themselves, rather than the means to a greater end. Thus evangelicals prefer to speak of 'praying to the Lord' rather than 'saying prayers'; the former focusses upon the end of prayer, which is an enhanced communion with the Lord, whereas the latter focusses upon a human activity. Indeed, one of the major evangelical concerns relating to 'spirituality' is that the emphasis often seems to fall upon human activities and practices as ends in themselves, rather than as a means to deepen a personal relationship with God. The

---

[36] Billy Graham, *Peace with God* (Kingswood: World's Work, 1954), pp 152-154.

evangelical will insist that emphasis falls upon the personal relationship between the believer and God, rather than upon spiritual disciplines in themselves.

The traditional Quiet Time must therefore not be allowed to become an end in itself. It falls to us to try to develop ways of reading Scripture or praying which are realistic in the modern period, are tailored to the personal rhythms of the individual, and yet retain a thorough grounding and immersion in Scripture. A respect for the past does not mean that we are wedded to that past; we owe it to our evangelical forebears to embody their vision in practices which are more suited to our changed situation. Above all, we need to take the sheer humanity of those to whom we minister much more seriously – a point which we may consider in more detail.

5.3 The Evangelical Neglect of the Human Factor

Many start the life of faith with great enthusiasm, only to discover themselves in difficulty shortly afterwards. Their high hopes and good intentions seem to fade away. The spirit may be willing, but the flesh proves weak. Fallen human nature all too often proves incapable of sustaining the high levels of enthusiasm and commitment which characterize the early days of faith. People need support, to keep them going when enthusiasm fades.

Catholic spirituality – as evidenced in the writings of Teresa of Avila, Brother Lawrence or Thomas à Kempis – has provided just such a support system for many in the past, precisely because it pays attention to the human side of the religious life, without neglecting the God-ward side of things. It is all very well to stress the total sufficiency of the gospel, and to focus on God as he has made himself known and available in Jesus Christ; but that gospel is addressed to sinful human beings, who need all the help that they can get to live by its precepts and harness its power in their lives. Evangelicalism, by too often stressing merely the God-ward side of the Christian life, has often been guilty of neglecting the human side of things.

Evangelicalism rightly insists that the quest for human identity, authenticity and fulfilment cannot be undertaken in isolation from God. But that is only half the story. What about ourselves? What about the needs and weaknesses of those to whom the gospel is addressed? Calvin states this principle with characteristic lucidity in the opening sentence of the 1559 edition of his *Institutes of the Christian Religion*: 'Nearly all the wisdom we possess, that is to say, true and sound wisdom, consists of two parts: the knowledge of God and of ourselves. And although they are closely connected, it is difficult to say which comes first.'[37] Precisely the same point is made in Jacques Bénigne Bossuet's *Traité de la connaissance de Dieu et de soi-même* (published posthumously in 1722), and is a leading theme of that major catholic writer's spirituality.

There are thus two aspects to the Christian life – knowing God, and knowing ourselves. ('Knowing' here designates 'knowing and experiencing', as one 'knows' a person). These cannot be separated, according to Calvin.[38] Thus any notion of spirituality as a quest for heightened religious experience as an end in itself is totally alien to the outlook of classic evangelicalism. 'Feel good' spiritualities are unacceptable, unless they are firmly grounded in scriptural passages which give us reasons to 'feel good'. The extensive appeal made to secular psychological and psychoanalytical disciplines in recent 'inner life' spirituality – such as Morton Kelsey's Christo-Psychology and much New Age material – needs to be criticized.[39] To draw upon insights concerning the human condition is only half of the story that Christian spirituality is concerned to tell; indeed, if only half of that story is told, it has not been properly and authentically told at all.

But perhaps evangelicalism in its turn has only told half the story. It has neglected to give weight to the human weaknesses and needs which make certain forms of spirituality so attractive an option for so many people. David Powlinson, who teaches at Westminster Seminary, Philadelphia, explains the attraction of psychology to many evangelical pastors along the following lines:

The church has become weak in the domain of personal and

---

[37] John Calvin, *Institutes of the Christian Religion* 2 vols (Grand Rapids: Eerdmans, 1975), vol. 1, p 37.

[38] For a full discussion, see W. Balke, 'The Word of God and Experientia according to Calvin', in W. H. Neuser (ed.), *Calvinus ecclesiae doctor* (Kampen: Kok Pharos, 1978), pp 19-31; Edward A. Dewey, *The Knowledge of God in Calvin's Theology* (New York: Columbia University Press, 1952); T. H. L. Parker, *Calvin's Doctrine of the Knowledge of God* revised edition (Edinburgh: Oliver & Boyd, 1969).

[39] The uncritical use of such psychological material in evangelical contexts has been documented by James Hunter, in his Evangelicalism: *The Coming Generation*, pp 64-71, and also his *American Evangelicalism: Conservative Religion and the Quandary of Modernity* (New Brunswick: Rutgers University Press, 1983), pp 91-99.

interpersonal problems. Evangelical churches and theologians have typically not grappled with the problems in living that Christian people have. The church has either misconstrued, oversimplified, or avoided facing the existential and situational realities of human experience in the trenches of life.[40]

Powlinson's analysis is highly suggestive. It points to a failure to address the realities of the human situation – the 'existential and situational realities of human experience in the trenches of life' which make spiritualities which centre upon human needs so attractive to many Christians, who feel that their spiritual lives are impoverished, and find evangelicalism unable or unwilling to offer them guidance.

Yet we have neglected our own heritage here. Calvin spoke of God 'accommodating himself to our abilities' – in other words, God, knowing our needs and abilities, revealed himself in a form suited and adapted to us.[41] Powlinson points out how the Puritans knew this, and developed pastoral strategies and approaches to spirituality to cope with it. But not, it seems, any more. Now others outside evangelicalism have addressed this issue better than we have; the result is that, in the long term, we are losing people to Christian traditions which address this problem, or to secular psychotherapies in which the 'human factor' is given pride of place. If we cannot change human nature, then we must ensure that forms of spirituality which are authentically evangelical are on offer in the religious marketplace.

It was concern over these issues which led my wife and myself to write a book relating to a major area of modern concern – self-esteem. Alarmed at the uncritical incorporation of secular notions of human nature, value and destiny into influential works such as Robert Schuller's *Self-Esteem*,[42] we decided to develop an approach to the issues surrounding self-esteem which was biblical, yet also responsive

---

[40] David Powlinson, 'Integration or Inundation?', in M. Horton (ed.), *Power Religion: The Selling out of the Evangelical Church?* (Chicago: Moody Press, 1992), pp 191-218; quote at p 200.
[41] Ford Lewis Battles, 'God was accommodating himself to Human Capacity', *Interpretation* 31 (1977), pp 19-38.
[42] Robert H. Schuller, *Self-Esteem: The New Reformation* (Waco, Texas: Word Books, 1982).

to helpful insights from psychology.[43] My wife studied experimental psychology at Oxford, before going on to undertake further studies at the Institute of Psychiatry in London, and currently is principal clinical psychologist in Oxford. Together, she and I were able to bring together psychology and theology in a responsible and thoroughly Christian manner. That needs to be done more often!

5.4 A Lack of Evangelical Role Models

Many people genuinely feel the need for a 'spiritual director', someone who will offer them spiritual guidance, discipline and support over a long period. And, sensing that this is not a real option within evangelicalism, they will look for this kind of direction outside. The result? Some evangelicals end up adopting both the theology and the spirituality of their more catholic colleagues. I have seen many of my students here in Oxford gradually lose sight of their evangelical roots in just this way. Yet in the past, evangelicals were aware of the vital role that experienced Christians could play in the spiritual formation of their younger colleagues. The 'letters of spiritual counsel' of great Christian pastors and leaders are a powerful reminder of the importance of this kind of nurturing and guidance in the past history of evangelicalism. Somehow, we seem to have lost sight of our heritage here.

I suspect that this situation will change as the years pass. However, at the moment, there are not enough active and credible practitioners of the craft of evangelical spiritual direction. One of the reasons why many seem to have lost confidence in evangelical spirituality is that there are relatively few individuals publicly available to embody that spirituality. We need national conferences, to identify resource people, books, approaches, methods and possibilities. We need international summer schools, to allow us to see what is happening at the global level in this field, in the hope that we may learn from what is going on elsewhere. We need local workshops, to allow all concerned with strategies for the deepening of faith to come together, and share our experiences, hopes and frustrations. In short: we need to get spirituality on the evangelical agenda, and make sure it stays there until we get this one sorted out.

---

[43] Joanna McGrath and Alister McGrath, *The Dilemma of Self-Esteem: The Cross and Christian Confidence* (Wheaton, Ill., and Cambridge, UK: Crossway Books, 1992).

5.5 Spirituality is still not a Core Element in Evangelical Theological Training and Education

Where are the evangelical institutions dedicated to promoting evangelical spirituality? Regent College, Vancouver, currently has two chairs of 'spiritual theology', occupied by the distinguished writers and speakers James M. Houston and Eugene H. Peterson. This development offers exciting possibilities for the development and consolidation of evangelical spiritualities; yet sadly, it is an exception, rather than the rule. All too often, there is a massive blind spot here in evangelical institutions, which serves only to perpetuate the neglect and devaluing of evangelical spirituality.

Equally, where are the journals of evangelical spirituality? There is now no shortage of such specialist journals devoted to evangelical theology. Yet evangelicalism has always had its greatest strengths in the pulpit, on the mission field, and on its knees. As I stressed earlier, its distinctive feature is not so much a theology, as a devotional ethos. There is an obvious need for a journal devoted to this theme. Evangelicalism can draw upon a variety of resources – the Reformation, the Puritans, the evangelical revivals of the eighteenth century, the holiness movement, and the charismatic movement – in seeking to confront and transform the future, aided and challenged by the resources of the past.

6. Rediscovering the Sacraments

One area of weakness in contemporary evangelical approaches to spirituality perhaps needs highlighting. This is the marginalization of the sacraments, especially the Lord's Supper or Holy Communion, from our ways of thinking. Evangelicalism has always been prone to treat the sacraments with suspicion. In a thoughtful essay, my Oxford colleague Peter Southwell identifies a number of reasons for this devaluation of the sacraments, not least a fear of superstition and a concern that services with a sacramental emphasis may hinder the proclamation of the gospel to outsiders.[44] Nevertheless, he concludes with a plea for evangelical attitudes to the sacraments to conform more closely to the characteristic evangelical reverence of Scripture and concern for evangelism:

> The proclamation of the Lord's death for our salvation inherent in [the Holy Communion] serves well the varied pastoral, theological and evangelistic needs of those who witness or participate in it. Physical things matter; Christ's incarnation proves it. The ways in which God has invited us to use some of these – water, bread, wine and oil among them – are to our own souls' health as we meet him and he meets us, when we use them according to his command, according to scriptural principles, and with all the love, imagination and care to which the church's Spirit-taught mind can rise.[45]

The modern evangelical suspicion of the sacraments contrasts sharply with the emphasis placed upon their kerygmatic, pastoral and spiritual role by leading writers of the Reformation, including Martin Luther and John Calvin.[46] While I do not have time to develop this point in this lecture, it seems to me to be imperative that we explore the enormous potential of the sacraments, supremely the Lord's Supper, for personal devotion and reflection.

For example, Luther appeals to the communion service to bring home in a powerful and tangible way that God's promises are both real and costly. The death of Christ is seen as a token of both the trustworthiness and the enormous price of the grace of God. Luther develops this point by using the idea of a 'testament', understood in the sense of a 'last will and testament'.

A testament is a promise made by someone who is about to die,

---

[44] Peter Southwell, 'Evangelicalism and the Sacraments', in R. T. France and A. E. McGrath (eds), *Evangelical Anglicans* (London: SPCK, 1993), pp 71-81.

[45] Southwell, 'Evangelicalism and the Sacraments', p 80.

[46] I stress this point in *Roots that Refresh*, pp 161-9 in which I explore the role of the sacraments for Reformation spirituality. For a more detailed analysis, see Alister E. McGrath, *Reformation Thought: An Introduction* (Oxford: Blackwell, second edition, 1993), pp 159-187. For a recent study of reflection on the role of the Communion service by evangelical Anglicans, see Christopher J. Cocksworth, *Evangelical Eucharistic Thought In the Church of England* (Cambridge: Cambridge University Press, 1993).

in which a bequest is defined and heirs appointed. A testament thus involves, in the first place, the death of the testator, and in the second, the promise of an inheritance and the naming of heirs ... We see these things clearly in the words of Christ. Christ testifies concerning his death when he says, 'This is my body, which is given' and 'This is my blood, which is poured out'. He names and designates the bequest when he says 'for the forgiveness of sins'. And he appoints the heirs when he says, 'for you and for many', that is, for those who accept and believe the promise of the testator.

Luther's insight here is that a testament involves promises which become operational only after the death of the person who made those promises in the first place. The liturgy of the communion service thus makes three vitally important points.

1. It affirms the promises of grace and forgiveness.
2. It identifies those to whom those promises are made.
3. It declares the death of the one who made those promises.

The mass thus dramatically proclaims that the promises of grace and forgiveness are now in effect. It is 'a promise of the forgiveness of sins made to us by God, and such a promise as has been confirmed by the death of the son of God.' By proclaiming the death of Christ, the community of faith affirms that the precious promises of forgiveness and eternal life are now effective for those with faith. The communion service thus reinforces both faith and devotion, by bringing home the reality and costliness of our redemption in a deeply evocative, memorable and moving manner. Perhaps we would do well to rediscover some of these approaches, which past fear and suspicion, however justified, have obscured.

7. Role Models for Evangelical Spirituality

One of the weaknesses which I pointed out earlier in this lecture is that there is something of an absence of role models for those concerned to foster evangelical approaches to the Christian life. This is not to say that there are none working in this area; it is to say there are not enough. But who are they? Last year, I decided to dip into the output of Christian publishing houses over the last few years, in search of writers whose approaches are genuinely evangelical. My selection is neither exhaustive nor definitive. It is simply illustrative, to indicate the kind of material that is already there, and which might point us in helpful directions as we seek to develop skills, tools and methods to meet the challenges of what lies before us. My concern is to identify possible role models for all of us wrestling with the issues noted in this lecture, as, a stimulus to further reflection. The individuals whom I shall identify are like landmarks, identifying positions of importance to travellers who wish to move on beyond the regions that have thus been marked. I must stress that many other individuals could be added to this list!

In the first place, such an evangelical spirituality will be Scripture-centred. However, this is a necessary yet not a sufficient condition. It is not simply that Scripture must be at the heart of evangelical spirituality; it must be approached and read in a certain manner. Scripture can be read with the cool critical detachment of the scholar, who treats this text 'as if it were any other book' (Benjamin Jowett). The distinction between a critical and a devotional commentary is well-founded. Scripture must be approached and read in the sure and confident expectation that God will speak to the reader. By meditating upon the scriptural text, the reader can deepen his or her relationship with God, forging a deeper bond of commitment, adoration, fellowship and love.

The importance of Scripture is easily stated. What is considerably more difficult, and arguably more important, is to develop methods of enabling readers to engage in a more satisfactory and fulfilling manner with the biblical text. One of the most satisfactory means of doing this, in my view, is that developed by Eugene Peterson. Peterson's technique, developed in works such as *A Long Obedience* – reflections on the 'Songs of Ascents' (Psalms 120-134), is to engage the reader's attention as he reflects on the meaning of biblical texts, and relates them to the situations of everyday life. He offers an extended meditation on the text, which makes a judicious appeal to the imagination – that vital human resource which has been so badly neglected by a generation of evangelicals who have soaked up the strongly rational spirit of the Enlightenment, and allowed such a rationalism to stifle our ability to imagine.[47]

In the second place, an evangelical spirituality will place considerable emphasis upon the transforming character of the knowledge of God. John Calvin stressed that 'knowledge of God' was no indifferent matter, but something which resulted in obedience on the one hand, and adoration on the other. This is a natural consequence of 'devotional' Bible study. 'When the death and resurrection of Jesus Christ have affected our lives in such a way, our transformed desires will immediately witness to the change within us.'[48] However, people need help and guidance as to how such study can transform their relationship with God, or their feelings and emotions.

James Houston has offered us invaluable guidance on how to address these issues in two recent works, *The Transforming Friendship* (1990) and *The Heart's Desire* (1992). In each case, Houston explores the way in which meditation and prayer can change our perception of God, our relationship with him, and our experience of him. Each work is richly illustrated with helpful quotations from the great writers of the past, and brief case studies of individuals to whom readers can relate. Throughout the works, there is a persistent and persuasive affirmation of the way in which knowing God changes things. Houston is perhaps one of the most lucid exponents of the dangers of allowing head and heart to go their separate and unrelated ways. Thus he writes of those whose experience of Christ is restricted to 'the top of their heads, with no substance to it at the bottom of their hearts.'[49]

And in the third place, evangelicalism – here drawing upon its Reformed roots – insists that spirituality must rest upon a solid and reliable foundation in the self-revelation of God. There is thus the closest of connections between spirituality and theology. This organic relationship prevents spirituality from degenerating into little more than a human-centred quest for heightened religiosity, by insisting that our spiritual lives rest securely upon the foundation of God's self-revelation. It also keeps a check on theology, inhibiting it from becoming abstract speculation about God, without any appreciation of the importance of

---

[47] Eugene H. Peterson, *A Long Obedience In the Same Direction: Discipleship In an Instant Society* (Downers Grove, Ill.: InterVarsity Press, 1980).
[48] James Houston, The *Heart's Desire: A Guide to Personal Fulfilment* (Oxford: Lion, 1992), p 156.
[49] Houston, *The Heart's Desire*, p 151.

'knowing God' for human devotion and personal fulfilment.

One of the finest exponents of this point is to be found in Jim Packer, whose *Knowing God* is a masterpiece of its kind. I wish, however, to consider here his seminal 1989 lecture 'An Introduction to Systematic Spirituality', noted earlier, in which he points out the utter impossibility of separating theology and spirituality:

> I question the adequacy of conceptualizing the subject-matter of systematic theology as simply revealed truths about God, and I challenge the assumption that has usually accompanied this form of statement, that the material, like other scientific data, is best studied in cool and clinical detachment. Detachment from what, you ask? Why, from the relational activity of trusting, loving, worshipping, obeying, serving and glorifying God: the activity that results from realizing that one is actually in God's presence, actually being addressed by him, every time one opens the Bible or reflects on any divine truth whatsoever. This ... proceeds as if doctrinal study would only be muddled by introducing devotional concerns; it drives a wedge between ... knowing true notions about God and knowing the true God himself.[50]

In particular, Packer draws attention to the need for 'more biblical and theological control' of spirituality, regretting the 'egocentric perspective' of many spiritual writers, who use radically subjective criteria in developing and commending spiritual practices. 'As I want to see theological study done as an aspect and means of our relating to God, so I want to see spirituality studied within an evaluative theological framework; that is why I want to arrange a marriage, with explicit exchange of vows and mutual commitments, between spirituality and theology.'[51] There is much wisdom to be gleaned from this great contemporary expositor of the Puritan ideal, just as there is much to be gained from the Puritan heritage which he so capably expounds.

---

[50] Packer, *An Introduction to Systematic Spirituality*, p 6.
[51] Packer, *An Introduction to Systematic Spirituality*, p 7.

8. Conclusion

Evangelical spirituality remains in its infancy. If there is any long-term threat to evangelicalism, this is it. Unless we can develop or rediscover forms of spirituality which are thoroughly evangelical in their roots and outlook, today's evangelicals may be tomorrow's ex-evangelicals. This is one of the most urgent tasks facing us today. We owe it to evangelicalism to get it right. And we owe it to the church at large, which is painfully aware of a gaping hole left by our failure.

Unless something is done to promote evangelical spirituality, the present growth of the movement may not be sustained in the longer term. It may be seen like a plant which goes through an initial surge of growth but thereafter needs to be supported. Yet I end on a note of justified optimism. In the past, evangelicalism has shown itself capable of rising to great challenges, and turning perceived weaknesses into opportunities to develop, grow and expand. I have every reason to suppose that the present weakness in spirituality will lead to a dedicated and sustained quest within evangelicalism to meet this deficiency. Evangelicalism is the slumbering giant of the world of spirituality. It needs to wake up. If it does, the new millennium could see some very exciting developments. We owe it to our future to do that right now.

For Futher Reading

T. R. Albin, 'Spirituality', in S. Ferguson and D. F. Wright (eds) *New Dictionary of Theology* (Leicester: InterVarsity Press, 1988), pp. 656-8.

Robert M. Banks, *All the Business of Life: Bringing Theology Down to Earth* (Sutherland, NSW: Albatross, 1987)

Owen Chadwick, 'Indifference and Morality', in P. N. Brooks (ed) *Christian Spirituality: Essays in Honour of Gordon Rupp* (London: SCM Press, 1975), pp. 203-30.

Christopher J. Cocksworth, *Evangelical Eucharistic Thought in the Church of England* (Cambridge : Cambridge University Press, 1993).

James Houston, 'Spirituality', in W. A. Elwell (ed) *Evangelical Dictionary of Theology* (Grand Rapids: Baker, 1984), p 1046.

James Houston, *The Heart's Desire: A Guide to Personal Fulfilment* (Oxford: Lion, 1992).

Gordon James, *Evangelical Spirituality* (London: SPCK, 1991).

Alister E. McGrath, *Roots that Refresh: A Celebration of Reformation Spirituality*

(London: Hodder & Stoughton, 1992).

James I. Packer, 'An Introduction to Systematic Spirituality', *Crux* 26 No. 1 (March 1990), pp. 2-8.

James I. Packer, *Among God's Giants: Aspects of Puritan Christianity* (Eastbourne: Kingsway, 1991).

David Parker, 'Evangelical Spirituality Reviewed', *Evangelical Quarterly* 63 (1991), pp. 123-48.

Eugene H. Peterson, *A Long Obedience in the Same Direction: Discipleship in an Instant Society* (Downers Grove, Ill.: Inter-Varsity Press, 1980).

Peter Southwell, 'Evangelicalism and the Sacraments', in R. T. France and A. E. McGrath (eds) *Evangelical Anglicans* (London: SPCK, 1993), pp. 71-81.

'But We Preach Christ Crucified':
The Cross of Christ in the Pastoral Theology of John Owen 1616 – 1683

Gavin J McGrath

1. Introduction: a message for all times 97
2. The Life of John Owen: A Brief Look at a Towering Figure 102
3. The Theological Battles of Owen's Times 105
   - *3.1 The Cross of Christ and God's Sovereignty*................... *108*
   - *3.2 The Cross of Christ and God's Judgement*.......................*111*
   - *3.3 The Cross of Christ and Christian Holiness*...................*116*
   - *3.4 The Cross of Christ and the Believer's Assurance*......... *120*
4. Conclusion: a message for our own times.......................122

For Further Reading...123

GAVIN J. MCGRATH was born in the United States but has lived in the UK since 1984. His PhD from Durham University was called *Puritans and the Human Will* and focused on the work of Richard Baxter and John Owen. Dr. McGrath was Vice-Principal of Trinity School for Ministry outside Pittsburgh, Pennsylvania and is an Adjunct Lecturer at Oak Hill Theological College, London. An ordained Anglican minister, he currently serves as Senior Pastor of Christ Church, Earlsfield, part of a network of Anglican church plants in the London area. He is the author of *A Confident Life in an Age of Change* and co-editor of *The New Dictionary of Christian Apologetics*.

1. Introduction: a message for all times

They were the best of times and the worst of times, to coin a phrase. The shockwaves of an earth-shaking message were spreading out from the middle-eastern epicentre. Through the Empire, ambassadors travelled with news of a great promise. Liberation and peace were available to all people, regardless of race, social status, sex or cultural background. A new age was dawning for a dark culture. Things were happening. These were exciting days.

They were demanding days too. Into the city of Corinth, one special herald arrived. Yet not without some problems. During the previous months of far-flung travel he had been welcomed by different peoples. Others, however, attacked him. On several occasions, in hasty, almost cloak and dagger style, he had been forced to flee from various cities for his life. Philippi, Thessalonica, Berea and Athens – after the events in these cities, Paul, an apostle of Jesus Christ, herald of an earth-shaking message, trembled himself. When he arrived in the city of Corinth it was not personally the easiest of times. He later wrote about his arrival, explaining to his Corinthian friends, 'I came to you in weakness and fear, and with much trembling' (1 Corinthians 2:3). Given the character of Corinth at that time, it is not surprising.

Corinth was a religious, economic, social and moral hodge-podge. As Gordon Fee writes, all the evidence 'suggests that Paul's Corinth was at once the New York, Los Angeles, and Las Vegas of the ancient world."[1] Understandably, Paul came to Corinth with some shaking. Yet he was certain of a crucial truth: the message of the cross of Jesus Christ. A person could feel intimidated by the cultural weight of Corinth, but one glorious reality blazed, 'For the message of the cross is foolishness to those who are perishing, but to us who are being saved it is the power of God' (1 Corinthians 1:18).

This is an astonishing association: the cross of Christ and the

---

[1] Gordon D. Fee, *The First Epistle to the Corinthians* in *The New International Commentary on the New Testament*, F.F. Bruce (gen.ed.) (Grand Rapids, MI.: Eerdmans, 1987), p 3.

power of God. The then popular Greek/Roman way of thinking considered death on a cross as a harsh but necessary way to deal with certain criminals. To associate this execution method, therefore, with the wisdom of the gods was seen as foolish stupidity. In the opinion of the Jewish people, some of whom were scattered through the Roman Empire, death on the cross was abhorrent. To relate this kind of death with the promised Messiah was offensive.

Not for Paul. The historical death of Jesus of Nazareth, and his subsequent resurrection from the dead, is God's powerful fulfilment of Israel's hopes. So too the cross of Christ is God's appointed way for non-Jews to enter into his promises and blessings. The cross and the power of God are not contradictory. In Paul's preaching, teaching and writing the two are inextricably linked. God's power is presented in the death of his Son on a Roman cross and his glorious resurrection two days later. Simultaneously, the ignominy and scandal of the cross are transformed by God's power into the means of peace.

The convergence of God's power and the cross of Christ provides men and women with what they cannot achieve on their own: salvation. Saved from what? From the inevitable consequences of our human rebellion and autonomy from the one true God. Those who respond to the news of Christ crucified, can be rescued from what we deserve: just, legitimate and fair divine judgement. In this gospel of Christ crucified and risen, God himself is pleased and powerful to free people in a way which upholds what is true and right and, at the same time, pardons and loves. With this message Paul entered Corinth with a confidence and boldness. He was convinced people should hear this good news, in the best of times and in the worst of times. Times like ours.

However, if the Greeks and Jews of first century Corinth were disturbed by the message of Christ crucified, our contemporaries are too. How can we explain this essential truth to our post-Christian society and non-Christian friends at the end of the twentieth century? In what ways can we help Christians know and experience on a moment by moment basis the life-giving power of the cross? We are thankful for the recent written contributions by Michael Green, John Stott and Joanna and Alister McGrath.[2] Their respective studies help us 'earth' our theological understanding of the cross with our day to day experiences. Likewise, the scholarly and technical works by Leon Morris, Martin Hengel and Jürgen Moltmann, while not univocal, aid our doctrinal comprehension.[3]

Still, in our present, post-modern society, we need all the help we can find. In this lecture I seek to recommend a resource who can facilitate the Church's proclamation, ministry and experience. Three reasons stand out. First, this resource understood how central and vital the cross of Jesus is in God's plan to rescue us to his praise and glory. Second, my recommended resource was able to explain the cross with a very impressive and incisive theological mind. We can find help in our present day's theological confusion and silliness, which sadly exists in too many evangelical churches. Thirdly, this resource knew not only the cross of Christ but also the human heart. Here is no detached guidance. It fits the realities, or we can say, the 'stuff' of life. Who would not want such help?

Help can come from one John Owen. He lived in the seventeenth century, and was in what people call the English Calvinist or puritan camp. Of course, I appreciate that some will decline the offer. Help from an old-time Calvinist? From an English puritan?

Admittedly, the word, puritan, is not normally regarded favourably. To call some one a puritan today is to suggest they are uptight, legalistic and particularly censorious. Puritans of old have received rather bad press in many circles. Not only is this unfortunate, it is erroneous. Let me explain by first defining puritan and then introducing puritan spirituality.

There is confusion about what exactly the word puritan means.

---

[2] Michael Green, *The Empty Cross of Christ* (London: Hodder and Stoughton, 1984); John R.W. Stott, *The Cross of Christ* (Leicester: Inter-Varsity Press, 1986); and Joanna and Alister McGrath, *The Dilemma of Self-Esteem: The Cross and Christian Confidence* (Wheaton, Ill, and Cambridge, England: Crossway Books, 1992).

[3] See Leon Morris, *The Apostolic Preaching of the Cross* (London: The Tyndale Press, 1955); *The Cross in the New Testament* (Grand Rapids: Eerdmans and Exeter, England: Paternoster Press, 1965) and *The Atonement: its meaning and significance* (Leicester: Inter-Varsity Press, 1983); Martin Hengel, *The Atonement*, John Bowden (tr.), (London: SCM, 1981); and Jürgen Moltmann, *The Crucified God* (London: SCM, 1974).

In the sixteenth century, it was a term of derision. Subsequently, it is not easy to define who and what were the puritans. There is no scholarly consensus about the precise meaning of puritan.[4] For our purposes, however, think of puritan as a way of classifying a conflict of conscience among certain English Protestants during the reign of Elizabeth I (1558-1603). This conflict was a struggle amongst basically like-minded Protestants, who had been influenced by certain Church Fathers, Augustine in the fifth century, the Reformation theology of Martin Luther and, especially, John Calvin.

The battle concerned the English Church: how far would it go to become a truly reformed church? Some thought it had gone far enough by the 1580s, others thought it was only 'halfly reformed'. Those who pushed for fuller reformation, and who were frustrated with Elizabeth's 'tarrying', became known as puritans. The protest came from a theological conviction that for the sake of the godly and the elect, which some saw as the nation, certain matters of church government and liturgics were unedifying.

Some puritans became Separatists, separating from the Elizabethan Church. During the subsequent reigns of James I (1603-1625) and Charles I (1625-1649) puritan sentiment and practice fragmented into different political and ecclesiastical expressions. The Independents and Congregationalists of the seventeenth century come to mind. In this sense, there is a continuity between Elizabethan puritanism and seventeenth century non-conformity. This means, therefore, that 'puritan' has a shifting meaning, describing a frustration born in the time of Elizabeth I and which continued in subtle ways into and through the seventeenth century. However, let me point out the driving force of what might look initially to be only a partisan protest movement. I refer to puritan spirituality. This is what should grab us and correct any misapprehensions.

As I have written elsewhere, puritan spirituality embraced life and sought a spirituality which honoured God in the whole of life.[5]

---

[4] See especially Paul Christianson, 'Reformers and the Church of England under Elizabeth I and the Early Stuarts', *Journal of Ecclesiastical History*, (31:4), 1980, pp 463-482 and in the same issue, Patrick Collinson, 'A Comment: concerning the name Puritan.'

[5] Gavin J. McGrath, *Grace and Duty in Puritan Spirituality* Grove Booklet Spirituality Series No.37 (Bramcote, Notts.: Grove Books, 1991).

Puritan spirituality was not quietistic, it was actively social and political. They were passionately concerned with doctrine and the purity of the church. Puritan preaching and writing displays a robustness and liveliness. Many longed for a society in which religious tolerance, better education, social welfare and democracy would be the outward manifestations of a godly society.

Their teaching on the individual Christian life was comprehensive and vigorous. Puritan preachers strove to integrate doctrine with experience. Members of puritan congregations were encouraged to take their experiences seriously, even analytically. The day-to-day life of faith was vital to understand. This theology is epitomized in the Westminster *Confession* and Catechisms.[6] Such practical theology was received in rural areas and in cities. It was not exclusively reserved for the wealthy or the poor. It stressed reading Scripture, hearing God's Word preached, meeting together with the 'godly', and measuring one's growth in grace and progress in the life of faith.[7]

Puritan theology gave considerable attention to the believer's experience. It was not just a case of knowing doctrine, a person had to experience the reality behind the doctrine. The puritan preacher and pastor was expected to help the 'godly' experience truth: he was to feed his flock, and in so doing become the physician of their souls. In addition to preaching and visiting, the pastor wrote books and pamphlets in order to give pastoral care to the greatest number of people.

---

[6] Both were produced by the Westminster Assembly, which met 1643-1649. The Assembly was a council summoned by Parliament to provide advice to the civil authorities. The *Confession* and two catechisms, as well as a *Directory for Public Worship*, were produced.

[7] The helpful books on puritan spirituality, covering a variety of aspects are: William K.B. Stoever, *'A Faire and Easie Way to Heaven'. Covenant Theology and Antinomianism in Early Massachusetts* (Middletown, Connecticut: Wesleyan University Press, 1978); Dewey D. Wallace, *Puritans and Predestination. Grace in English Protestant Theology 1525-1695* (Chapel Hill: The University of North Carolina Press, 1982); Paul Seaver, *Wallington's World. A Puritan Artisan in Seventeenth Century London* (London:Methuen & Co., Ltd., 1985); John Von Rohr, *The Covenant of Grace in Puritan Thought.* American Academy of Religion, Studies in Religion, Number 45 (Atlanta: Scholars Press, 1986); and Charles Lloyd Cohen, *God's Caress: The Psychology of Puritan Religious Experience* (Oxford: Oxford University Press, 1986).

With this preliminary explanation of puritan, let us proceed to one of the giants of the puritan period, John Owen. We want to stand on his shoulders, and for some very good reasons.

2. The Life of John Owen: A Brief Look at a Towering Figure

John Owen was born in 1616 in Oxfordshire. Little is known about Owen's early days. There are few autobiographical insights gained from his published works or the correspondence that survives. We do know his father, Henry, was a clergyman sympathetic to puritan sentiment and exercised a non-conformist ministry in Stadham.

In 1631 John followed his older brother, William, to Oxford. A student at Queen's College, he was admitted to the degree of B.A. in 1632 and his M.A. in 1635. Oxford at that time underwent changes, largely due to the influence and reforming concerns of William Laud.[8] What Owen thought about the growing influence of what some contemporaries believed to be Laud's Arminianism (a term I will explain shortly), is difficult to ascertain. It is known that he eventually left Oxford in 1637, and in all probability this had much to do with the implications of Laudianism and Arminianism.

After leaving Oxford Owen spent time in the private service of first, Sir Robert Dormer, as a tutor for his son, and then as chaplain to one Lord Lovelace. In 1643 he accepted the living at Fordham in Essex, a living offered to him by Parliament. Already Owen's non-conformist inclinations were evident.

Owen was forced to leave Fordham by the patron in 1646 and became minister to a gathered church at Coggeshall, Essex. St. Peter's was a puritan stronghold: the Earl of Warwick, to whom Owen dedicated his work on the atonement, *Salus Electorum Sanguis Jesu*

---

[8] Nicholas Tyacke provides the best overview of Arminianism at Oxford during this period. Tyacke details how Oxford was different from Cambridge during this period: Oxford Arminians were far more assertive. Nicholas Tyacke, *Anti-Calvinists. The Rise of English Arminianism c. 1590-1640* (Oxford: Clarendon Press, 1987), pp 78-86.

(1648) was the patron. His immediate predecessor was Obadiah Sedgwick, a member of the Westminster Assembly. It was here that Owen's Independency developed. Furthermore, his preaching at Coggeshall must have been impressive, for one record reports that on some Sundays close to 2,000 came to listen to him.[9]

John Owen's ministry and influence grew beyond the boundaries of Fordham and Coggeshall. His first publication, *A Display of Arminianism* (1643) was dedicated to the Parliamentary Committee of Religion. Furthermore, at the close of the first Civil War, he was invited to preach before Parliament, at one of its fast-day meetings on 29 April 1646.[10]

In 1647 he was introduced to Henry Ireton, Oliver Cromwell's son-in-law, and other officers of the New Model Army at the time of the battle of Colchester. As the second Civil War ensued, Owen too was involved in ministry to the Army, beginning with those under the command of General Fairfax. He continued to gain the favourable regard of Parliament, culminating, if we can put it this way, in his call to preach after the execution of Charles I on 30 January 1649.[11]

Owen's influence upon the affairs and leaders of the nation reached its apex through his relationship with Oliver Cromwell.[12] Undoubtedly his preaching skill, manifested on those occasions when he preached before Parliament, was noted by Cromwell. Cromwell met Owen, in April/May of 1649 through General Fairfax.

In 1651 Oliver Cromwell appointed Owen Dean of Christ Church, Oxford, an appointment he held until 1659.[13] In 1652 he

---

[9] John Asty, "Memoirs of the Life of John Owen," in *A Complete Collection of the Sermons of the Reverend and Learned John Owen D.D.* (London: 1721) p vii. Quoted in Toon, *God's Statesman*, p 26.

[10] Owen, *A Vision of Unchangeable Free Mercy* (1646). Goold : 8, pp 5-41.

[11] This was later published as *Righteous Zeal Encouraged by Divine Protection* (1649), Goold: 8.

[12] Toon, *The Correspondence of John Owen (1616-1683)* (Cambridge and London: James Clarke & Co. Ltd., 1970) provides a total of seventeen items of correspondence between Cromwell and Owen: 13 from Cromwell to Owen, 4 from Owen to Cromwell. These letters are predominately concerned with practical matters regarding Oxford.

[13] See Toon, *Correspondence*, #3, pp 52-53.

became Vice-Chancellor.[14] His years at Oxford were not idle. Besides exercising a number of reforms to student life and attempts to enhance lecturers' pay, he joined forces with Thomas Goodwin, then president of Magdalen College, in a preaching ministry at St. Mary's Church.[15] From this shared preaching ministry, during 1652-57, Owen produced some of his more significant pastoral works, eventually published for a wider audience as *On the Mortification of Sin* (1656) and *Of the Nature and Power of Temptation* (1658). When we think of today's university Christian gatherings, it is amazing to note that both of these works were first preached mainly to young Oxford students!

With the return of the monarchy, Owen's political influence diminished. In 1659/60 he was removed from Christ Church and subsequently moved to Stadhampton. Apart from his involvement in 1667 to persuade Parliament to pass a Toleration Act, his life and ministry shifted more towards matters of church polity and to his theological writing. There was the notable invitation from the First Congregational in Boston, New England, to become their pastor. This church, earlier led by John Cotton and latterly by John Norton, was well known to Owen, but for reasons known only to himself he declined the offer.[16] His ministry moved to London, and by 1673 his Congregational flock combined with the Leadenhall church formerly led by the recently deceased Joseph Caryl.

In this final period of Owen's life a large proportion of his works were published; he was a prodigious writer. Equally, Owen's leadership role amongst Congregationalists was at its height. Sadly, he experienced the personal loss of his first wife, Mary, who died in 1675. A year later, however, he married Dorothy D'Oyley. In supposed retirement at Ealing, yet in failing health, Owen produced his *Meditations on the Glory of Christ*, which perhaps tells us something of his thoughts and concerns in those last months. John Owen died on 24 August 1683.

---

[14] See Toon, *Correspondence*, #13, pp 62-63; #24, p 74; #35, pp 84-85; and #45, p 94. It was a position which had to be renewed each year.

[15] Goodwin was appointed president of Magdalen by Cromwell at the same time Owen was recommended to Christ Church. Toon, *Correspondence*, #3, p 53.

[16] Toon, *Correspondence*, #71, pp 135-136 is a transcription of a letter from the General Court of Massachusetts affirming and ratifying this invitation to Owen. Later in 1671 Owen was invited to become President of Harvard: this too he declined.

3. The Theological Battles of Owen's Times

If we are to read Owen properly, and understand the specific context of his practical writings, we must briefly explain the theological battles of his day. I refer to some of the terms I introduced earlier: Arminianism and Antinomianism.

Remember, puritan theology originated out of Reformed theology. The history of Christian theology, however, is rarely cut and dried; this is the case when we try to understand seventeenth century Reformed theology. By the seventeenth century the theological scene on the Continent and in England began to change. Principally, there was a reaction against a rigid a view of predestination. Most noteworthy was the criticism by the Dutch thinker, Jacobus Arminius (1560-1609).

Arminianism, as it was later called, has been described as a 'protest against those tenets in the theology of the Reformed Church that dealt with God's Election and Reprobation of individuals to eternal life or death.'[17] Arminianism spread on the Continent as a counter-reaction to Calvinist orthodoxy. Jim Packer identifies its main contentions:

1. Though sinful, it is not beyond the ability of humans to respond 'savingly' to the gospel when it is presented to them.

2. Humans are not so controlled by God that they cannot, if they so choose, reject the gospel.

3. God does not elect those who will be saved through sovereign predestination but foresees that certain people will become Christians in their life-time.

4. Christ's death did not, in and of itself, establish the salvation of anyone, but created the possibility of salvation for everyone if they believed.

5. It is up to the believer to continue in faith, trusting in God; but if a person chooses to turn from God, he or she can fall away, ultimately losing salvation.[18]

Orthodox Calvinism responded to Arminianism, particularly in the

---

[17] A.W. Harrison, *Arminianism* (London: Duckworth, 1937), Preface.
[18] J.I. Packer, *Among God's Giants* (Eastbourne: Kingsway, 1991), p 166.

Synod of Dort (1618-19): pushing further the ideas of supralapsarianism (God chose his elect before the Fall of Adam and Eve), limited atonement, unconditional and irresistible grace, total human inability, and the assurance of the final perseverance of the elect. The battle lines were drawn, and the ensuing theological debates became fierce.

Arminianism in England was not merely an English reaction to a Dutch conflict. By the time of the Synod of Dort there was already a reaction against orthodox Calvinism. The battle had begun, and with the reluctance of James I and Charles I to embrace the canons of Dort conflict continued the next twenty years. The Arminian theology of Richard Neile, Bishop of Durham, Lancelot Andrewes, Bishop of Winchester and John Cosin, Neile's successor to Durham stressed a dislike of predestinarian language. By 1628 the Arminian faction had gained significant ecclesiastical power within the English Church: clear Arminians such as Richard Neile and William Laud were in positions of leadership. In 1633 the death of Archbishop Abbot made way for Laud to move to Canterbury. Thus, even before Owen began his ministry, Arminianism was an important element in the theological and ecclesiastical context.

What does this tell us? We need to appreciate the practical implications of Arminianism. The puritan pastor wanted his congregation to be active and responsible. At the same time he would not want them to think that it was their activity, including their response in faith, which instigated their life in Christ. Arminianism challenged rigid predestinarianism. English Calvinists accused English Arminians of giving too great an emphasis to human freedom, choice and response. Some puritans, notably Owen, accused them of exalting human capability over divine grace.

Another aspect of the context in which Owen pastored, preached and wrote was Antinomianism. This was a movement within English Protestantism which rejected orthodox Calvinism's use of the law.[19] It was a reaction against Orthodox Calvinism just as much as Arminianism, but in an entirely different direction. Whereas Arminianism argued that the Orthodox Calvinists minimized human ability, Antinomians challenged the Orthodox for giving too much attention to human choice and responsibility.

---

[19] See Von Rohr, *Covenant of Grace*, p 50.

Antinomians criticized the idea that a person's faith and repentance somehow qualified him or her to enter the covenant. This would be to give too much importance to the human side of regeneration. Antinomians like John Saltmarsh (1612-1647), Tobias Crisp (1600-1643) and John Eaton (dc.1575-1642)[20] claimed that the act of justification was not dependent upon the performance of the believer's faith. They insisted that Christ's death alone procured the salvation of the elect unconditionally: the believer's faith in no way merited justification, Christ satisfied all.

Antinomianism was threatening. It seemed to some critics of Antinomianism that if Christ believed and repented for the elect, then it did not matter what the elect did – either before or after they came to faith. Extreme Antinomian sects only made things worse with their moral laxity and extreme permissiveness: done in the name of liberty from the law. This was alarming, especially when the country was caught up in a civil war and the world appeared upside down.

Arminianism and Antinomianism, then, were the two poles between which Owen's theology was expressed, and he has to be read with an eye on these movements. Often his practical theology and spirituality responded to either Arminian emphasis on human activity or Antinomian excesses. Of course, a believer's experience is never an either/or situation. Owen tried to define a middle ground, and this was no easy task. At various points in his arguments we may wonder if some of his views are extreme. Provided we appreciate his concern to integrate doctrine with experience we will see the fuller significance. Owen's theology was rarely abstract; it was forged in the heat of theological battles and people's struggles. This is apparent as we now turn to his understanding of the cross of Christ. Four main and vital themes are all we have space to present. Each relates to up-to-date issues and concerns facing us in our experience and ministries as we work to preach Christ crucified.

---

[20] Of importance are the following illustrative works: Saltmarsh, *Free Grace; or, the Flowings of Christ's Blood freely to sinners* (1645); Eaton, *The Honey-Combe of Free Justification by Christ alone* (1642); Tobias Crisp, *Christ Alone Exalted, in Fourteen Sermons* (1643).

3.1 The Cross of Christ and God's Sovereignty

Have you been to St. Paul's Cathedral in London and seen the famous painting by Holman Hunt? It vividly conveys the sense of Revelation 3:20, 'Here I am! I stand at the door and knock. If anyone hears my voice and opens the door, I will come in and eat with him, and he with me.' Hunt's painting portrays a lantern-carrying Jesus, knocking on a door. There is no handle on the outside of the door. Presumably only the owner of the house can open the door and let Jesus inside. The painting seems to ask, 'Will the door open, or will it remain closed and Jesus move on?'

It is a powerful and emotive image of the reality Christians know from personal experience. While Revelation 3:20 does not *directly* or *contextually* relate to unbelievers, many of us became Christians in response to an evangelistic talk or explanation which employed this passage. 'Christ is waiting. He wants to have a personal relationship with you', we were told. 'He won't force himself on you. It's up to you.'

Do you and I preach like this, when we preach the cross of Christ? I hope we do preach for a decision, for a response. However, much of today's evangelism places a premium on a person's ability to decide for Christ or 'inviting Jesus into your heart'. As a result, either Jesus is one of life's many spiritual options or the God of the universe is just as uncertain as the evangelist and organising committee. No wonder our evangelism and preaching lacks a little something. What would John Owen tell us?

He would remind us that men and women are invited by God to enter into the new covenant through faith in the Lord Jesus Christ. This is a work of God's mercy. He summons all people to repentance. Yet it is always a *sovereign* mercy and summons. Too easily we lose sight of this. Consequently, our evangelism is deficient and our pastoral theology is inadequate.

Owen stressed the absolute certainty of God's will: a certainty not at all because of mere foreknowledge regarding human agency, but a foreknowledge of that which he decreed. He wrote, 'whatever God doth in time bring to pass, that he decreed from all eternity so to do: all his works were from the beginning known unto him.'[21] Owen insisted that this is the basis of the believer's confidence and assurance:

> It is no small comfort to be assured that we do, nor can, suffer nothing, but what his hand and counsel guides unto us: what is open, and naked before his eyes, and whose end and issue he knoweth long before: which is a strong motive to patience, a sure anchor of hope, a firm ground of consolation.[22]

God's immutable character defines his will and thus guarantees the certainty of his will for the future. What is Owen driving at here?

Owen's understanding of the divine initiative shaped his view of the death of Christ. He argued that Christ's death was not universal – for all men and women. Rather, Christ only died, according to the will of the Father, to save the elect. He was not questioning the sufficiency of Christ's death. Instead, the issue was with the end of his death. We would today call it the purpose or aim of Christ's death. As he put it in 1648:

> The summe of all is: the death and bloodshedding of Jesus Christ hath wrought, and doth effectually procure, for all those that are concerned in it, eternal redemption, consisting in grace here, and glory hereafter.[23]

The death and intercession of Christ could not be said to have been in vain or merely to establish a conditional covenant of pardon; it had a specific and absolute end:

> To save sinners; not open a door for them to come in, if they will or can; not to make a way passable, that they may be saved; not to purchase reconciliation and pardon of his Father, which perhaps they shall never enjoy; but actually to save them from all their guilt and power of sinne, and from the wrath of God for sinne, which if he doth not accomplish, he fails of the end of his coming; and if that ought not to be affirmed, surely he came for no more than towards whom that effect is procured.[24]

---

[21] Owen, *A Display of Arminianism* (1643), Russell: 5, pp 19-20.
[22] Owen, *Arininianism*, p 29.
[23] Owen, *Salus Electorum Sanguis Jesu or the Death of Death in the Death of Christ* (1648), p 3.
[24] Owen, *Death of Death*, p 151; cf. pp 61-64.

Yet does not all this talk of sovereign election only lead to an impossible position concerning evangelism? If people are elected, and this is God's will, then what is the point of evangelistic preaching when we urge people to hear and respond to the gospel? However logical these questions seem, they are absurd and unhelpful. We never know from the outset who the elect are.

> We say, though God hath chosen some only to salvation by Christ, yet that the names of those some are not expressed in Scripture; the doing whereof would have been destructive to the main end of the word, the nature of faith, and all the ordinances of the gospel; yet God having declared that whosoever believeth shall be saved, there is sufficient ground for all and every man in the world, to whom the gospel is preached, to come to God by Christ, and other ground there is none, nor can be offered by the assertors of the pretended universality of God's love.[25]

Furthermore, it is *through* Spirit-anointed preaching and teaching of the Bible, which is at the heart of sound evangelism, that the elect are called, converted and begin the life of faith. As Owen put it, 'For they [preachers] are used and employed in the work it self by the Spirit of God, and are by him made instrumental for the effecting of this new birth and life.'[26]

To be sure, an individual is not regenerate and pardoned until he or she believes and repents. In this sense Owen was denying a justification from eternity. Christ's death accomplishes God's sovereign purposes while, simultaneously, there is no actual completion or fulfilment of this purpose for the individual until the time he or she repents and believes. 'Things have their certain fruition,' wrote Owen, 'not instant actual existence, from the eternal purposes of God concerning them.'[27] Even the elect are very much under the wrath and judgment of God for sin until they are converted.

> The state or condition of those for whom Christ died, is not actually and really changed by his death in itself; but they lie under the curse, whilst they are in the state of nature,

---

[25] Owen, *Vindicae Evangelicae* (1655), Russell: 9, p 197
[26] Owen, *Πνευματολογια ; or a Discourse Concerning the Holy Spirit* (1674), p 188.
[27] Owen, *Of the Death of Christ, the Price He Paid, and the Purchase He Made* (1650), Russell: 5, p 611.

unregenerate, and all the effects of sin whatever. That which is procured for them, is left in the hand of the Father; they are not in the least intrusted with it, until the appointed time do come.[28]

Their faith and trust are established not merely by the decree of election but through the death of Christ. By his death Christ actually procures the fruit of his death.[29]

In other words, in the covenant of works God commanded perfect obedience but in the covenant of grace God himself promises that the elect will be given the faith which the covenant demands. No one can ever, on their own, repent and believe; only God can bring about this. Owen insisted that even the faith required was given absolutely through the death of Christ. It was this absolute provision which Owen argued made the covenant of grace superior to the first covenant.[30] Let us move on to the second main theme to see what he meant. Again, our goal is to strengthen our commitment to proclaim the crucified Saviour in our generation.

3.2   The Cross of Christ and God's Judgement

At the heart of Christianity is the death of Jesus on a cross.[31] Certainly, his resurrection speaks of life and hope, but why do the New Testament writers link his exaltation with his death? They claim his lordship and kingship are predicated upon his willingness to die (Philippians 2:9-9). Why then did Jesus of Nazareth have to die? Why is his death so important?

---

[28] Owen, *Doctrine of the Saints' Perseverance Explained and Confirmed* (1654), Goold: 2: pp 403-404.
[29] Owen, *Death of Death*, pp 87, 101-112 and 163.
[30] Owen, *Death of Death*, pp 103-104.
[31] Many would prefer to stress the life of Jesus, and his teaching. I certainly do not seek to reduce the life of Christ Jesus. On the other hand, I argue that the crucial importance of Jesus' earthly life and ministry is his death. This is the New Testament writers' primary, although not sole, focus. Leon Morris' point is well made, 'But our examination of the evidence leads us to think that the view that 'the blood' directs our attention primarily to 'the life' is erroneous, and that, in point of fact, the Scriptures of both Old and New Testaments stress the death when they make use of this expression... the impression left by those biblical passages which refer to the blood of Christ is that they are pointing us to the death of the Lord considered as the means whereby sin is dealt with, not merely the means whereby man may be inspired to deal with it.' Morris, *The Apostolic Preaching of the Cross*, pp 276-277.

Fundamentally, it was the will of God. Quite understandably, the modern mind recoils in horror and distaste at the proposition that God demanded the innocent sufferings of Jesus to be appeased and satisfied. Stated this baldly it has a discordant ring. However, it was according to the *good, loving and gracious purpose of God.*

The shedding of blood was required, and there was a divine necessity for satisfaction; both are inextricable in God's loving and merciful plan.[32] The New Testament writers weave the various emphases on Jesus' death around God's glory and love. The different words and expressions used concerning Christ's death speak of a multi-faceted significance and accomplishment: ransom, redemption, to buy out of slavery, an example, to bear away or to take away sin, a sacrifice of atonement or propitiation, and the means to disarm the powers of evil. Throughout history these different themes have been underlined. The death of Christ has been explained in the light of example, substitution and rescuing power. All are present in the New Testament. It is *normally* wise not to stress unduly one over against the other. There is a unity.

Nevertheless, it is common among many today to play down the idea of substitutionary atonement. Yet, to dismiss outright the idea of substitution and satisfaction is to raise more problems than it attempts to displace. Powerlessness and oppression are not our only problems, we face the moral dilemma of guilt. Apart from the substitutionary death of Jesus, the holy justice of God and the seriousness of human sin cannot be *justly* reconciled.

Why accent justice? It is because of the glory and majesty of God. If there is no justice, God is not a God whom we can trust or worship. We would live in a universe of indifference. Even on a human level we know that justice is a necessity. Without justice societies fall either into anarchy or oppressive totalitarianism. Our awareness of this importance is a reflection of God's character. He is a God of holy justice.

Modern people risk missing the ultimate issue: humanity's standing before a particular God. The one true and only God with whom we must deal is pure, true, majestic, holy and just. This is why sin,

---

[32] See the following passages: Mark 8:31 and 9:12; Luke 24:45, 46; John 3:16; Acts 2:23 and 3:18; and 1 Corinthians 15:3.

human rebellion against God, matters. Our generation denies this constantly. Before we come to faith, we may think this is irrelevant. Surely, God's business is to forgive and let live! The Bible, however, focuses on the greater issue of justice, what is right. Why should God forgive without dealing with the transgression of his law and standards? It is not simply a question of conforming to an external code; it is congruity to truth, the very character of God.

This is why the Bible frequently speaks of the wrath of God against sin.[33] Sin is non-truth in an active, relational and moral sphere: the relationship of humanity with its creator. Accordingly, a right verdict is delivered by a holy God against all that is the opposite of his nature. At the same time, the Bible tells us God wills to save people from this just consequence. What is God's solution, one both just and loving? The better we understand this the sounder our evangelism will be and the richer our pastoral care will be. Allow John Owen to help us.

According to Owen, the punishment due to men and women demanded in the law (the old covenant, or the covenant of works) was real. Christ, however, paid the penalty in substitution for the elect (Galatians 3:13). The punishment was a full condemnation of sin; God did this in Christ (Romans 8:30) and the condemning of sin was the infliction of the penalty. Christ underwent actual death (cf. Genesis 2:11 and Hebrews 2:14). It is not just that an angry God chose to punish his pure and innocent Son. Most importantly, in him, as the substitute ransom, believers are joined or incorporated. Faith joins believers with Jesus, the crucified and risen Saviour. The mystical, but real, union Christ has with his people enables them to see and experience Jesus as *the accepted Saviour.*

In 1653 John Owen published *De Diatriba Justitia*, the English title, *A Dissertation on Divine Justice.* This work was a response to a line of thought called Socinianism. Following the views of the rationalist, Lelio Sozzini (1525- 62), Socinianism essentially viewed the cross of Christ as a morally persuasive means to demonstrate God's love and pardon to sinners. The idea of God demanding Christ's death for divine satisfaction of justice was denied. Socinian writers with whom

---

[33] See Deuteronomy 9:8; Psalms 21:9; 85:3; 90:11; Isaiah 9:19; 26:20; Jeremiah 3:5; 7:29; Ezekiel 22:20-31; Habakkuk 3:2; Matthew 3:7; John 3:36; Romans 1:18; 3:5; Ephesians 2:3; 1 Thessalonians 1:10; and Revelation 6:16-17.

Owen battled, notably one John Biddle, did not accept the notion of divine necessity for appeasement and atonement. Owen argued that God must punish sin, not because he is compelled by some law outside of himself. Rather, God cannot co-exist with sin. Accordingly, punitive judgment is from God, not only because of his will but in accordance with his nature. To quote Owen:

> That justice is not a free act of divine will, which God may use or renounce at pleasure; nor is sin only a debt of ours, which as we were unable to pay, he might forgive, by only freely receding from his right: for what reason then could be assigned why the Father of mercies should so severely punish his most holy Son on our account, that he might, according to justice, deliver us from our sins ... for sin is that ineffable evil, which would overturn God's whole right over his creatures, unless it were punished.[34]

Owen insisted that Christ did not endure eternal death, because of the dignity of his person. He is the Son of God. Yet the obligation that death occur under the first covenant was met fully by Christ. 'He charged upon him, and imputed unto him all the sins of all the elect, and proceeded against him accordingly.'[35] He went on to argue,

> Christ underwent not only that wrath, (taking it passively) which the elect were under, but that also, which they should have undergone, had not he borne it for them. He delivered them from the wrath to come.[36]

His substitution was not just an acceptable sacrifice, it was in strict terms a full satisfaction. In another work, entitled, *Of the Death of Christ, the Price he Paid, and the Purchase He Made* (1650), he wrote, 'There is a sameness in Christ's sufferings with that in the obligation in respect of essence, and equivalency in respect of attendencies.'[37] Faith, then, joins us with this substitute — who, in his incarnation, identified with his people. It is this second Adam, the Lamb of God, in whom we find legitimate forgiveness, ransom and the hope of resurrection life.

---

[34] Owen, *Diatriba de Divina Justitia seu Justitiae Vindicatricis Vindicae*, or *A Dissertation on Divine Justice* (1653), Russell: 9, pp 500-501.
[35] Owen, *Death of Death*, p 160.
[36] Owen, *Death of Death*, p 160.
[37] Owen, *Death of Christ*, p 448.

In our generation, when Christians speak of the cross the tendency is to explain Christ's death as an act of love for us. It most certainly was! Furthermore, it is often explained Christ identifies himself with our weaknesses and pain. This is true! However, if this is all we show when we ask our contemporaries to 'look' at the cross of Christ, it is a short-sighted perspective. In a subtle and insidious manner, it elevates our humanity and minimises the superior character of God. Christ did not die for us only because we are weak, hurting and broken people (which of course we are!), but because a holy God sought to reconcile himself with those whom he would save. Today we need this balance and precision, for as Owen reminds us: '... in dying for us Christ did not only aim at our good, but also directly died in our stead. The punishment due to our sin and the chastisement of our peace was upon him ...'[38]

What does this mean for the believer? An overwhelming sense of joyful assurance. As Owen explained,

> ... the main foundation of all the confidence and assurance whereof in this life, we may be partakers, (which amounts to joy unspeakable, and full of glory) ariseth from this strict connexion of the oblation and intercession of Jesus Christ, that by the one he hath procured all good things for us, and by the other he will procure them to be actually bestowed; whereby he doth never leave our sinnes but follows them into every court, until they be fully pardoned, and clearly expiated, Heb. 9:26. He will never leave us until he hath saved, to the utter most, them that come unto God by him ... [39]

Owen has much to teach us here. His aid could well strengthen our evangelism and, equally, our pastoral counselling. There will be a final day of accountability for the entire human race. On the other hand, when we repent and believe in the gospel, we are truly and justly pardoned. We need not fear the condemning accusations of either our conscience or Satan, the enemy of our souls. When God pardons us in Christ, we are free indeed. How great a proclamation this is for all of us. For some, the past suggests too many errors and wasted moments in wrong living. Others find their present battles almost overwhelming.

---

[38] Owen, *Death of Death*, p 19.
[39] Owen, *Death of Death*, p 34.

Their guilt screams too loudly. Yet, a louder, more dominant declaration resonates from heaven. On that day when we stand before the judgement throne of God, if we are a Christian now in this life, no one will justly condemn us before God. God will not, Satan cannot, even our conscience may not. This is why we preach Christ crucified.

3.3 The Cross of Christ and Christian Holiness

If I may be allowed a homely illustration, have you ever tried your hand at making soup? Part of the skill is the occasional tasting and adding of additional herbs and seasoning. Experience yields knowledge which results in good flavour. A good cook can taste and know what is missing.

Do we have the relative skill in Christian living? When we look at our personal lives, and the life of our churches, can we tell what crucial ingredient is not present? Here is my point. If we are honest about ourselves, a character trait easier to claim than to possess, we must confess that as Christians today there is something vital missing in our life. We sense an absence of a 'something' when we consider the overall consistency of our faithfulness to the gospel. There is, to use a different metaphor, a poor connection between the splendour of the gospel and the day-to-day character of our life. What explains this?

We lack holiness. It is not that we do not exhort one another to live holy lives or even long for holiness. Rather our understanding of holiness, true holiness, is poor. With a poor understanding of holiness what we long for and exhort to see in Christian communities is always inadequate. Yet, here too John Owen can aid us, and his assistance is remarkably up-to-date. As he helps us understand the nature of holiness and its necessity, he offers us encouragement with a state-of-the-art pastoral skill.

Owen's view of holiness is comprehensive. Holiness encompasses and fills the whole of Christian experience and practical living. 'Holiness, whereof faith is the root, and obedience the body,' he wrote, 'is that whereunto, and not for which, we are elected.'[40] But what precisely is holiness, or as Owen also called it, sanctification?

---

[40] Owen, *Arminianism*, p 119.

> Sanctification is an immediate work of the Spirit of God on the soul of Believers, purifying and cleansing of their natures from the pollution and uncleanness of sin, renewing in them the image of God, and thereby enabling them from a spiritual and habitual principle of Grace to yield obedience unto God according to the Tenor and Terms of the New Covenant, by vertue of the Life and Death of Jesus Christ.[41]

As this quote reveals, Owen focused on the internal working of the Holy Spirit. It is his work in our lives, by which he changes us progressively into conformity with Jesus. Notice holiness has to do with combating sin and growing into renewal; holiness also concerns the whole of our humanity.

At the same time, do not miss the foundation of Owen's argument. Holiness is established and according to Christ's atoning toil on the cross for his people. In his major study on the atonement, Owen insisted,

> So that our sanctification, with all other effects of free grace, are the immediate procurement of the death of Christ. And of the things that have been spoken this is the summe, sanctification and holiness, is the certain fruit and effect of the death of Christ, in all them for whom he dyed...[42]

Owen was writing at a time when it was far too easy for people to think that holy living was a matter of willpower and self-resolution. Moralism, namely the tendency to strive for the marks of a Christian character without entering a personal relationship with Christ, was a threat in Owen's generation.

We might think this danger is non-existent in our society. Nonetheless, as voices decry our modern moral breakdown, listen closely to their assumptions. Moral improvement, or a return to so-called traditional values, faces a major obstacle: the sinful hearts of men and women. Christian morality (which is true, authentic human living), without reverence for Christ is impossible.

Only as a man or woman is converted, filled with the Holy Spirit, is holiness possible. The point of reference is not human

---

[41] Owen, *Holy Spirit*, p 338.
[42] Owen, *Death of Death*, p 121.

morality but conformity to Christ. Only the Lord brings about this supernatural work in us.

> And this belongs unto the Establishment of our Faith, that he who prepared, sanctified, and glorified the human nature, the natural body of Jesus Christ, the head of the Church, hath undertaken to prepare, sanctifie and glorifie his mystical body, or all the Elect given unto him of the Father.[43]

To quote Owen at length:

> No person therefore, whatever, who hath not been made partaker of the washing of regeneration and the renovation of the Holy Ghost, can possibly have any union with Christ. I do not speak this as though our purifying were in order of time or nature antecedent unto our union with Christ, for indeed it is an effect thereof. But it is such an effect as immediately and inseparably accompanyeth it; so that where the one is not, there is not the other. The act whereby he unites us unto himself, is the same that whereby he cleanseth our natures.[44]

Does this mean, however, that we simply sit back and do nothing in our personal growth in holiness? Are we meant to 'let go, let God'? John Owen's answer was no. In no way are we to see ourselves totally passive. Owen reminds us, we are called to a Spirit-prompted active involvement.

> He that thinks to please God, and to come to the enjoyment of him without holiness, makes him an unholy God, putting the highest indignity and dishonour imaginable upon him. God deliver poor sinners from this deceit. There is no remedy, you must leave your sins, or your God.[45]

Assuredly, this is the most pertinent point in our analysis of our contemporary predicament. Whether it be in the area of our sexuality, understanding of power, use of money and sets of relationships, holiness is our calling. This is hard work, demanding from us a willingness to say no to ourselves. Temptations, both internal and external, abound; and in this respect I cannot urge too strongly getting

---

[43] Owen, *Holy Spirit*, p 155.
[44] Owen, *Holy Spirit*, p 406.
[45] Owen, *Holy Spirit*, p 505.

hold of Owen's work on indwelling sin and temptation. I owe John Owen a great debt for his sober, realistic and profoundly hopeful counsel. I have not yet discovered any contemporary Christian writer who knows better the human heart, the power of the indwelling Spirit, and the sufficiency of Christ's finished work on the cross. There is no other legitimate basis for a sane holiness than the liberating news of Christ crucified.

Owen reminds me of this. He knew that only the atoning death of Christ can triumph over our failures and weaknesses in the Christian life. 'For even those who have this real spiritual principle of holiness, may be surprized into actual omission of duties, commission of sins, and a temporary indulgence unto corrupt affections.'[46] As Owen told students at Oxford, and later wrote in his 1658 study on temptation, 'Even the best of saints, being left to themselves, will quickly appear to be less than men, to be nothing.'[47] Likewise, in a work on the call to mortification, namely fighting sin, he wrote: '... sin is always acting, always conceiving, always seducing and tempting ... there is not a day but sin foils, or is foiled; prevails or is prevailed on: and it will be so whilst we live in this world.'[48]

Where then is our hope? How can we prevail in this life? Listen to the pastor's care of John Owen:

> I shall freely say, this one thing of establishing the soul by faith in expectation of relief from Jesus Christ, on the account of his mercifulness as our high-priest, will be more available to the ruin of thy lust and distemper, and have a better and speedier issue, than all the rigidest means of self-maceration, that ever any of the sons of men engaged themselves into. Yea, let me add, that never any soul did, or shall perish by the power of any lust, sin or corruption, who could raise his soul by faith to an expectation of relief from Jesus Christ.[49]

Here is why we must preach Christ crucified. It is the only life-giving alternative to a foolish superficiality or, at the other extreme, an

---

[46] Owen, *Holy Spirit*, p 426.
[47] Owen, *Of Temptation* (1658), Russell: 7, p 438
[48] Owen, *Of Mortification of Sin in Believers* (1656), Russell: 7, p 338. All further references to this work are simply, *Mortification*.
[49] Owen, *Mortification*, p 424.

oppressive and fearful legalism.

In the Preface to his book, *A Passion for Holiness*, Jim Packer, with characteristic insight, commands our attention.

> ... the shift of Christian interest away from the pursuit of holiness to focus on fun and fulfilment, egomassage and techniques for present success, and public issues that carry no challenge to one's personal morals, is a fact. To my mind it is a sad and scandalous fact, and one that needs to be reversed.[50]

How can this reversal start and continue? It involves sober and realistic self-understanding. Yes, change takes place as we take seriously the call and challenge of holiness. At the same time, this reversal can only start and continue when we preach to others and to ourselves Christ crucified. Only as believers know the fullness of the gospel of Christ crucified will they be able to know and experience the essential power of holiness. This is why we must preach Christ crucified to Christ's people today.

3.4 The Cross of Christ and the Believer's Assurance

Let us conclude this study with realism along with legitimate hope. Owen superbly provides us both. We can see this as we draw together the previous points and show how each contributes to a justifiable assurance.

First, Christ died on the cross in accordance with the Father's sovereign will. The will of God assures the salvation of those for whom Christ died. There is an unbreakable link between the atonement and a believer's assurance. Owen insisted that because of God's character his work in salvation was infallible and certain.

> The main foundation of that which we plead for, is the eternal purpose of God, which his own nature requireth to be absolutely immutable and irreversible. The eternal act of the will of God designing some to salvation by Christ, infallibly to be obtained,'for the praise of the glory of his grace', is the bottom of the whole ...[51]

---

[50] J. I. Packer, *A Passion for Holiness* (Nottingham: Crossway Books, 1992), p 9.
[51] Owen, *Perseverance*, p 22, Preface to the Reader.

Owen never denied that some who make professions of faith apostatise, but are they, he asked, truly faithful and of the elect? While believers at times yield to indwelling sin and even have seasons of backsliding, nevertheless, they will persevere to the end. How was this? Perseverance was rooted in the work of grace. The sin of believers was not like that of non-believers.[52] A believer was one who had received the converting work of God, which included an infused habit of grace. Accordingly, this work of God had to produce infallibly a new creation consistent with itself. God would not abandon his work of regeneration and sanctification. Sin would not triumph. Believers belonged to Christ and were children of the Father; though they sinned, and were accountable for this sin, they never ceased to be his children.[53] 'Until he hath taken away his Spirit and grace, although they are rebellious children, yet they are his children still.'[54]

Second, because the death of Christ involved not only the Father's love and mercy to sinners but also the way of satisfied reconciliation, believers can find assurance despite their guilty conscience, the demands of the Law and Satan. Jesus is the substitute victim, whose death is our pardon. As Owen put it, '... his wounding and our healing, impetration, and application, his chastisement and our peace are inseparably associated.'[55] Accordingly, Owen saw an inextricable inter-association between Christ's death and his present, on-going, intercession for his church. Jesus is our great high-priest.

> ... his intercession in heaven, is nothing but a continued oblation of himself. So that whatsoever Christ impetrated, merited or obtained, by his death and passion, must be infallibly applied unto, and bestowed upon them, for whom he intended to obtain it; or else his intercession is vain, he is not heard in the prayers of his mediatorship ...[56]

Third, it is the cross of Christ which assures us in our growth in

---

[52] Owen, *Perseverance*, pp 85-86.
[53] Owen, *Perseverance*, pp 97-98.
[54] Owen, *Perseverance*, p 98.
[55] Owen, *Death of Death*, p 90. By impetration, Owen means, 'the meritorious purchase of all good things made by Christ for us, with and of his Father.' (p 87). The term, *application*, means, 'the actual enjoyment of those good things upon our believing...' (p 87).
[56] Owen, *Arminianism*, p 148.

holiness. The promises of the gospel flow out of our union with Christ. According to Owen, perseverance in holiness is not dependent upon the faithfulness and obedience of the saints, for this would be foolishly illogical. 'Now what one drop of consolation can a poor, drooping, tempted soul, squeeze out of such promises, as depend wholly or solely upon any thing within themselves ...?'[57] The answer is the complete satisfaction of Christ's substitution on the cross. Owen reminds us,

> Set faith at work on Christ for the killing of thy sin. His blood is the great sovereign remedy for sin-sick souls. Live in this, and thou wilt die a conqueror. Yea, thou wilt through the good providence of God, live to see thy lust dead at thy feet.[58]

Sadly, we will struggle with the continued presence of what Owen called indwelling sin. A greater, clearer and more realistic perspective would help us all in these days.[59] The more we are engaged in biblical preaching, pastoring, apologetics and counselling, the more we will deal with the rough realities of our human fallenness. People need assurance, legitimate confidence. There are many tempting ways to provide this need; however, Owen can help us to see that in contrast to so much superficial counsel, '... but we preach Christ crucified.'

4. Conclusion: a message for our own times

In his magisterial study of the cross of Christ, John Stott writes, 'There is no greater cleavage between faith and unbelief than in their respective attitudes to the cross. Where faith sees the glory, unbelief sees only disgrace.'[60] Stott's point is apt. To the cross men and women throughout the ages have come in faith and trust. Over the cross many, many others have, figuratively speaking, tripped in their disbelief and rejection of the gospel. The message of the risen Lord and Saviour, who is so because he went to the cross out of obedience to the Father, is divisive.

---

[57] Owen, *Perseverance*, pp 238-239; see also pp 235-239.
[58] Owen, *Mortification*, p 420.
[59] I attempt to provide this in my work, *A Confident Life in an Age of Change*, published by Inter-Varsity Press (1995).
[60] John R.W. Stott, *The Cross of Christ* (Leicester: Inter-Varsity Press, 1986), p 40.

If it divides, nevertheless, it is essential. In the reality of our Lord's death and resurrection, believers find true life. The cross of Christ is at the heart of our preaching, pastoring, worship, community life and total Christian experience. To be sure, Christ is no longer on the cross, he is risen. The cross of Christ is an empty cross. However, we can never rightly divorce our present blessings and future hopes from the once for all death of Jesus on a Roman cross.

This study on John Owen is a call for contemporary Christians, facing an immediate task of gospel ministry, to turn back to help from Owen. Naturally, we need to interpret Owen carefully and cautiously. He wrote into his own, specific cultural context. Things have changed since the seventeenth century! However, there is a freshness to his counsel. It can fit the best of times and the worst of times; in other words, times like ours. Days in which we must determine to preach Christ, and him crucified into the Corinth of our contemporary society and culture.

For Further Reading

The Works of John Owen are still available in the 16 Volume, William H. Goold (ed.), edition reprinted by The Banner of Truth Trust, 3 Murrayfield Road, Edinburgh EH12 6EL or Po Box 621, Carlisle, PA. 17013, USA.

Sinclair B. Ferguson, *John Owen on the Christian Life* (Edinburgh and Carlisle, Pa.: Banner of Truth, 1987).

Michael Green, *The Empty Cross of Christ* (London: Hodder and Stoughton, 1984).

Joanna and Alister McGrath, *The Dilemma of Self-Esteem – the Cross and Christian Confidence* (Wheaton, Ill, and Cambridge, England: Crossway Books, 1992).

Gavin J. McGrath, *Grace and Duty in Puritan Spirituality* (Bramcote, Notts: Grove Books, 1991).

James I. Packer, *Among God's Giants: Aspects of Puritan Christianity* (Eastboume: Kingsway, 1991).

John Stott, *The Cross of Christ* (Leicester: Inter-Varsity Press, 1986).

Peter Toon, *God's Statesman: the life and work of John Owen* (Exeter: Paternoster Press, 1971).

Using the Shield of Faith: Puritan Attitudes to Combat with Satan

Peter Jensen

Introduction: Contemporary Dualism 127
1. The Work of Satan 129
    1.1 *The Power of Satan* *130*
    1.2 *The Power of God* *131*
2. The Shield of Faith 132
    2.1 *Faith and Justification* *133*
    2.2 *Faith and Adoption* *133*
    2.3 *Faith and Truth* *134*
3. Faith and Conflict 135
4. Scripture and Conflict 137
Conclusion 139

PETER F. JENSEN is the Archbishop of Sydney, Australia. His DPhil from Oxford was on the life of faith in the teaching of Elizabethan Protestants and from 1973 until his consecration as Archbishop in 2001 he was first Lecturer and then Principal of Moore Theological College in Sydney. He is the author of several books including *The Revelation of God* and *The Future of Jesus* and also serves as General Secretary of the worldwide *Fellowship of Confessing Anglicans* (GAFCON/FCA).

Introduction: Contemporary Dualism

Charismatic Renewal, The Search for a Theology is the title of a recent book by Tom Smail, Andrew Walker and Nigel Wright. All three authors owe a great deal to the pentecostal/charismatic movements, but all express their reflective criticisms. Andrew Walker, who has now become a Russian Orthodox Christian, writes perceptively on 'The Devil You Think You Know: Demonology and the Charismatic Movement.'

In this chapter he suggests that the fundamental dualism of the charismatic movement, with the world divided between God and the devil, has led its adherents to a sort of paranoia. He argues that this was not true in classic pentecostalism, but that it has become true in the post-second world war charismatic movement. He traces the way in which the demonic is regarded as a spiritual infestation, resulting in a paranoid universe.

Satan's attacks are thought to take the form of the spirits of lust, anger, jealousy and even nervousness and nicotine. Certain teachers have

> pioneered a belief in the prevalence of witchcraft in our societies and the danger of amulets and charms, which they saw as demonically infused, or at least under the dominance of Satan. They talked not only of demons trying to control individual bodies, they also talked of "strong men," super-demonic powers that dominated – along with the lesser devils – churches, cities and whole nations.[1]

Social groups, such as world religions, homosexuals or feminists can be demonised.

To this way of thought, everyone needs deliverance, Christian or not. Indeed, in the thinking of some teachers, demons can enter a human being 'through abortion, sexual intercourse, the womb during

---

[1] Andrew Walker, 'The Devil You Think you Know: Demonology and the Charismatic Movement' in *Charismatic Renewal, The Search for a Theology* (London: SPCK, 1995) p 91.

pregnancy, a traumatic birth, genetic inheritance.'[2] Walker quotes Bill Subritzky, a leader in the demonic warfare, as claiming, 'On occasions I have seen spirits like flies attached to the back of a person's head.'[3] Not surprisingly, Walker observes that the paranoid universe favours the rise of 'men and women of power' who can protect us from this malign potency. It also leads to fear: 'Ironically, what is demonic about the paranoid universe is not that it is a world that suddenly sees demons everywhere, but that it is a world in bondage to fear.'[4]

It is not possible to make a simple transfer from the present moment to the world of the reformers and the puritans. But the first Protestants also had to give serious theological attention to the demonic.[5] The 1590s, for example, saw a major controversy about exorcism. The earlier Protestant belief had been that it was not open to post-apostolic Christians to exorcise persons allegedly possessed by the devil. The example of Christ did not constitute a charter for us. Indeed, the devil would be only too pleased if we were to chat with him, and may even do our bidding as a way of deceiving us about his real power. All traces of exorcism were removed from the Prayer Book, and the Christian was exhorted to use prayer alone if assailed by the devil.

Roman Catholics continued the practice of exorcism, however, and in 1597, a well-known puritan preacher, John Darrell (fl. 1562-1607) spent several months in Nottingham endeavouring to exorcise a man named William Sommers. The ecclesiastical authorities became involved, and a legal and literary struggle ensued, with John Deacon and John Walker the chief theological adversaries of Darrell.[6]

In the end, we can detect three points of view about possession and exorcism. There was first what may be called a 'sceptical' position adopted by Deacon and Walker. They emphasised both the possibility of

---

[2] p 94.
[3] *Ibid.*
[4] p 93.
[5] I do not propose to enter into the discussion of what constitutes a puritan. Suffice to say that I believe that there are strong theological links between much early Protestantism and late puritanism, and that I have focused most attention on persons generally acknowledged at the time and later to be 'puritans.'
[6] R A Marchant is willing to identify Deacon as a puritan. See *The Puritans and the Church Courts in the Diocese of York* 1560-1642 (London: Longmans, Green & Co., 1960), p 145.

fraud, and also God's sovereignty and the power of Christ's death to deal with Satan. On philosophical grounds they doubted the ability of Satan to possess people, and they saw his influence as spiritual rather than physical.

Second, Darrell and others were clearly attracted by the possibility that demonic power could be overcome by demonstrations of divine power through human hands. They were countering the Roman Catholic appeal to a religion which could be seen to 'work,' with their own experiential efforts. Darrell showed great interest in combing the text of scripture for the smallest details of possession and exorcism in order to get guidance about what he needed to do.

Third, men like the leading puritan thinkers William Perkins and George Gifford (although not directly involved in the Darrell controversy) accepted the physical power of the devil, but by emphasising God's sovereignty turned the attention away from human power to divine. They accepted the view that the day of miracles was passed, and that no-one should attempt to exorcise by speaking to the devil. Our proper response is prayer.[7]

Many contemporary Christians regard the Darrell approach as the only tenable one. But there are important theological elements to the Perkins/Gifford view which we would do well to observe and learn from. I am going to argue that, although they failed to sustain their position rigorously enough, we can learn from their failures as well as from their insights. Indeed, it was the emphasis of Deacon and Walker on the Christ's victorious death which would have helped to sustain the logic of this third position.

1. The Work of Satan

One way of explaining what early puritans taught about Satan and the demonic is to explore the riches of the Geneva Bible. The marginal notes give us an insight into early Protestant and puritan teaching.

---

[7] I ought to add that Gifford, Perkins and others were involved in a major way with the debate about witchcraft, but there is no space to discuss their response to that matter here.

There are two great themes to consider: the power of Satan, and the power of God.

1.1   The Power of Satan

At Satan's instigation, God was disobeyed, the world ruined and mankind corrupted. Satan acquired for himself 'the power of sinne and death' (Genesis 3:15). As a result he exercises a certain rule over mankind: 'All townes and countries whence Gods worde, and good living is banished, are the throne of Satan, and also those places where the word is not preached syncerly, nor maners a right reformed' (Revelation 2:13).

The devil is aided in this by his 'wonderful nature' (Romans 8:38). As the head of a vast horde of demons he is virtually ubiquitous (see Luke 8:30), and is capable of enough foreknowledge to give accurate predictions (Acts 16:16, Titus 1:12).[8]

Since he has already secured some dominion over unbelievers, his chief antagonism is to the church. He seeks to make Christians doubt God's word. He does this in the first place by sheer guile. He is a past-master of the lie, and will sometimes even tell the truth in order to pervert a deeper truth. One method of approach is through 'suggestion' or temptation to do the wrong thing. The Christian must watch, 'lest Satan steals on you un-awares' (1 Corinthians 16:13). His 'chiefest subtiltie' is 'to cause us not to feare Gods threatenings' (Genesis 3:4). The temptation of Adam and Eve, and the temptation of Jesus provide the only descriptions of the mechanism of temptation in scripture. The Geneva Bible draws conclusions from the text about what we are to do: 'It is not enough twise or thrise to resist Satan: for he never ceaseth to tempt: or if he relent a little, it is to the end that he maye renewe his force and assaile us more sharply' (Luke 4:13).

But Satan is not restricted to guile. As the case of Job demonstrates, he is able to make us suffer through violence in the physical world. Satan is by nature 'ever ranging for his pray' (Job 1:7), seeking to destroy the Christian, just as Job had been destroyed. In particular, he assaults the faith of the man of God: 'This is the most

---

[8] The biblical texts all refer to the relevant marginal notes of the first (1560) edition of the Geneva Bible.

grevous temtation of the faithful, when their faith is assailed, and when Satan goeth about to persuade them that their trust in God is vaine' (Job 2:9).

The extent of Job's sufferings indicated that Satan is capable of exercising considerable power in the world. The Geneva Bible is cautious about Satan's might, but it attributes cases of pestilence and paralysis to him (Psalm 91:3, Luke 13:11), it agrees that Satan may possess, and it accepts the Bible's teaching that Satan can do miracles (see Revelation 13:13, and 2 Thessalonians 2:10). It also regards him as responsible for the success of magic. Thus, in the case of Saul and the witch of Endor, the apparition is actually Satan who 'toke upon him the forme of Samuel' (1 Samuel 28:14).

Satan's violence is especially apparent through the persecution of Christians and it is linked specifically with the papacy. The Catholic claims for miracles are 'according to the operation of Satain ... with all power, signes and miracles of lies' (Revelation 13:15). Protestants, as we have seen, made no claims for contemporary miracles. Any such experience was immediately greeted with suspicion. Protestantism was a religion in which the word had power.

1.2 The Power of God

The Geneva Bible describes Satan as the 'prince of this world (who) almost hathe the universal government' (Revelation 12:3). But there can be no doubt that the power of Satan is not absolute. The notes are at pains to emphasise that God's providence overrules the devil: 'although Satan be adversarie to God, yet he is compelled to obey him, and do him all homage, without whose permission, and appointment he can do nothing' (Job 1:6). Satan cannot even leave God's presence without permission, and he 'can go no further in punishing then God hathe limited unto him' (Job 2:6). There is, therefore, no dualism in the Geneva Bible's treatment of Satan; if he does harm, it is at God's command.

The New Testament reveals the second important check to Satan's power, the victory of Christ: 'The Messias came downe from heaven into the earth, to triumph over Satan, deathe and sinne and led them as prisoners and slaves, which before were conquerors, and kept all in subjection' (Ephesians 4:8).

When Jesus predicted that the prince of this world would be cast out, the marginal note comments, 'The crosse is the meane to gather the Church of God together, and to drawe men to heaven' (John 12:31). As this gospel is preached, and people believe it, so the hold of Satan is broken (Luke 10:18).

It is not surprising, therefore, that the Geneva Bible as a whole is moderate in its references to Satan. Certainly he does not dominate its pages, and there are very few marginal references to the devil where the text is silent. Nor can it be maintained that the notes substantially inflate what can already be seen in the text. Indeed, much care is taken to bring the power of God and the victory of Christ into close connection with references to the demonic. Nonetheless, when all that is said, the picture is quite formidable: Satan has power to bring sickness and to possess; he can control the forces of nature in order to afflict; all occult happenings, good or bad, and contemporary miracles are his work; he blinds, dominates and rules unbelievers; he inspires those who persecute the church; he is the moving force behind the papacy. He is a 'moste dangerous' enemy. And yet, who was the real enemy?

I have noted already that God ruled Satan. In a sense, therefore, God himself is the supreme 'enemy.' It is the sovereign Lord who upholds the basic order and harmony of the universe, and the notion of an independent malevolent force was denied as strenuously as the notion of luck or astral influence. God is the one with whom we had to do. The Protestants denuded the world of miracles, of exorcisms, of sacramental protection, of charms and relics and holy water, of holy men and holy times and holy places, and they denuded the universe of the crowds of saints thronging the church to counterbalance the demons. In the end they reduced spiritual reality to the One great power, God himself, and at the same time pressed home the sinfulness and alienation of human beings. What if God is not for us?

2. The Shield of Faith

George Gifford wrote extensively on matters to do with Satan. According to him, 'Faith apprehendeth the power of God and armeth us with it.'[9] Three key issues were involved in this bold claim.

2.1 Faith and Justification

In so emphasising the sovereignty of God and the sinful impotence of man, the Protestants left their hearers and readers with the agonising problem of the angry God. But the heart of the reformation message, the heart of the puritan message, was Jesus Christ. Christ, to use the words of William Perkins, was the 'sum of scripture' and the 'scope and drift' of the Old and New Testaments. The devil, at God's behest, assaulted men by tempting them to do wrong or by sending them trials and afflictions. He held sway over those who were unforgiven, because their sins put them into his power, and so Christ's death to free sinners was the supreme victory over Satan. By it, Christ released his people from the devil's tyranny; those who were being saved had no further cause to fear or serve the devil, although he would continue to attack them. Simple faith in Jesus Christ brought the power of God in forgiveness.

2.2 Faith and Adoption

Not only did faith bring forgiveness, it brought to the believer a filial relationship with God and, as a result, a new and positive relationship with creation. The Lord who ruled heaven and earth was now his most precious Father, who would do all things for good. The temptations suffered by Christ were evidence that he would sympathise with any who were similarly tried, and his afflictions enabled him to console any who were suffering. The believer was adopted by God, and so was safe from Satan's power over him, a fact of which the death of Christ was the sure pledge. Furthermore, the power of Christ's spirit in mortification and the new life gave the believer strength to defeat temptation and to withstand trials. When a person placed his trust in God, all the resources of God were his; as a justified sinner he could have complete confidence in God's fatherly care, and so in God's control of Satan for his good. He knew this because of the love of God shown in Christ. The believer's duty, therefore, was to exercise himself in prayer to God for relief (since God ruled the devil), and to give himself to follow the

---

[9] G Gifford, *Two Sermons on 1 Peter 5, verses 8 and 9* (1597) p 47.

precepts of scripture and thus resist the devil. The world ruled by this sovereign God was cleansed of other spiritual forces and became both the simple and good arena of the Christian life.

2.3 Faith and Truth

True faith is based on the truth alone. Faith has no power of itself – it draws all its power from its object. Faith is trust in Jesus Christ, but it involves confidence in all of God's word. It was, therefore, absolutely vital that scripture be rightly apprehended in order to defeat Satan. As William Perkins observed, it was 'the written word of God rightly wielded by the hand of faith' which was 'the most sufficient weapon for the repelling of Satan and the vanquishing of him in all his temptations.'[10] He is not speaking here of the attitude which simply throws texts at the perceived source of temptation; that, too, is conferring with the devil. Rather our proper recourse is to turn to God himself, in his word, to trust him and to obey him. Relate to God! A faith based on other than scripture was not faith but superstition. Faith and superstition are identical when thought of subjectively or experientially; they divide sharply from one another according to their object.

It was on the basis of this understanding of faith and truth that other means of fighting the devil were repudiated as superstitious. Methods in common use such as the sign of the cross, or ringing church bells, or employing spoken formulae had no genuine effect, and pandered to man's self-confidence. Such methods were felt to attribute too much authority to Satan for they assumed that he was able to come and go without God's specific direction.

Most important of all, as I have already indicated, exorcisms were abandoned by most puritans, despite the fact that they were described in the New Testament. It was regarded as not being within the rights of the ordinary person, including ministers, to talk directly to the devil. The precedents of scripture, even those involving Christ, were not regarded as implying promises or commands for later disciples. To quote another Elizabethan puritan, Henry Holland,

I see no warrant we have to talke or question with Sathan: for

---

[10] W Perkins, *The Combat betweene Christ and the Divell displayed* (1606), p 19.

hee is the Lord's executioner, hee hath sent him, what authoritie then wee have to commaund him to depart, where God has sent him ... the onely way, no doubt, is to entreat the Lord to be pacified, and (for the Lord) to rebuke Sathan."

As was felt to be the case with a whole range of superstitions, an appeal to scripture could simply cloak an attack on the sufficiency of what God was offering the Christian in Christ.

The power of faith, then, was regarded as considerable, since it was the power of God in the gospel. It depended for its success on a proper attitude to scripture, seeing Christ as its sum and its theme, seeing Christ's victory at the cross as its decisive moment. How well did the power of faith fare?

3. Faith and Conflict

If anything, the power attributed to Satan increased through the Elizabethan period. One author maintained that the devil is 'neere our elbowes at all times;'[12] Henry Holland believed that Satan used secret poisons to cause incurable diseases;[13] others spoke of the way in which he deceived the senses, moved bodies through the air and performed other wonders. Indeed, all contemporary marvels including such things as ghostly appearances and miracles were attributed to either fraud or the devil. Gifford warned that 'hee hath a thousand wayes, a thousand occasions, yea ten thousand sleights and crafty meanes for to winde in himself.'[14] So incessant were his assaults thought to be that he rivalled God in the intimate nearness of his personal relationship. Good influences seemed feeble by comparison.

While such things were being said about the devil, faith was undergoing a crisis. We have already seen how Gifford isolated faith as the crucial point. But he himself (rightly) insisted on faith being genuine. To establish this he further insisted that faith be tested by its

---

[11] H Holland, *Spiritual Preservatives against the Pestilence* (1603) pp 69-70.
[12] T Bentham, *A notable and comfortable exposition* (1578) signs. E6.
[13] *Op cit*, pp 68-73.
[14] *Op cit*, p 46.

fruit. According to Gifford,

> Such onlie as by a lively faith doe feel the power of Christ in them mortifying and slaying sinne, and quickening them with righteousnesse and true holinesse even to walke in the light, and to bring forth the fruites and vertues of the spirite, have the strong consolation.[15]

By making sanctification the test of faith, Gifford was trying to give an access to an area of incontrovertible experience which would reassure. But he then made this reassurance almost impossible to find, by also teaching that 'the reprobate receive a kinde of faith and zeale, which yet is not the true and lively faith.'[16] By linking sanctification so firmly to assurance, while allowing that the reprobate showed some of the signs of sanctification, Gifford made it far more difficult for a person of sensitive conscience to feel that he had the 'stedfast faith' necessary to defeat the devil. The puritan Andrew Kingsmill, who adopted the same approach, was even bold enough to declare that sinners were beyond Christ's help if they continued to entertain sinful thoughts: 'If thou have a pleasure and delight in sinne, if there were a thousand Christs in heaven, they could not save thee.'[17]

William Perkins was another whose treatment of faith had the effect of discouraging assurance. His strategy was to lower the standards of faith. 'To see and feele in ourselves the want of any grace pertaining to salvation, and to be greeved therefore, is the grace itselfe,' became enough.[18] Indeed, Perkins allowed the possibility that Satan may have such a hold over even a pious mind that the result may be blank despair. There was a real danger that Satan himself would become the dominant figure in Christian experience.

There were, in short, considerable difficulties in the way in which these Protestants handled the theme of faith. The introspective search for evidence of sanctification, and the ambiguous nature of the evidence when it was discovered, made assured faith difficult to sustain. It will be remembered, however, that there was a second aspect of their defence against Satan, namely 'the written word of God, rightly wielded

---

[15] *Ibid*, p 83.
[16] *Ibid*, p 108.
[17] A Kingsmill, *A Conference, containing a Conflict had with Satan* (1577) sig. Aiii.
[18] *Op cit*, p 23.

by the hand of faith.' How was the 'sword of the Spirit' to be rightly wielded?

4.   Scripture and Conflict

There are three great temptation narratives in the Bible, those of Eve, Job and Christ. Commentaries and sermons on them came from a substantial number of puritans and other writers, including Henry Smith, William Perkins, John Udall and Henry Holland. Despite the differences in skill and insight which characterise the different authors, they share four features in common.

First, there is a careful attention to the details of scripture. In the attempt to gain exact knowledge of the ways of Satan, the text is subject to a minute examination, and anything which it may be thought to yield about Satan and his methods is drawn out and applied. Bishop Babington, for example, commented that if we think that Satan is absent from our rich houses, then remember that Eve was tempted even in Paradise: 'even in our Princely Pallaces, our glistening Chambers, our dainty and delicate Gardens, the divell will be chatting with us.'[19]

Second, Satan becomes the most lively figure in the exposition, with the result that he seems closer and more active than God. There is, for example, the revelatory role he assumes, 'chatting with us' as Babington put it. Whereas the word of God has to be laboriously recalled by the believer, the devil is always whispering and cajoling. According to Henry Smith, Satan is 'like the circumference, and man is, as it were, in the Centre: that is, temptations goe around about them, and he dwelleth in the midst of them.'[20] Henry Holland attributed great winds, comets, sicknesses, blazing stars, and 'meteor, of all sortes, and in all partes of the ayr' to the work of evil spirits.[21]

Third, the need to provide practical spiritual counsel shaped the exposition of all the writers. The professed aim was to give an

---

[19] G. Babington, 'Comfortable Notes on the Five Bookes of Moses' from *The Workes* (1615) pp 17-19.
[20] H Smith, *The Sermons of Master Henrie Smith* (1592) pp 986-987.
[21] H Holland, *An Exposition of the First and Second Chapter of Job* (1596) pp 183, 186.

understanding of contemporary satanic attack, with directions about how to defeat it. Was Christ fasting? Udall points out that the devil comes 'when, or where man is weakest and most like to bee most easely overthrowne.'[22] Was Christ in the desert? Perkins claimed that the church, too, 'is in this world as in a wildernesse.'[23] Was Christ on the temple pinnacle? Bentham warned that those in high office are 'most egged on by the devil.'[24] In short, it was perfectly clear that the chief purpose of the exposition was to cater for the needs of practical religion rather than to concentrate on the natural meaning of the text.

Fourth, there are inevitable uncertainties attendant upon such a use of scripture. On the face of it, this may be the opposite of what could be expected; indeed, to read this material is to be impressed with the authority with which the pastors spoke about the methods and powers of the devil. But this authority masked a real difficulty in coming to assured results. The very nature of the subject matter contributed to this, since almost no exaggeration was impossible when the power of Satan was being spoken of. If a person was spiritually downcast, it was supposed that Satan would find this an ideal time to attack; but if the opposite pertained, Satan was just as likely to tempt. Virtually anything was possible with so fiendish an adversary. The result was that the appearance of precision was given when he was spoken of, but the demand for clear and precise information was thwarted.

Taken together, these four features of the Protestant exposition of the temptation narratives have an important bearing on the use of the scriptures. Just as in the doctrine of faith there was a tendency to obscure the role of Christ, so in the treatment of the Bible there was a distinct tendency to neglect Christ's place as the 'sum' of scripture. This tendency manifested itself in a detailed interest in Christian spirituality at the expense of the work of Christ. Each of those who wrote on the temptation of Christ mentioned his final victory at the cross, but the overwhelming stress fell on the 'use' of the doctrine in instruction for the Christian. Perkins started well, noting that 'in the temptation Christ stood in our room and stead.' Even he, however, had a greater interest in the practical use of the story. The thrust of these tracts precluded the

---

[22] J Udall, 'The Combate betwixt CHRIST and the Devill,' *Certain Sermons* (1596) sig. B 6 ii.
[23] W Perkins, *The Combat betweene Christ and the Divell displayed* (1606) p 11.
[24] *Op Cit,* sig. E 6.

theology of redemption from dominating, invited the reader to put himself at the centre of the picture, and inflated the significance of Satan. The result was an intense interest in moralising conclusions which could only be obtained by ensuring that every detail of the text served the desire for practical relevance.

Conclusion

I referred in my introduction to Andrew Walker's phrase 'the paranoid universe,' and his observation that 'what is demonic about the paranoid universe is not that it is a world that suddenly sees demons everywhere, but that it is a world in bondage to fear.'

What we have seen in the reformed religion of puritanism are the resources to put the devil firmly in his place. The chief resource is the gospel itself. Through faith in the gospel we are justified and adopted as God's children. We do not have to deal with other spiritual entities such as saints or demons. At a fundamental level, the created world is cleansed of spirit, and such things as charms lose all their power to bless or harm. The natural world is accorded its proper place in the scheme of things, and we are left to focus on God. If we fear God, we need not fear the devil.

It is true, as we have seen, that these insights were endangered when faith become introspective and when the scriptures began to be used primarily for spirituality and moralism. Even so, all was not lost; the gospel's work continued as people read the scriptures. The world of frightening spiritual phenomena became less significant as it was recognised to be both demonic and unimportant, and the world of nature came to be studied in a new, positive and helpful way. Faith continued to be assured of the fatherly goodness of God towards us in Christ Jesus, and so to release us from fear of the occult and especially fear of the devil.

The contemporary recurrence of these fears and the accompanying adherence to powerful human leaders is deeply troubling. What are we to make, then, of the advice of Wayne Grudem in his recent *Systematic Theology?* To him, God wants Christians to speak directly to a demon who is allegedly troubling someone, rather than just to pray. He likens this to evangelism, where God wishes us to speak and not merely to pray. He says, 'the New Testament pattern seems to be that God ordinarily expects Christians themselves to speak directly to unclean spirits.' This he sees as resisting the devil. He even suggests that children troubled by dreams of witches or goblins or other frightening images should be taught to say, 'In Jesus' name, go away!'[25]

At the very least, the judgement of our Reformation ancestors that such practices are wrong should make us think hard. To my mind, Grudem's advice is most unhelpful. It puts the focus where it does not belong, by encouraging young people to talk to Satan and to believe that dreams may be caused by him when they are far more likely to have an entirely natural explanation. God does want us to relate to the people we are evangelising; does he want us to relate, even negatively, to demonic forces?

When the Gospels describe the great encounter between the Lord Jesus and Satan, their primary purpose is not to lead us to follow Christ's methods. We see in this encounter his glory, in that he did battle with Satan on our behalf and put the evil one to flight. We see here our own weakness and his great strength. Ultimately, we see here the cross at which his supreme victory was won. It is by faith, and wielding the shield of faith, that we ourselves will gather the marvellous fruit of his victory, and so put the devil to flight.

---

[25] Wayne Grudem, *Systematic Theology* (Grand Rapids, Mich.: Zondervan, 1994) p 430.

An Anglican to Remember
William Perkins: Puritan Popularizer

J. I. Packer

1. Meet William Perkins 143
2. Perkins' Ministry 147
3. Precepts for Spiritual Progress 156
4. Perkins the Theologian 162

JAMES I. PACKER began his ministry as Curate of St. John the Baptist, Harborne Heath in Birmingham. After several years in England as Principal of Tyndale Hall, Bristol and Warden of Latimer House, Oxford he moved in 1979 to Regent College, Vancouver (Canada). He is arguably the most significant and influential Reformed Evangelical Anglican writer of the last 100 years, and has played a key role in the revival of interest in Reformed and Puritan theology over the last six decades. His 1955 DPhil from Oxford was on redemption in the thought of Richard Baxter. He has since published a large number of books including the classic *Knowing God* and *Among God's Giants: The Puritan Vision of the Christian Life*. He is also General Editor of the English Standard Version.

1. Meet William Perkins

The name of William Perkins is hardly known today outside a small circle of professional historians and theologians. It may therefore come as a surprise to learn that during the half-century from 1585 to 1635 Perkins was both the best-known English international theologian, being classed with Calvin and Beza as third in what someone called 'the trinity of the orthodox,' and was far and away the best-known and best-selling English writer of Christian books for ordinary people. But so indeed he was. No Puritan author save Richard Baxter ever sold better than Perkins, and no Puritan thinker ever did more to shape and solidify historic Puritanism itself.

Many nowadays know that the real Puritanism was not the eccentric and combative Protestant Pharisaism that nineteenth-century novels and history books imagined. Many know that the real Puritanism was an evangelical holiness movement seeking to implement its vision of spiritual renewal, national and personal, in the church, the state, and the home; in education, evangelism, and economics; in individual discipleship and devotion, and in pastoral care and competence. Many know that real Puritan piety centred upon regeneration and repentance, self-suspicion and self-examination, rational biblicism and righteous behaviour, discursive meditation and rhetorical prayer, faith in and love to Jesus Christ as Saviour and Lord, recognition of the sovereignty of God in providence, grace, and judgment, the comfort and joy of a well-grounded assurance, the need to educate and cherish one's conscience, the spiritual war against the world, the flesh, and the devil, the ethic of discipline and duty, and the saints' hope of glory. Few however know as yet that it was Perkins, quite specifically, who established Puritanism in this mould.

Who was this man William Perkins? He is a somewhat shadowy figure, but the main facts of his life are not in doubt. He was an Elizabethan in a very precise sense, for he was born in 1558, the year in which Elizabeth became queen, and he died of unrelieved gallstones at the age of 44, in 1602, shortly before Elizabeth's death in 1603. He was a Warwickshire man who in 1577, aged 19 – late in the day, by Elizabethan standards – went up to Christ's College, Cambridge, the most Puritan-minded house in the University at that time, where

Laurence Chaderton, a well-known gospel preacher, later to be master of Emmanuel and Perkins' lifelong friend, became his tutor. At first Perkins ran wild, but then was converted (details not known); a passion for theology now replaced the devotion to astrological studies that had marked him hitherto, and he impressed his peers by the thoroughness and speed with which he mastered the things of God. In 1584, having graduated M.A., he was elected to a fellowship at Christ's, and before the year was out, following a few months of strikingly effective evangelism on a volunteer basis in Cambridge gaol, he was also installed as lecturer (that is, endowed preacher) at Great St. Andrews, a poor and needy parish that brought in to its vicar the less than princely stipend of 10 pounds per annum. Perkins as lecturer was not the vicar, and whatever he received for his preaching would have come from private sources. We learn that when in 1595 he left Christ's to marry a lady named Timothye Cradock of Grantchester, parishioners and wealthy supporters augmented his income to ensure that his ministry at St. Andrews would continue; which it did, till Perkins died seven years and seven children later. When Thomas Goodwin, twelve years old and not yet a Christian, matriculated in 1613, so he tells us, 'the Town was then filled with the discourse of the Power of Mr Perkins, his Ministry still fresh in Mens Memories,' even though Perkins had been more than ten years in his grave.[1]

Nor was this the whole story, or even the main part of it. During the years that Perkins preached his pen was busy, and he left behind him almost separate treatises of various kinds, covering the whole range of theology, spirituality, and ethics, and including several major pieces of biblical exposition. Perkins' special strength both in preaching and on paper was to be systematic, scholarly, solid and simple at the same time. No one else in world Protestantism had hitherto produced material of Perkins' type and range at Perkins' level of lucidity, and soon Perkins' books were appearing in French, Dutch, Italian, Spanish, Czech, German, Hungarian, Latin, and Welsh. Ian Breward, writer of the best survey of Perkins' work to have appeared so far, explains Perkins' international popularity and influence as 'due to an attractive and practical piety, ability to popularise and an extraordinarily wide range of

---

[1] Thomas Goodwin, *Works* (Edinburgh: James Nichol, 11 vols., 1861-65), II.lviii (from 'The Life of Dr. Thomas Goodwin; compos'd out of his own papers and memoirs' by Thomas Goodwin, Jr.)

theological activity,' and observes that 'translating and publishing Perkins was a minor industry,' listing 29 translators and 28 publishers outside England to prove his point.[2] 'After his death,' writes William Haller, 'his disciples ... gathered up for publication or republication three tall volumes of his polemics, treatises and sermons ... No books, it is fair to say, were more often to be found upon the shelves of succeeding generations of preachers, and the name of no preacher recurs more often in later Puritan literature. 'As for his books,' Fuller observed half a century later, 'it is a miracle almost to conceive how thick they lye.'[3] It was these books that determined seventeenth-century Puritanism's profile and priorities, and that led the Dutch theologian Voetius in his treatise *Concerning Practical Theology*, in which many Puritan pietists are commended, to call Perkins 'the Homer [that is, the magisterial classic], of practical Englishmen.'[4]

We speak of George Stephenson as the Father of Railways because in designing the Rocket and in laying out first the Stockton and Darlington and then the Liverpool and Manchester lines he got everything basically right, albeit at a rudimentary level, so that the development of steam traction world-wide could and did proceed most successfully by following the guidelines he had established. In the same way we should call William Perkins the Father of Puritanism, for it was he more than anyone else who crystallised and delimited the essence of mainstream Puritan Christianity for the next hundred years. This makes it ironical, first, that Perkins detested and refused the word 'Puritan' as a label for himself and those like him, and, second, that among the forty or so Puritan writers who have been reprinted for the common Christian reader during the past forty years nothing by Perkins

---

[2] Intro, and ed., Ian Breward, *The Work of William Perkins* (Abingdon: Sutton Courtenay Press, 1969), pp xi, 130.
[3] William Haller, *The Rise of Puritanism* (New York: Columbia University Press, 1938), p 65; quoting Thomas Fuller, Abel Redevivus, 1651, p 434.
[4] Tr. and ed. J.W. Beardslee, *Reformed Dogmatics* (New York: Oxford University Press, 1966), pp 274-275.

has yet appeared.[5] To be sure, the irony diminishes on closer inspection, for the word 'Puritan' in Perkins' day carried implications of both a revolutionary spirit and a separatist purpose, and Perkins' plain-glass treatments of basic themes were all superseded by later Puritan treatments that were fuller and had more punch. But the key fact remains as stated: Perkins was the pioneer who shaped Puritanism in a decisive way, imparting to it the qualities that were to characterise it for the next hundred years.

Before Perkins, Calvinistic Anglicans seeking change in the national church had not been at one on their goals and priorities, and a strident hotheadedness had marked their public style. Some had sought Prayer Book revision, so as to get further away from Roman-type worship, and had flaunted their nonconformity to the established liturgical order. Some had sought a workable pattern of parochial church discipline, and had flung themselves into the crypto-Presbyterian classis movement, which had this as one of its aims. Not many had yet focused their goal in evangelistic terms, as the conversion of England to real godliness through teaching, preaching, and pastoral care. Perkins' example and influence, however, along with that of parish clergymen like Richard Greenham and Richard Rogers, Arthur Hildersam and John Dod, established mainstream Puritanism as a movement majoring on evangelism and spiritual life, bearing with ecclesiastical inconvenience for the time being in order to fulfil in the Church of England a full-scale soul-saving ministry. Puritanism, with its

---

[5] The major reprinters of Puritans have been Banner of Truth Trust (Edinburgh) and Soli Deo Gloria (Morgan, PA). English Puritans whose works have been reprinted in whole or in part include Thomas Adams, Henry Ainsworth, William Bates, Richard Baxter, Lewis Bayly, Robert Bolton, Samuel Bolton, William Bridge, Thomas Brooks, Jeremiah Burroughs, John Bunyan, Joseph Caryl, Thomas Case, Arthur Dent, Thomas Doolittle, John Downame, John Flavel, Thomas Goodwin, William Gurnall, Matthew Henry, Oliver Heywood, Ezekiel Hopkins, John Howe, James Janeway, Christopher Love, Matthew Mead, Walter Marshall, John Owen, Matthew Poole, John Preston, Nathanael Ranew, Edward Reynolds, Ralph Robinson, Richard Sibbes, Henry Scudder, Obadiah Sedgewick, George Swinnock, Robert Traill, Thomas Vincent, Thomas Watson. Likeminded Scotsmen whose work has reappeared include Hugh Binning, David Dickson, William Guthrie, George Hutcheson, Samuel Rutherford and Thomas Boston. Reprinted American Puritans include Thomas Hooker, Thomas Shepard, Solomon Stoddard, and (a Puritan born out of due time) Jonathan Edwards. Breward's volume of extracts from Perkins is a selection designed for scholars rather than the general Christian reading public.

complex of biblical, devotional, ecclesiastical, reformational, polemical and cultural concerns, came of age, we might say, with Perkins, and began to display characteristically a wholeness of spiritual vision and a maturity of Christian patience that had not been seen in it before.

2. Perkins' Ministry

How, we may now ask, did Perkins himself approach his own ministerial work? We are told that in daily life he was a man of peace, studied moderation, and a personal sanctity that impressed everyone. He was faithful in fulfilling his role as a professional academic and a college tutor, but it is clear that his wider ministry at Great St. Andrews, and the popular writing that went with it, were his chief concerns. We are told that at the head of the title-page of each of his manuscripts he would write this message to himself: 'Thou art a Minister of the Word: Mind thy business.' That, certainly, is what he did.

Here is Benjamin Brook's account of Perkins as a preacher. It goes back to Thomas Fuller, who though a royalist in politics was a Puritan in his Christianity, and was fascinated by Perkins, who died six years before he was born; Fuller researched Perkins, wrote a brief life of him, and introduced him as a model of faithfulness in ministry in several of his own writings. Drawing on Fuller, Brook pinpoints Perkins' pulpit strengths as follows:

> His hearers consisted of collegians, townsmen, and people from the country. This required those peculiar ministerial endowments which providence had richly bestowed upon him. In all his discourses, his style and his subject were accommodated to the capacities of the common people, while, at the same time, the pious scholars heard him with admiration ... Mr. Perkins' sermons were all law, and all gospel. He was a rare instance of those opposite gifts meeting in so eminent a degree in the same preacher, even the vehemence and thunder of Boanerges, to awaken sinners to a sense of their sin and danger, and to drive them from destruction; and the persuasion and comfort of Barnabas, to pour the wine and oil of gospel consolation into their wounded spirits. He used to apply the terrors of the law so directly to the consciences of his hearers,

that their hearts would often sink under the convictions; and he used to pronounce the word damn with so peculiar an emphasis, that it left a doleful echo in their ears a long time after.[6]

His preaching was as erudite and edifying as it was authoritative and clear. 'In a word,' declares Fuller, 'the Scholar could have no learneder, the Townsmen no plainer Sermonds.' And again: 'Our Perkins brought the schools into the Pulpit, and unshelling their controversies out of their hard school-terms, made thereof plain and wholesome meat for his people.'[7] Majestic and magisterial, expository and evangelical, informal and applicatory, Perkins' preaching set standards for the whole Puritan movement thereafter, just as it brought benefit to great numbers in the Cambridge of his own day.

But this was not the whole of his ministry. Like his older contemporary, Richard Greenham of Dry Drayton, just outside Cambridge, Perkins became known as an expert in spiritual pathology, and he fulfilled a notable counselling mininstry to confused and tormented souls who for one reason or another feared themselves spiritually ruined and lost. Here is one example from Perkins' gaol ministry of 1584, narrated by Samuel Clarke in a book dated 1654.

> A young felon mounting the scaffold looked panicky and half-dead. Perkins, attending the execution as chaplain laboured to cheer up his spirits, and finding him still in an agony, and distress of mind, he said to him, What man? What is the matter with thee? Art thou afraid of death?
>
> Ah no (said the prisoner, shaking his head) but of a worser thing.
>
> Sayest thou so (said Master Perkins) come down again man, and thou shalt see what God's grace will do to strengthen thee: Whereupon the prisoner coming down, Master Perkins took him by the hand and made him kneel down with himself at the ladder foot ... when that blessed man of God made such an effectual prayer in confession of sins ... as made the prisoner

---

[6] Benjamin Brook, *The Lives of the Puritans*, 1813, (repr. Pittsburgh: Soli Deo Gloria, 1994), II. p 130.
[7] Thomas Fuller, *op.cit.*, p 434; *The Holy State*, 1642, p 89.

burst out into abundance of tears; and Master Perkins finding that he had brought him low enough, even to hell gates, he proceeded to the second part of his prayer, and therein to show him the Lord Jesus ... stretching forth his blessed hand of mercy ... which he did so sweetly press with such heavenly art ... as made him break into new showers of tears for joy of the inward consolation which he found ... who (the prayer being ended) rose from his knees cheerfully, and went up the ladder again so comforted, and took his death with such patience, and alacrity, as if he actually saw himself delivered from the hell which he feared before, and heaven opened for the receiving of his soul.[8]

Nor was it only to persons of the criminal class that Perkins ministered in this way. It is well known that at the end of the sixteenth century many serious souls were troubled and often desperate about their condition and prospects before God, and this is sometimes seen as the unhealthy fruit of injudicious and excessive Puritan preaching about predestination and hellfire. That the Puritans were never mealy-mouthed on these two topics is certainly true, but all the evidence shows that they presented them in a pastorally responsible way, and a more adequate explanation of the distresses people felt centres upon four other factors.

First, uncertainties and anxieties about the future pervaded late Elizabethan community life, partly as a reaction to what seemed to be the permanent embattled hostility to England of the whole Roman Catholic world, partly at least as a spin-off from the enterprising but often anarchic and calamitous individualism that had developed during Elizabeth's reign on the economic and political fronts; and this mood of anxiety naturally infected English religion.

Second, as in the modern West, a quarter of the population needs treatment for depression at some point in their lives, so in Puritan times depressive tendencies, linked as so often today with obsessive-compulsive neuroses, were widespread; indeed, it was an era in which a measure of 'melancholy,' as depression was then called, was expected and even cultivated among the cultured, so naturally problems of spiritual depression were widespread.

---

[8] Samuel Clarke, *The Marrow of Ecclesiastical History*, 1654, pp 416-417; quoted from Breward, *op.cit.,* p 9-10, with modernized spelling.

Third, in that age of compulsory church attendance Puritans like Perkins rightly laid stress on the need for self-suspicion and self-search in order to arouse the complacent among their hearers to the possibility of their still being unconverted and hell-bound, and such teaching has a naturally traumatic and anxious-making effect, as of course it is intended to.

And, fourth and most important of all, the Holy Spirit worked in power in England throughout the Puritan period, so that the impact of gospel preaching, conviction of sin, demands for repentance, and the fear of divine rejection, went very deep.

I venture to affirm that there was nothing intrinsically unhealthy about any of this from a spiritual standpoint; much unhealthier was, and is, the unconcern of those who refuse to care about the issues of eternity as the gospel sets them out and who ridicule preachers and people who do in fact care about them. That persons convicted of sin, and those whom we would label clinically depressed, should feel hopeless and helpless should not cause us surprise. And anyhow, the record states that many troubled souls came to Perkins one on one, and he was able to help them to faith, hope, confidence, and devoted discipleship. As Fuller quaintly puts it: 'An excellent Chirurgeon *[surgeon]* he was at joynting of a broken soul, and at stating of a doubtful conscience.'[9] In Perkins' pastoral counselling, no less than in his pulpit expositions, wisdom about the paths God opens to conversion and the peace God gives to troubled hearts flowed abundantly, and there was joy in Cambridge as a result.

The many businesslike laymen's books on principles and problems of Christian living that came from Perkins' pen were part of this same ministry. They were written, not to advance the author's reputation and career, but to build up Englishmen in the Christian faith. When Perkins' ministry began, Protestant England had no devotional literature of its own at popular level at all. Literate clergy – a minority at that stage in Anglican history, be it said – could enlarge their overall Christian understanding by reading Calvin, his successor at Geneva Beza, the *Decades* of Bullinger, and the two official Anglican books of Homilies. If questions of church order captured their interest, they could pursue them via the keen though dryish writings of

---

[9] Thomas Fuller, *The Holy State*, p 90.

Cartwright, Whitgift, and Travers. If they wanted anti-Roman reinforcing, Jewel's Apology and Foxe's Acts and Monuments were available. But there was nothing whatever as yet for their literate parishioners to read, to build them up in the faith. Perkins set himself to fill this gap. If you think of him as in this respect a forerunner of J.C. Ryle, C.S. Lewis, and John Stott, you will not be far wrong. Perkins devoted his first-class mind and his flair for simple forceful statement to the production of popular nurturing literature for laypeople. Let us now survey his achievement.

The Apostles' Creed, the Lord's Prayer and the Ten Commandments were, and are, the three classic formulations on which mainstream Christianity rests, and around which the Prayer Book Catechism and countless other sixteenth and seventeenth century catechisms were constructed. Perkins composed expositions of all three: *An Exposition of the Symbol, or Creed of the Apostles* (1595); *An Exposition of the Lord's Prayer* (1592), and chapters 19-29 of *A Golden Chain: or, The Description of Theology* (1590 in Latin, 1591 in English), where the Decalogue is systematically laid open.[10] Starting with the dictum, 'Theology is the science of living blessedly for ever,' this latter work analyses all God's purposes and procedures in relation to human destiny. It sold well, running through nine editions in 30 years. In addition, Perkins composed *The Foundation of Christian Religion, Gathered into Six Principles: And it is to be Learned of Ignorant People, that they may be fit to hear Sermons with Profit, and to Receive the Lord's Supper with Comfort* (1590). This was a question-and-answer evangelistic catechism on the contents of the gospel. Beginning with an address to the ignorant, listing 32 'common opinions' in which their ignorance found expression, it showed them in simplest form (1) God's triunity; (2) man's sin and lostness; (3) Christ's saving work (4) the individual's salvation 'by faith alone apprehending and applying Christ with all his merits to himself;'[11] (5) the means to faith, namely the Word preached, backed by sacraments and prayer; and (6) the prospect of heaven for the godly and hell for unbelievers. In writing this work, Perkins became the spiritual ancestor of moderns like Michael Green and Nicky Gumbel, and alerts us today, four centuries after, to the need

---

[10] *The Workes of that Famous and Worthy Minister of Christ in the Universitie of Cambridge Mr William Perkins, 1616*, I. pp 32-69.

[11] Breward, p 147.

for initial knowledge of the Christian ABC if one is to get the best out of expository preaching. These pieces by Perkins were the first significant resources for the Puritan discipling of England, and the catechism in particular was very widely used for half a century after its composer's death.[12]

Producing these basic items was only, however, a small part of Perkins' labour as a formulator and popularizer of Puritan faith and practice. Consider the following series of books (all fairly small, despite their titular fulsomeness), which Perkins wrote with a lay readership directly in view.

> (1) *A Treatise Tending unto a Declaration whether a Man be in the Estate of Damnation, or in the Estate of Grace: and if he be in the first, how he may in time come out of it; if in the second, how he may discern it, and persevere in the same to the end* (1588). Described by Perkins himself as 'a Dialogue of the State of a Christian Man Gathered Here and There Out of the Sweet and Savoury Writings of Master Tyndale and Master Bradford' [William Tyndale the Bible translator and John Bradford the Marian martyr], this item, in the words of Ian Breward, 'sums up in brief form what were to become the classical concerns of puritan piety'[13] – that is, in a nutshell, saving grace, saving faith, and holy life.

> (2) *A Case of Conscience, the Greatest that Ever Was: How a Man may Know whether he be the child of God, or no: Resolved by the Word of God* (1592). This is an ingenious dialogue between the apostle John and his interlocutor, 'Church,' in which every verse of 1 John is presented as the answer to some error, uncertainty, or confusion about assurance of salvation that was abroad among English churchmen in the late sixteenth century.[14]

> (3) *A Grain of Mustard Seed: Or, The Least Measure of Grace that is or can be Effectual to Salvation* (1597). Viewing conversion as a life-process which the Holy Spirit works in sinners by stages once he has united them to Christ, Perkins here argues that the

---

[12] Breward, pp 137-167; from *Workes* I. pp 1-8.
[13] Breward, p 355.
[14] *Workes*, I. pp 421-438.

desire for full conversion, that is, for strong faith and thorough repentance, is itself a sign that one is already accepted by God, even though faith and repentance have hardly begun to appear in one's actual performance.[15]

(4) *Two Treatises: 1. Of the nature and practice of Repentance. 2. Of the combat of the flesh and spirit* (1593). For the Puritans, as for the Reformers, repentance was a fruit of faith and a lifelong discipline of the Christian life. Perkins' presentation is a searching analysis of what repentance involves. In his preface to it he affirms his solidarity with Protestants who preceded him as follows:

> And whereas there have been published heretofore in English two sermons of repentance, one by Mr. Bradford Martyr, the other by Mr. Arthur Dent; sermons indeed which have done much good: my meaning [intention] is not to add thereunto, or to teach another doctrine, but only renew and revive the memory of that which they have taught.
>
> Neither let it trouble thee that the principal divines of this age, whom in this treatise I follow, may seem to be at difference in treating of repentance. For some make it a fruit of faith, containing two parts, mortification and vivification: some make faith a part of it, by dividing contrition, faith, new obedience [marginal reference to Melanchthon]: some make it all one with regeneration [marginal reference to Calvin, who also proposed the mortification-vivification analysis]. The difference is not in the substance of doctrine, but in the logical manner of handling it ... repentance ... is taken two ways ... Generally for the whole conversion of the sinner, and so it may contain contrition, faith, new obedience ... and be confounded with regeneration. It is taken particularly for the renovation of life and behaviour: and so it is a fruit of

---

[15] *Workes*, I. pp 637-644; with some abbreviation, Breward, pp 397-410.

faith. And this only sense do I follow in this treatise.[16]

The treatise on repentance includes an elaborate scheme for self-examination by the light of the decalogue and the gospel, and both treatises hit out hard at the Tridentine teaching on meritorious human acts.

(5) *How to Live, and that Well, in all Estates and Times, Specially, When Helps and Comforts fail* (1601). This is an extended sermon on Habakkuk 2:4, showing how Bible-based faith brings peace, joy, godliness, and good hope.[17]

(6) *A Salve for a Sick Man: or, a Treatise containing the Nature, Differences, and Kinds of Death: As also the Right Manner of Dying Well. And it may serve for Spiritual Instruction to 1. Mariners when they go to sea; 2. Soldiers when they go to battle; 3. Women when they travail with child* (1595). That preparation for dying is a duty and discipline of the Christian life may sound strange in modern Christian ears, but the Reformers, Puritans, and earlier evangelicals, like the mediaevals, were clear about it, and Perkins handles the theme in a forthright gospel-based and down-to-earth way, which since death is the one certain fact of life seems entirely appropriate.[18]

(7) *The Whole Treatise of the Cases of Conscience... Taught and Delivered by Mr. W Perkins in his holyday Lectures* [= Sunday sermons], *examined by his own briefs* [manuscripts], *and published for the common good by T Pickering* (1606). This posthumous publication was the pioneer attempt to work out a full-scale Protestant casuistry for the moral guidance of all God's people. Starting from the assertion that there is 'a certain and infallible doctrine, propounded and taught in the Scriptures, whereby the consciences of men distressed, may be

---

[16] *Workes*, I. p 454; spelling modernized, as in all quotations from Perkins' text. The treatise runs from pp 453-474. Bradford's sermon is in *Works of John Bradford: Sermons and Treatises*, (Cambridge: Parker Society, 1848, repr. Edinburgh: Banner of Truth, 1988), pp 29-81. The sermon by Arthur Dent, author of *The Plain Man's Pathway to Heaven* (1601), one of the two books that formed the dowry of Mrs. John Bunyan, has not been reprinted.
[17] *Workes*, I. pp 475-486.
[18] *Workes*, I. pp 487-513.

quieted and relieved,'[19] the treatise deals in order with three sets of questions: first, those relating to personal salvation, assurance, and various forms of spiritual distress; second, those relating to the knowledge and worship of God; and third, those relating to the practice of Christian virtues (prudence, clemency, temperance, liberality, justice is Perkins' list) in the family, the church, and the commonwealth.

These seven items, taken together, point us to the concerns that were central in Perkins' ministry. As a professional theologian of the Church of England, he used his gifts of lucid analysis and straightforward exposition to fill gaps in the Church's pastoral resources as he saw them, and so to provide Englishmen, both from the pulpit and on paper, with guidance on godliness from the cradle of conversion to the grave. The guidance he gave was Bible-based, according to the principles of literal and contextual interpretation established by the Reformers; it was Calvinistic, in the second-generation Aristotelian manner of Beza, Calvin's successor at Geneva for forty years, and of Zanchius, the converted Italian Thomist, with his colleagues Ursinus and Olevianus, who taught and wrote Reformed theology at Heidelberg; it was practical, being attuned at every point to the business of finding and following the path of eternal life; and it was experiential, in the sense that it focused constantly on motives, desires, distresses, graces and disgraces in the heart and inner life, as the source from which both obedience to God and its opposite take their rise.

Perkins gave prime attention throughout his ministry to the religious concerns already indicated – each person's need of regeneration; the quest for the peace and joy of assurance; the duty and discipline of self-examination to uncover one's sins, and of invoking Christ constantly by faith to cover them by his blood; the experience of flesh-spirit conflict; the reality of falls and recoveries as one travels the path of obedience; battles against doubts, discouragements and depression; the practice of lifelong repentance, and conscientious avoidance of wrongdoing. By concentrating on these things Perkins earned from the German writer August Lang the description, 'father of pietism,' inasmuch as reading Perkins' practical works sparked and fed the continental movement, particularly in Holland and Germany, that

---

[19] *Workes*, III. p 1f. (1613). The Treatise occupies pp 1-152.

went by this name. We should at once note here that the anti-intellectual, anti-cultural, anti-national-church attitudes, plus the emotionalistic and legalistic and individualistic inclinations, that marked and marred some later pietists represent deviations from, and indeed contradictions of, Perkins' Puritan humanism. With that (admittedly, rather heavy!) qualification, however we should accept 'father of pietism'[20] as a true label for Perkins, and treat the phrase as a title of honour. The first note in any definition of pietism, after all, is that it gives priority to piety. Perkins did this, insistently and robustly; and so, I venture to say, should we all.

3. Precepts for Spiritual Progress

In *A Grain of Mustard Seed* Perkins depicted the sinner's conversion through the Holy Spirit as typically a complex unitary process involving the whole person over a period of time, and urged that the only final proof that it has started is that it advances – in other words, that the personal change from natural sinfulness to supernatural godliness continues. At the end of the book he speaks his mind on the way to ensure growth in grace, in a passage so striking that I cite it at length and claim for it classic status in the literature of Western spirituality. Here, then, is Perkins explaining his assertion that 'the ... beginnings of grace are counterfeit unless they increase,'[21] and showing us as he does so what for him constitutes health in the Christian's inner life.

> The wickedness of man's nature and the depth of hypocrisy is such that a man may and can easily transform himself into the counterfeit and resemblance of any grace of God. Therefore I put down in this last conclusion a certain note whereby the gifts of God may be discerned, namely that they grow up and increase as a grain of mustard seed to a great tree and bear fruit answerably. The grace in the heart is like the grain of mustard seed in two things: first, it is small to see at the beginning; secondly, after it is cast into the ground of the heart, it

---

[20] A. Lang, *Puritanismus und Pietismus*, Neukirchen Kreis Moers, 1941, pp 126-131; reference taken from Breward, p 131.
[21] Breward, p 404.

increaseth speedily and spreadeth itself. Therefore, if a man at the first have but some little feeling of his wants, some weak and faint desire, some small obedience, he must not let this spark of grace go out, but these motions of the Spirit must be increased by the use of the word, sacraments and prayer: and they must daily be stirred up by meditating, endeavouring, striving, asking, seeking, knocking (Matthew 25:26; 2 Timothy 1:6). As for such motions of the heart that last for a week or a month and after vanish away, they are not to be regarded. And the Lord by the prophet Hosea complains of them saying, 'O Ephraim, thy righteousness is like the morning dew (Hosea 6:4).'

Therefore, considering grace unless it be confirmed and exercised is indeed no grace, I will here add certain rules of direction that the more easily we may put in practice the spiritual exercises of invocation, faith and repentance, and thereby also quicken the seeds and beginnings of grace.

(1) In what place soever thou art, whether alone or abroad, by day or by night, and whatsoever thou art doing, set thyself in the presence of God. Let this persuasion always take place in thy heart, that thou art before the living God: and do thy endeavour that this persuasion may smite thy heart with awe and reverence and make thee afraid to sin. This counsel the Lord gave Abraham (Genesis 17:1). This thing was also practised by Enoch who for this cause is said to walk with God.

(2) Esteem of every present day as the day of thy death: and therefore live as though thou wert dying and do those good duties every day that thou wouldest do if thou wert dying. This is Christian watchfulness; and remember it.

(3) Make catalogues and bills of thine own sins, specially of those sins that have most dishonoured God and wounded thine own conscience. Set them before thee often, specially then when thou hast any particular occasion of renewing thy repentance, that thy heart by this doleful sight may be further humbled. This was David's practice when he considered his ways and turned his feet to God's commandments, and when he confessed the sins of his youth (Psalm 119:59; Psalm 25). This was Job's practice, when he said he was not able to answer one of a thousand of his sins unto God (Job 9:3).

(4) When thou first openst thine eyes in a morning, pray to God and give him thanks heartily. God then shall have his honour and thy heart shall be the better for it the whole day following. For we see in experience, that vessels keep long the taste of liquor with which they were first seasoned. And when thou liest down, let that be the last also, for thou knowest not whether fallen asleep, thou shalt ever rise again alive. Good therefore it is that thou shouldest give up thyself into the hands of God, whilst thou art waking.

(5) Labour to see and feel thy spiritual poverty, that is to see the want of grace in thyself, specially those inward corruptions of unbelief, pride, self-love, etc. Labour to be displeased with thyself: and labour to feel that by reason of them thou standest in need of every drop of the blood of Christ to heal and cleanse thee from these wants. And let this practice take such place with thee, that if thou be demanded what in thine estimation is the vilest of the creatures upon the earth, thine heart and conscience may answer with a loud voice, I, even I, by reason of mine own sins: and again, if thou be demanded what is the best thing in the world for thee, thy heart and conscience may answer with a loud and strong cry, one drop of the blood of Christ to wash away my sins.

(6) Shew thyself to be a member of Christ and a servant of God, not only in the general calling of a Christian, but also in the particular calling in which thou art placed. It is not enough for a magistrate to be a Christian man, but he must also be a Christian magistrate. It is not enough for a master of a family to be a Christian man, but he must also be a Christian in his family and in the trade which he followeth daily. Not everyone that is a common hearer of the word and a frequenter of the Lord's table is therefore a good Christian, unless his conversation in his private house, and in his private affairs and dealings be suitable. There is a man to be seen what he is.

(7) Search the scriptures to see what is sin and what is not sin in every action. This done, carry in thy heart a constant and resolute purpose not to sin in anything, for faith and the purpose of sinning can never stand together.

(8) Let thine endeavour be suitable to thy purpose and therefore do nothing at any time against thy conscience, rightly informed by

the word. Exercise thyself to eschew every sin and to obey God in every one of his commandments that pertain either to the general calling of a Christian, or to thy particular calling. This did good Josiah, who turned unto God with all his heart, according to all the law of Moses and thus did Zechariah and Elizabeth, that walked in all the commandments of God without reproof (2 Kings 23:25; Luke 1:6).

(9) If at any time, against thy purpose and resolution, thou be overtaken with any sin little or great, lie not in it, but speedily recover thyself, confessing thine offence and by prayer intreat the Lord to pardon the same, and that earnestly: till such time as thou findest thy conscience truly pacified and thy care to eschew the same sin increased.

(10) Consider often of the right and proper end of thy life in this world, which is not to seek profit, honour, pleasure, but that in serving of men we might serve God in our callings. God could, if it so pleased him, preserve man without the ministry of man, but his pleasure is to fulfil his work and will, in the preservation of our bodies and the salvation of our souls, by the employment of men in his service, every one according to his vocation. Neither is there so much as a bondslave, but he must in and by his faithful service to his master, serve the Lord. Men therefore do commonly profane their labours and their lives by aiming at a wrong end, when all their care consisteth only in getting sufficient maintenance for them and theirs, for the obtaining of credit, riches and carnal commodities. For thus men serve themselves, and not God or men, much less do they serve God in serving of men.

(11) Give all thy diligence to make thy election sure and to gather manifold tokens thereof. For this observe the works of God's providence, love and mercy, both in thee and upon thee, from time to time: for the serious consideration of them and the laying of them together when they are many and several, minister much direction, assurance of God's favour and comfort. This was the practice of David (1 Samuel 17:34, 36; Psalm 23).

(12) Think evermore thy present estate, whatsoever it be, to be the best estate for thee, because whatsoever befalls thee, though it be sickness, or any other affliction or death, befalls thee of the

good providence of God. That this may be better done, labour to see and acknowledge a providence of God as well in poverty as in abundance, as well in disgrace as in good report, as well in sickness as in health, as well in life as in death.

(13) Pray continually, I mean not by solemn and set prayer, but by secret and inward ejaculations of the heart; that is by a continual elevation of mind unto Christ sitting at the right hand of God the Father, and that either by prayer or giving of thanks, so often as any occasion shall be offered.

(14) Think often of the worst and most grievous things that may befall thee, either in this life or death, for the name of Christ. Make a reckoning of them and prepare thyself to bear them, that when they come, they may not seem strange, but be borne the more easily.

(15) Make conscience of idle, vain, unhonest and ungodly thoughts, for these are the seeds and beginnings of actual sin in word and deed. This want of care in ordering and composing our thoughts is often punished with a fearful temptation in the very thought, called of divines *tentatio blasphemiarum*, a temptation of blasphemies.

(16) When any good motion or affection ariseth in the heart, suffer it not to pass away, but feed it by reading, meditating, praying.

(17) Whatsoever good thing thou goest about, whether it be in word or deed, do it not in conceit of thyself or in the pride of thy heart, but in humility, ascribing the power whereby thou doest thy work and the praise thereof to God. Otherwise thou shalt find by experience, God will curse thy best doings.

(18) Despise not civil honesty: good conscience and good manners go together. Therefore remember to make conscience of lying and customable swearing in common talk. Contend not either in deed or word with any man, be courteous and gentle to all, good and bad. Bear with men's wants and frailties, hastiness, forwardness, self-liking, curiousness, etc., passing them by as being not perceived. Return not evil for evil, but rather good for evil. Use meat, drink and apparel in that manner and measure that they may further godliness and may be, as it were, signs in which thou mayest express the hidden grace of thy heart. Strive not to go beyond any, unless it be in good things. Go before

thine equals in the giving of honour, rather than in taking of it, making conscience of thy word, and let it be as a bond. Profess no more outwardly than thou hast inwardly in heart, oppress or defraud no man in bargaining, in all companies either do good, or take good.

(19) Cleave not by inordinate affection to any creature, but above all things quiet and rest thy mind in Christ; above all dignity and honour, above all cunning and policy, above all glory and honour, above all health and beauty, above all joy and delight, above all fame and praise, above all mirth and consolation that man's heart can feel or devise beside Christ.

With these rules of practice, join rules of meditation: whereof I propound six unto thee, as I find them set down by a learned divine called Victor Strigelius.

i. We must not fall away from God for any creature.

ii. Infinite eternity is far to be preferred before the short race of this mortal life.

iii. We must hold fast the promise of grace, though we lose temporal blessings, and they also in death must needs be left.

iv. Let the love of God in Christ and the love of the church for Christ be strong in thee and prevail against all other affections.

v. It is the principal art of a Christian to believe things invisible, to hope for things deferred, to love God when he shews himself to be an enemy and thus to persevere unto the end.

vi. It is a most effectual remedy for any grief to quiet ourselves in a confidence of the presence and help of God, and to ask of him, and withal to wait either for some easement or deliverance."[22]

---

[22] Breward, pp 405-410; *Workes*, 1. pp 642-644. Victor Strigelius was a Lutheran divine who taught at Heidelberg. Perkins, after saying he will quote six 'rules of meditation' [guidelines for devotional reflection] from Strigelius, adds a seventh, 'All the works of God are done in contrary means,' which is apparently a way of saying that as God works out his purpose, things are regularly not what they seem.

4. Perkins the Theologian

Educationalist, popularizer and gap-filler, rapid reader, lightning writer, and master crafter of simplicity without shallowness, father both of pietism as a European ethos and of Puritanism as an English ideology, Perkins produced luminous didactic treatments of many subjects that I have not yet mentioned, among them the callings of Christian people; Christian family life; 'the virtue of equity, or moderation of mind';[23] the role of the professional ministry; the principles of homiletics; the functioning of conscience; the worship of God; the control of the tongue; the errors of Rome; and the doctrine of predestination. Clearly, however, the realities of religion in the regenerate – in other words, conversion, assurance, devotion, and biblically-ordered behaviour – were always central to his interest. Kendall's statement that Perkins 'devoted himself primarily to showing men that they must, and how they can, make their calling and election sure to themselves' is too narrow;[24] Perkins' first concern was that people should be Christians, and his aim of helping them to know they were Christians came second. The passage just quoted brings together the main things he had to say about the believer's inner life, which is the touchstone of Christian reality, and this profile of the growing saint gives us a vantage-point from which to review Perkins' theology as a whole, asking as we go how each aspect of it bears on what we now see to be its author's major focus.

Basic to all Perkins' work is a desire to maintain continuity with the Reformational heritage, both at home and abroad, and to disciple people in it. As Kendall truly states, 'he saw himself as being in the mainstream of the Church of England, which he often defended.'[25] He had no sympathy with the advocates of separation over questions of church order; as long as the Church was committed to Reformation orthodoxy and he himself was free to teach, preach, and apply that orthodoxy, his Anglican loyalty would not be in doubt, even when he had to endure harassment from within the system. (An example of this was that in 1587 he had to answer to the University Vice-Chancellor for saying in a sermon that the Prayer Book requirements of kneeling at

---

[23] Breward, p 481. The title of the treatise is *Epieikeia*. It is based on Philippians 4:5.
[24] R.T. Kendall, *Calvin and English Calvinism to 1649*, (Oxford: Oxford University Press, 1979), p 54.
[25] *Ibid.*

communion and having the celebrant administer the elements to himself were not the best options.) Nonetheless, loyalty to the established system was integral to the Christianity he taught.

As for the wider Protestant heritage, it is important to see that Perkins who identified himself as a Calvinist, absorbed the teaching not only of Calvin but of other Reformed writers also, such as, apparently, Bucer, Bullinger, Musculus, and Peter Martyr, and particularly Beza of Geneva and Zanchius of Heidelberg. A long appendix from Beza rounds off *A Golden Chain* (the basic material of which had been borrowed from Beza in the first place), and a digest of Zanchius' thoughts about assurance fills more than half of *A Case of Conscience*, and Perkins' own account of faith and assurance clearly reflects the influence of these two giants. Generically, Reformation theology conceived faith as the Christian's whole-souled reliance on the Christ of the biblical promises for a right relationship with God. Calvin had defined faith as a Spirit-taught persuasion of God's favour for Christ's sake,[26] in other words as an assured confidence of mind and heart, and he had explained Peter's summons in 2 Peter 1:10 to 'make your calling and election sure' as a simple plea for behaviour consistent with one's Christian profession.[27] Perkins, however, extended the definition of faith to include both the will (that is, the desire and longing) to believe which precedes active trust, and the act of the soul applying the Christ of the promises to one's own troubled heart and guilty conscience; and he follows Beza and Zanchius in understanding 2 Peter 1:10 as telling Christians to make their standing 'in the life,' as the Welsh phrase it, sure and certain to themselves, by noting how grace has already changed them.

Perkins linked this view of the verse with his own clearly focused Thomistic concept of conscience as the mind working its way through what he called 'practical syllogisms' for either disapproval and condemnation or approval and comfort. In a practical syllogism the major premise would be a moral or spiritual rule, ideally a biblical declaration; the minor premise would be a factual observation; and the

---

[26] 'Now we shall possess a right definition of faith if we call it a firm and certain knowledge of God's benevolence toward us, founded on the truth of the freely given promise in Christ, both revealed to our minds and sealed in our hearts through the Holy Spirit': *Inst. III.ii.7*.
[27] Kendall, p 25, quotes the passage.

conclusion a moral judgment. A simple example, which Perkins actually uses, as many of us also do today, is:

> Everyone that believes is the child of God;
> But I believe;
> Therefore I am the child of God.[28]

Kendall finds Perkins' account of faith confused and his path to assurance illusory, but his criticisms seem to depend on reifying the mind and the will in a way that Perkins never did, on equating biblical self-examination with introspection, and on forgetting Perkins' axiom that real grace grows, and proves its reality thereby.[29] In my opinion, Perkins was right, first to analyse conscience as operating, in however compressed a way, by practical syllogisms, and second to affirm that scriptural self-examination will ordinarily yield the Christian solid grounds for confidence as to his or her regeneration and standing with God.

Basic too to all Perkins' work was his insistence that Holy Scripture must be received as the teaching and testimony of God, and that interpretation must take the form of applying biblical principles to the interpreter's own times and needs. Breward states this well, highlighting the Christocentric focus of Perkins' hermeneutic. He begins by citing Perkins' contention that Holy Scripture 'agrees with itself most exactly and the places that seem to disagree may easily be reconciled,' for the simple reason that 'the scope of the whole Bible is Christ with his benefits.' If diverse opinions about the meaning of scripture existed:

> in this diversity of opinions ... we must still [always] have recourse to Christ, and that in the scripture alone: for although there were a thousand diverse expositions of one place, yet by the circumstances thereof, conferring [comparing] it with other like places of scripture, a man shall be able to find out the true sense: *for Christ in Scripture expoundeth himself.*[30]

---

[28] *Ibid.*, p 71.
[29] *Ibid.*, p 74f.
[30] Breward, p 47, drawing on Perkins, *Workes*, II. p 55f., I. p 484, III. p 220; my italics. Breward's review of Perkins' interpretative procedures, as set forth in his pioneer homiletical handbook, *The Art of Prophecying* (1607; in Latin, *Prophetica*, 1592), and illustrated by his printed expositions, should by all means be consulted.

Of the supralapsarian version of Calvinism that Perkins learned from Beza and Zanchius, set forth in *A Golden Chain*, and defended in Latin in *De Praedestinatione* (1598) and in English in *God's Free Grace and Man's Free Will* (1602), little need be said here. Supralapsarianism is the view that in God's initial, pre-mundane decision-making with regard to mankind his purpose of electing some and reprobating the others envisaged human beings not yet created, as distinct from the infralapsarian view that in decreeing this double predestination God envisaged human beings as both created and fallen. Perkins embraced supralapsarianism out of a desire to maintain the absolute sovereignty of God in our salvation against Lutherans, semi-pelagian Roman Catholics like Bellarmine, and anti-predestinarians in England like Peter Baro, Samuel Harsnet and William Barrett. By embracing it, however, he surrounded the good news of the redeeming love of God to lost sinners with a forbidding rationalistic framework which, like all versions of the supralapsarian formula, seemed to imply that God is an arbitrary decision-maker with an abstract interest in having two sorts of people, one justly saved and one justly condemned, and that he willed the fall in Eden as a means to this end.[31] Most seventeenth-century Puritans, like most Reformed theologians since their time, were infralapsarian, and it is in order, I think, to express quiet regret that Perkins the Elizabethan Puritan pioneer took a different line. The sovereignty of God in salvation must surely be maintained, but dogmatic supralapsarianism is not the best nor the most scriptural way to do it.

But the supralapsarianism in Perkins' head did not in any way inhibit the expressing of his evangelistic and pastoral heart, and it is to this that I return as I close. From an exposition of Zephaniah 2:1-2, 'preached at Stourbridge Fair, in the field; taken from his mouth'[32] – that is, recorded, presumably in shorthand, as he spoke, apparently in 1593, and published posthumously in 1605 – I draw two extracts, both characteristically Puritan (by which I mean that any Puritan preacher over the next hundred years might have said the same; indeed, we know

---

[31] The clearest statement of this defect is that of B.B. Warfield, *The Plan of Salvation*, revised ed., (Grand Rapids: Eerdmans, 1966), p 88: 'That (God) has any creatures at all they (the supralapsarians) suppose to be in the interest of discrimination, and all that he decrees concerning his creatures they suppose that he decrees only that he may discriminate between them.'

[32] Breward, p 279.

that very many did). The first extract shows us Perkins the evangelist, proclaiming the whosoever-will invitation of the gospel. Speaking of the gospel promise as a 'precious jewel,' Perkins says:

> ... never allege that it is above thy compass and being a jewel is too dear and costly for thee, for I offer it freely unto you and to every one of you. I pronounce unto you from the Lord that here this blessed doctrine is offered unto you all in his name freely and that you may buy it without money (Isaiah 55:1). Happy is that day when thou, coming so far to buy things for thy body and paying so dear for them, dost meet with so precious a jewel, the virtue whereof will save thy soul, and payest nothing for it.[33]

The second extract is pastoral, prophetic, and in the best sense patriotic. It has to do with England, England's Church, and the threat of national judgment.

> The common sins of England ... are ... First, ignorance of God's will and worship ... The second main sin of England is contempt of Christian religion ...
>
> Our church doubtless is God's cornfield and we are the corn heap of God and those Brownists [followers of Robert Browne who wanted separation] are blinded and besotted who cannot see that the Church of England is a goodly heap of God's corn. But withal we must confess that we are full of chaff. ... therefore God will winnow us to find out the corn ... the way to escape God's trial is to try thyself ... and so the way to escape the fearful fan of God is to fan thine own heart by the law of God ... Once a day put thyself and thy life under the fan of God's law ... Once a day keep a court in thy conscience, call thy thoughts, thy words, thy deeds to their trial. Let the ten commandments pass upon them, and thy sins and corruptions which thou findest to be chaff, blow them away by repentance ... Our long peace, plenty and ease have bred great sins ...When we have renewed our repentance, let us then every one of us deal with the Lord by earnest prayer for this church and nation, that the Lord would show his mercy upon it and continue unto it this peace and the

---

[33] *Ibid.*, p 300.

gospel.[34]

In the title of this lecture I rated William Perkins, theologian, preacher, and pastor four centuries ago, an Anglican to remember; and I trust that what we have learned has justified that estimate. I now ask: is there not an uncanny relevance for us in the thoughts about England and the Church of England that we have just found Perkins expressing? That is a question that I hope we shall all ponder.

---

[34] *Ibid.* pp 293, 297-302.

Pilgrim's Progress and Contemporary Evangelical Piety

Bruce Winter

1. Introduction 171
2. Putting Pilgrim's Progress in Context 171
   2.1 *Pilgrimage* 171
   2.2 *Progress* 174
3. Putting Evangelical Piety in Context 176
   3.1 *'Preserve the gold'* 178

BRUCE W. WINTER began his working life in the Australian Public Service before training for ordination at Moore Theological College (Sydney) and entering parish ministry in Singapore in 1973. A highly respected New Testament scholar, his PhD from Macquarie University, Sydney was published as *Philo and Paul Among the Sophists*. From 1987 until 2006 he served as the Warden of Tyndale House, Cambridge. As well as now being Principal of Queensland Theological College (Australia), Dr. Winter is also the Director of the Institute for Early Christianity in the Graeco-Roman World.

1. Introduction

With the rise and subsequent demise of the Utopian aspirations of the Commonwealth, the mood of the Puritans changed from that of warfaring to wayfaring. The Christian Commonwealth had failed. The Act of Uniformity of 1662 saw the eviction of some of the best theological minds from the Established Church. Among these were two thousand Puritans who were deprived of their livings. Those, such as John Bunyan, who continued to preach, were to find themselves in prison for holding 'non-conformist' worship services. For the writer of *The Pilgrim's Progress from this World to that which is to Come*, the famous Christian classic, it involved incarcerations from 1660-72, and again from 1676-7, with occasional remissions. That the concept of the Christian life as a pilgrimage should so capture the pious minds of those who first read Bunyan's famous work should not surprise us. This was a traumatic reversal for the Puritans from Commonwealth to Restoration both ideologically and personally, for those who had fought for, and temporarily enjoyed life in a 'Christian' nation.

2. Putting Pilgrim's Progress in Context

This great classic was written in the context of the imprisonment of 'that illiterate tinker prate' as Charles II pejoratively described Bunyan to John Owen.[1] While it used a particular theological concept and was part of a literary genre, it captured the hearts of many in its day because, as we have already noted, it reflected a particular moment in Puritan history.

2.1 *Pilgrimage*

Because *Pilgrim's Progress* became a classic and the most read book apart from the Bible, it can easily be overlooked that the image of

---

[1] The former Dean of Christ Church and Vice-Chancellor of Oxford University replied, 'Please, your majesty, could I possess that tinker's abilities for preaching, I would gladly relinquish all my learning.'

pilgrimage which Bunyan so effectively used had its roots in Roman Catholicism. From the time of the Canterbury Tales in 1387 we learn that, with the arrival of the month of April, 'thanne longen folk to goon on pilgrimages.' They were an essential image and a pious act of the Christian life by which indulgences were secured. Chaucer's work shows this to be so for all walks of life. By the sixteenth century the English idea of pilgrimage had changed. No longer was it 'from every shires end of Engelond to Caunterbury they wende, the hooly blisful martir for to seke.'[2] Popular Puritan preachers were not averse to making use of what was a 'popish' theme to express important aspects of their piety and practice. Christopher Hill has demonstrated that the theme of pilgrimage in the early seventeenth century became a 'common-place.'[3] He suggests that there was a reason for this–'The idea of abandoning all for Christ, including one's own family, had especial relevance to the mobile world of vagrant soldiers and ex-soldiers of the 1640's and 1650's.[4] This may provide a partial explanation of why this portrayal of the Christian life as a pilgrimage struck a chord in the heart of the pious Puritan–but there were other reasons as well.

It must not be forgotten that the sixteenth century had already baptised this theme into the piety of the Reformation–S. Batman, *The Travayled Pilgrim* (1569), and W. Bronup, *St Peter's Path to the Joyes of Heaven* (1598) both wrote on this theme. More importantly, Bunyan's contemporaries also found this concept of pilgrimage a very congenial theme. W. Denny wrote *The Pilgrim's Passe to the Land of the Living* in 1653, and V. Powell, *A Christian Pilgrimage in the Bird in the Cage, Chirping* was published in 1661 while he also was in prison. The Latitudinarian attempted take-over of the theme by S. Patrick in 1664 in his *The Parable of the Pilgrim,* written to show the superiority of the Established Church, shows how popular this perception of the Christian life had become.

Tracing the antecedents of Bunyan's great work, or putting it in its historical context, does not in any way denigrate the importance and originality of Bunyan's distinctive and lasting contribution to Christian spirituality. We know that John Calvin was influenced by the *Devotio*

---

[2] G. Chaucer, 'General Prologue,' *The Canterbury Tales*, 11. lines 12, 15-18.
[3] C. Hill, *A Turbulent, Seditious and Factious People: John Bunyan and his Church* (Oxford, OUP, 1989) pp 204-206.
[4] *Ibid. p* 202.

Moderna of Thomas à Kempis through the Augustinian order, although he did not endorse aspects of the theological framework which gave rise to it. In the same way, John Owen was himself an inheritor of Augustine's doctrine of human sinfulness and divine grace and Calvin's work on mortification.[5] Theological reflection seldom arises *de novo*.

Given the commitment of the Puritans to framing their discussion in biblical categories, it may come as a surprise to learn that the concepts of 'pilgrim' and 'pilgrimage' were not technically biblical ones. The Puritans themselves may not have believed that to be the case, for William Tyndale had translated the term παρεπιδήμους [*parepidēmous*] in 1 Peter 2:11 as 'pilgrem' and the King James Version followed his rendering, but not his spelling.[6] This also happened in Hebrews 11:13 where ξένοι καὶ παρεπίδημοί [*xenoi kai parepidēmoi*] as a self description of Christians was translated as 'strangers and pilgrims.' In the Old Testament in Genesis 47:9, Exodus 6:4 and Psalm 119:54, 'pilgrimage' was the word supplied. However, the two terms in Greek do not describe someone who is on the move. On the contrary, the biblical words (which are drawn from legal terminology) describe one's status as a person who is sojourning in a place as a resident alien.[7] He or she does not possess local citizenship but is nevertheless domiciled in a city. The biblical concept of the Christian life is not stated in terms of a pilgrimage to heaven, but rather is described as that of a person residing in this world, but not really belonging to it, waiting here for the grace that shall be revealed at the revelation of Jesus Christ (1 Peter 1:13).

---

[5] R.C. Gleason, *John Calvin and John Owen on Mortification: A Comparative Study of Reformed Spirituality*, Studies in Church History (Berlin and New York, P. Lang, 1995).

[6] The translators were not the first nor the last to mistake the concept of pilgrimage for sojourning. See D.J. Estes, *From Patriarch to Pilgrim: The Development of the Biblical Figure of Abraham and its Contribution to the Christian Metaphor of Spiritual Pilgrimage*, Ph.D. dissertation, University of Cambridge, 1988. For a discussion of the theme in the second to the fifth centuries AD see 'Abraham and Spiritual Pilgrimage in the Early Christian Literature' in chapter 6 of this dissertation.

[7] The K.J.V. and R.V. translated the latter term παρεπιδήμους [*parepidēmous*], as pilgrim. For a discussion of the use of these terms see M. M. Chin, 'A Heavenly Home for the Homeless: Aliens and Strangers in 1 Peter,' *Tyndale Bulletin* 42.1 (1991) pp 96-112.

'Pilgrimage' as a theme of biblical theology with a journey to the Promised Land (or Zion) and an Exodus and return from Babylonian Exile, is not a biblical construct, for the theme of salvation has not been unfolded thus.[8]

2.2 Progress

What did Bunyan mean by progress? It had nothing to do with the Council of Trent's formulation of a concept of an 'increase in justification,'[9] nor had it anything to do with progress in holiness which can be erroneously seen as the meaning of the doctrine of sanctification.[10] The progress to which Bunyan refers was not an upward one in terms of becoming a better Christian, but rather a description of the experiences and difficulties of being in the midst of turbulent as well as tranquil periods, or – as the writer of Ecclesiastes designates them – 'the seasons of life' (3:1-15). Bunyan's work, then, is not a reflection on the Christian life in terms of progressive improvement. Rather, in his own inimitable style, it is about the trials and temptations that the Christian can expect to face – and inevitably faces – as he or she lives in this world before departing from it. It is about being resilient in the face of 'all disaster,' not being deflected from being a pilgrim, and knowing that, at the end, the celestial gates will open. The Christian life is about the 'tribulations' which we can expect to experience and which were promised by Jesus himself.

Bunyan's *Pilgrim's Progress* was not strictly a discussion of the Christian life from the theological perspective of 1 Peter or any other New Testament book. They have an overarching eschatological framework in which the Christian life is to be seen, i.e., as eschatological sojourning and not progressive pilgrimage. Bunyan's theology draws upon the theme of a coming judgement as the basis for repentance, but the hope of Christ's second coming to the Christian

---

[8] O. Lutand, *Des Deux revolutions d'Angleterre: Documents politiques, sociaux religieux* (Paris, 1978), p 80.
[9] Decree on Justification, chapter 10, the Sixth Session of the Council of Trent.
[10] For an extremely important discussion of this doctrine which rejects the idea of sanctification as progress in holiness or a process see D. Peterson, *Possessed by God: A New Testament theology of sanctification and holiness*, New Studies in Biblical Theology (Leicester: IVP, 1995).

does not really feature; rather he discusses the Christian's journey towards heaven.

John Bunyan himself anticipated that portraying the Christian life as he did in his allegory would draw critics. He therefore took the initiative and produced an Apology which is set forth as the beginning of his book and in which he seeks to answer them. He records that when he showed his finished work to others opinions were divided.

> Some said, John, print it; others said, Not so:
> Some said, It might do good; others said, No.

In hindsight it was good that he ignored the negative advice and it was printed for, as a Christian classic, it has done much good. Of the method adopted he also felt it necessary to defend his approach by citing biblical precedents.

> The Prophets used much by metaphors
> To set forth Truth; Yea, who so considers
> Christ, his Apostles too, shall plainly see,
> That Truths to this day in such Mantles be.

In seeking to put *Pilgrim's Progress* in its social and theological context, one sees that it represented a radical theological departure from the idea of going on pilgrimages in order to secure indulgences.[11] This seventeenth century concept was embraced partly as a reaction to the failed millenarianism of the Commonwealth. It is therefore in part a reflection of the uncertain times in which he, and those who were ejected from the Established Church, lived and sought to integrate a Christian understanding of what had happened to those who, in the Restoration, had been made outsiders. Wayfaring had become a dominant theme of the rejected. One of the abiding legacies of *Pilgrim's Progress* is that it epitomised a biblical perspective which brought home the fact that problems and difficulties, trials and temptations were, and always will be, part and parcel of what it means to be a Christian in any generation.

---

[11] On twentieth century Roman Catholic teaching on them, see the *Apostolic Constitution on the Revision of Indulgences*, Second Vatican Council.

3. Putting Evangelical Piety in Context

Unlike thirty or forty years ago, *Pilgrim's Progress* is no longer a best seller in Christian bookshops. The choice of editions available is now limited. True, there have been some excellent children's editions, and this reflects that those most unlikely to appreciate the full impact of the work, i.e., young children, are seen as the most appropriate audience by publishers. Why is it that *Pilgrim's Progress* no longer strikes a chord in contemporary piety, and one seldom hears it commended as a book to young Christians? In theological colleges it can no longer be assumed that allusions to some of the great characters in John Bunyan's work would be understood. It does not appear on the list of those Christian classics that ought to be read – even for discussions of 'spiritual formation' or 'spirituality.'

It is suggested that one of the reasons for this rests in a very substantial sea change in Western society which began at the turn of the century and has gained force at important stages. Just as the collapse of the Commonwealth gave rise to a wayfaring theology, so too, there have been secular changes which have quietly affected the perception of the Christian life in our day.

It could be said that it began with a play that was considered scandalous in its own day – J.M. Synge's *Playboy of the Western World* – and which at one time was banned in England and America. Reading it at the *end* of the century one might wonder what the fuss was all about. It made hedonism respectable – although it had long operated under the surface of Victorian values. In the 1920's psychological hedonism became a fashionable explanation of human behaviour, but it was also commended, i.e., one ought to avoid pain and pursue those things that are pleasurable. What was an explanation of human behaviour became a 'scientific' base for conduct. It was left until after the Second World War for Hugh Heffner to promote the hedonistic lifestyle. This came in the form of a soft core pornographic magazine which, next to the *Readers Digest*, sold more copies from the 1950's to the 1970's than any other magazine. Its popularity rested not only in the voyeurism, but also in the lifestyle it presented. This glossy magazine even had a religious editor who, within the context of hedonism, was able to dispense advice and to provide a religious justification for the playboy's philosophy. While Walter Lippman argued that the pursuit of happiness was a most unhappy pursuit, Hugh Heffner not only ran his 'bunny' clubs as an extension of the playboy's world, but strongly defended his playboy's philosophy in a series of articles in the magazine in the late 1960's. Aspects of his arguments were reminiscent of the Greek philosophical hedonism but it was his treatment of women as 'objects' that was to draw intense flak, especially in the rising tide of feminism. It is interesting to note that some Asian countries banned *Playboy Magazine* and in the 1960's and 1970's the question asked by customs officers in such countries was whether or not the traveller was carrying a copy of *Playboy Magazine*. While this drew derision from some who wrongly assumed that it was because of its pornography, it was not the point at issue. Rather it was that some Asian governments recognised the pernicious philosophy this magazine packaged with such style – it was a philosophy in which individual happiness was to be secured at the expense of responsibilities.

This growing tide of hedonism did not end with the collapse of Heffner's clubs or a drop in circulation because of more hard core pornographic publications. Rather the pursuit of happiness in more affluent times post war was to move onto the political scene with promises of the 'feel good' factor to the acquisitive spirit.

The Christian church itself was not unaffected, although the doctrine of hedonism tended to present itself more in the calculated guise of Greek philosophical hedonism which argued that one should pursue one's own happiness, but never beyond certain boundaries, for then it ceases to be happiness. Its quiet infiltration through the subliminal programming of men and women via the media, etc. meant that for many Christians the biblical concept of 'joy' came to be equated with 'happiness.'[12] Aspects of church services and Christian books were meant to meet this need for 'happiness' or a 'feel good' factor about oneself and being a Christian. Such a feeling was thought to be appropriate for evangelical Christians within their denomination or the Christian scene generally. Many Christian parents articulate their hopes for their children not in terms of their contribution to the Kingdom of God in its widest biblical understanding, but rather in the categories of

---

[12] The word for 'happiness' or 'pleasure,' ἡδονή which transliterates as *hēdonē*, is condemned in the New Testament (Luke 8:14; Titus 3:3; James 4:1, 3; 2 Peter 2:13), but the concept of 'joy' as one of the fruits of the Spirit is not.

the good life with an appropriate spouse who shares similar Christian values and aspirations. In some circles the Christian life is seen more as a Mediterranean stopover before the final destination for which tickets are underwritten by the gilt-edged security of the death of Christ. Perceptions of the Christian life and evangelical piety in particular, are more at the mercy of trends in the secular world than we would care to own.

One of the acid tests of our contemporary piety is the place that biblical words and concepts such as 'discipleship,' 'cross bearing,' 'denying oneself and 'losing one's life' play in our vocabulary or even our perceptions of the Christian life. These are clearly the conditions upon which Jesus offered discipleship in his 'if any man would come after me' teaching in Mark 8:34. Suffering and adversity are not seen as something of a disaster in the Christian life.

3.1   'Preserve the gold'

In the conclusion to his *Pilgrim's Progress* Bunyan expresses the belief that although what he had written was 'a dream,' yet it would be 'helpful to an honest mind.' He was also a humble enough writer to invite an assessment of his work.

> What of my dross thou findest there, be bold
> To throw away, but yet preserve the gold.
> What if my gold be wrapped up in ore?
> None throws away the apple for the core.

Attention has already been drawn to a particular theological deficiency in *Pilgrim's Progress*, namely the absence of the New Testament's expectation of the second coming of Christ to the sojourning Christian. One cannot be too critical for it is a biblical perspective that is all too lacking in contemporary evangelical theology and affects our piety. If that is 'the dross,' one would not want to throw away 'the gold' from this great Christian classic, for it is necessary for those who stand as Evangelicals in the Puritan tradition to be self-critical of aspects of contemporary evangelical practice and piety. Some of these will occupy the remainder of this lecture. There are four important areas – Scripture, judgement, mortification and death which, if they appear to be rather sterile issues in our brave new world, may point to the problem of our spirituality, namely that we are more the subjects of our secular culture than we would care to recognise. That we could be so should not surprise us for we live in an age unprecedented for its speed of media communication and sophistication for the subliminal transformation of human values and wants. Hopefully an examination of these four vital areas of Christian teaching will whet the appetite to re-read *Pilgrim's Progress* and compel us to ask whether the insights of Bunyan are solely a reflection of his own situation. Was he a wise pastor who laid hold of biblical truths which have in some cases become obscured not by our subsequent skills in biblical and theological discussions but by the spirit of our own age?

Firstly, note the breadth of Scripture cited by Bunyan. He does not construct his view of the Christian life upon a smattering of New Testament texts, nor a single text such as Romans 7:25, nor indeed from the New Testament alone. Of the three hundred and forty-nine texts cited by Bunyan there are one hundred and fifty-seven drawn from twenty books from the Old Testament canon. The Psalms predominate containing the highest number of citations, followed closely by Isaiah and Proverbs which feature as many times in this work as do the books of Matthew, Hebrews and the Revelation.[13] This reflects not only Bunyan's intimate knowledge of the Bible, but also his theological commitment to the use of the whole of it as the Word of God. From this, contemporary evangelical theological practice could learn much. Our worship today is often dominated by music in many forms – hymns, and more recently repetitive spiritual songs – and unlike the church in the first or the seventeenth century, the reading of Psalms (and sometimes Scripture in general) finds little or no place in teaching and admonishing the congregation (Colossians 3:16). For Bunyan the theology of the Psalms (indeed of all the Old Testament books) was central to his understanding of the Christian life. He did not give notional assent to them as Holy Scripture, or simply ignore them as possessing no abiding truth, but they were merely part of the economy of salvation. One voice spoke from the two Testaments. The Old Testament was not first draft and the New the final, definitive edition.

Secondly, we note that his preaching of the gospel to Christians was not framed in terms of its present benefits. Its motivation was to

---

[13] Psalms 25, Isaiah 23, Proverbs 21, Revelation 24, Matthew 23 and Hebrews 23. The only books he omitted are Joshua, 2 Samuel, 1 Kings, Lamentations, Joel, Obadiah, Jonah, Nahum, Haggai.

flee from the coming judgment of God upon the inhabitants of the city of destruction. His Christian theology had yet to be subjected to the powerful onslaught of the secular utilitarianism of Jeremy Bentham and others whose emphasis was on the greatest happiness for the greatest number in this life. This later philosophical shift meant a change in the theory of justice propounded by William Paley who held to the biblical view of retributive justice – that it was not inappropriate for God to hold every person accountable for his works. Bentham's shift to 'remedial' justice has

> proved historically momentous. For the Benthamite view had and still has a wide currency. With it comes a difficulty in understanding the wisdom and justice of the cross. Surely it is immoral for God to judge and punish, rather than to educate and rehabilitate...And if there is a world to come beyond this present one how can God be just if such a world provides no opportunity for reform.[14]

These questions which arose from the philosophical move from Paley to Bentham were felt keenly by the Victorians and still pose a difficulty even for some contemporary evangelicals in the proclamation of the New Testament's presentation of the gospel in our own day and generation. That it does so means that

> the Christian communicator seeking to spread the gospel of the cross to societies greatly affected by secular utilitarianism would need to be aware of the historical change that has taken place in the understanding of justice from retribution to reform, that makes the traditional doctrines of the cross and the wrath of God so conceptually problematical and morally unappealing to so many...[15]

There is perhaps something of an unnecessary embarrassment on the part of contemporary gospel proclamation which fails to take account of the fact that, on the day of judgement, each will agree with the verdict for 'one's own conscience will either excuse or accuse' (Romans 2:15-16). The view that the pleading of an able QC might well be able to secure another verdict based on the promise of reform, or that there will

---

[14] See G. Cole, 'Utilitarianism and the eclipse of the theistic sanction,' *Tyndale Bulletin* 42.2 (1991) pp 226-244 and citation on p 243.
[15] *Ibid.*, p 244.

be no such moment of accountability, will be seen to be foolish. Today's evangelist might have been somewhat coy to have called upon Bunyan's Christian to flee the coming judgement as the reason for embracing the gospel of grace, or that Jesus delivers from the wrath to come those who turn from idols to serve the true and living God (1 Thessalonians 1:10). Repentance, not reform, was Bunyan's biblical gospel.

Thirdly, Bunyan reminds us, as did his predecessors and his contemporaries, that the Christian life is a fight and that the one battle that has to be fought constantly is that within our hearts. One of the most chilling and salutary descriptions comes from the chapter on 'The Interpreter's House' where a Christian is held in bondage to his lusts to which he has yielded. This has resulted in his being trapped in 'despair in an iron cage.' The imagery might not appeal but the problem of denying all that cries out day by day to be satisfied immediately remains. In contemporary reflection on the Christian life there seems to be little, or no, place for what the Puritans called mortification. In 1656 Bunyan's contemporary, John Owen, preached a series of sermons in the declining days of the Commonwealth *On the Mortification of Sin in Believers* to young undergraduates in his charge at Christ Church. The vulgarity of the Restoration comedies and their conscious parodying of biblical virtues shows with what lightening speed the ethical shift to permissiveness had taken place. Bunyan discussed 'passion' over against 'patience' where the former is portrayed by its demand for immediate satisfaction but was self-deceived, being left with nothing but rags. Having pointed out the futility for the Christian of caving into his wants, he looks at the example of one who as a good believer had set out on the same path for the Celestial city as Christian, with the same quiet confidence and joy that he would arrive at his destination, but was now a man of despair who was entrapped by his own actions in 'the passions, pleasures and advantages of this world' and from which he is now unable to escape. In citing passages such as Hebrews 6:6 and 10:26-9, Bunyan gives full weight to the enormous dangers that self-indulgence creates. In our age it is somewhat unfashionable in preaching to face head on the warning passages of Hebrews because of their theological untidiness for some and their unpalatable implications for a more open approach by Christians to 'freedom' and their 'unhappy search for happiness.' The playboys' theology is more alive than we would care to acknowledge and even Hugh Heffner in his old age could give more than notional assent to its validity without thought for its consequences. The Puritans firmly believed that a crucial aspect of the work of the Spirit was the help given in the fight against indwelling sin which no longer has absolute dominion in the life of the Christian but, on the other hand, requires the daily commitment of the Christian to engage in a healthy battle against its ravages. The reminder of Colossians 3:5-14 that certain things must be put to death, other things must be put off, and in their place new things must be put on, has become somewhat alien to evangelical piety.

All young preachers affirm to young and old alike, believers and unbelievers that they are not afraid to die. As life proceeds, the thought and possible pain of death modifies their confidence. In latter years even Dr. Billy Graham has publicly confessed that the thought of death itself is not relished. Is this simply a capitulation to the great concern to speak of the Christian life solely in terms of its present benefits and to ignore, like the rest of society, the reality of the coffin?

It is the mark of the great pastoral insight of John Bunyan that in his final chapter, 'The Land of Beulah, the Fords of the River, At-Home,' the end of the pilgrimage is no jolly jaunt to the gates of the celestial city. It reflects the wisdom and experience of those Christians who have in the final stages of life 'hesitated' at the gates of death. 'Was there no other way to those gates?' Christian was to ask. 'Only for Enoch and Elijah and those who are there when the last trumpet sounds,' is the reply. Perhaps in that hour the immediate thought of Christ's return is a straw to clutch on to, but not the lively hope that it ought to have been as the mainspring throughout life as the Scriptures teach. Christian experienced a great conflict at the hour of death when we read how his mind is filled with horror and his heart with dread as he recalls the sins he has committed both before and since he has become a Christian. It may come as a shock to the reader that Christian needs the encouragement of Hopeful at that moment when, in the words of Wordsworth, he is 'putting out to sea.' It should not surprise us that at that moment we will feel the need for the forgiveness of Christ as much then, if not more so, than we feel the necessity of it today. That hesitation and the recollection of the past life of the Christian should throw him or her daily on the promised clemency of Christ secured though his death and passion. Perhaps it shows us that at times Evangelical piety is in danger of feeling, and even teaching, that it has passed beyond Calvary to Pentecost for the cross has done its work, and that the Spirit must now do his. While that is partially true, there is the deep need to stir up our minds to the continual remembrance of the inestimable benefits given to us by the Judge of all men who has been judged in our place.

While the children's song that 'Heaven is a wonderful place' is true, those who stand this side of heaven have to remind ourselves that we have not yet entered into our rest. We cannot live as if there is no need to make our calling and election sure. We are to deny ourselves, taking up our cross and following the One who set down the conditions alone upon which any person could follow him.

In *Pilgrim's Progress* we rightly asked what part the Bible and external circumstances played in the moulding of Bunyan's piety. If the concept of pilgrimage was 'the principle metaphor running through Puritan spirituality' as Hambrick-Stowe suggested,[16] what is that which contemporary evangelicalism has embraced? For the Puritans the Christian life was a joyful and serious business which demanded their daily thought and on which they continually saw the need to concentrate their energies. This work by 'that illiterate tinker prate' has been a formative part of our spiritual heritage. Its removal from the shelf of recommended Christian classics[17] should warn us that its message of struggle and discipleship may indicate a serious deficiency in the articulation of our contemporary Evangelical piety and lifestyle which may have more to do with the ethos of our age than a reflection of a biblical portrayal of it. This great Christian classic does provide a helpful yardstick for measuring our own understanding of the Christian life.

Evangelical scholarship, both biblical and theological, has earned its right to speak in academic forums, and has reached a level of sophistication comparable to that of the Puritans with their exegetical commentaries and theological works. It would be a foolish Christian generation indeed which failed to give a hearing to important ancestors by refusing to read the 'Puritan School of Divinity' before joining with the secular world in the perfunctory dismissal of it. In 1616 it was the wisdom of Richard Vane, the parish of St Antholin and other far-sighted parishioners that the contribution of the Puritan divines should not be lost, and that though dead, they should yet speak to future generations. It was the prudence of some of our own generation that the lectures

---

[16] C. Hambrick-Stowe, *The Practice of Piety* (Chapel Hill, University of North Carolina Press, 1982) p 54.
[17] It is readily available, even on the Internet for those Christians who 'surf' it.

should be revived lest those who ignore the theological wisdom of the past should be doomed to fall into the very errors that the Puritans saw and sought to correct.

A Church 'Halfly Reformed': The Puritan Dilemma

Peter Adam

1. Introduction 187
2. Reform 'From Above' 190
3. Reform 'From Below' 193
   - 3.1 *Bibles and Christian books* *193*
   - 3.2 *Preachers of the Word* *194*
   - 3.3 *Biblical training for ministry* *195*
   - 3.4 *A new style of preaching* *196*
   - 3.5 *In-service training for ministers* *197*
   - 3.6 *New models and opportunities for ministry* *198*
   - 3.7 *Committed and trained lay people* *199*
   - 3.8 *Godliness in daily lives* *201*
   - 3.9 *Gospel and Church* *202*
   - 3.10 *Prayer and suffering* *204*
   - 3.11 *Gospel outreach* *205*
   - 3.12 *Planning for the future* *205*
4. Evaluation 206
5. Conclusion 211

Bibliography 214

PETER J. H. ADAM served several curacies in Melbourne, Australia and studied in England at both London and Durham Universities, gaining a PhD from the latter on the practice of the imitation of Christ with special reference to the theology of Dietrich Bonhoeffer in 1981. After several years as a tutor at St. John's College, Durham he returned to Australia and was minister of St. Jude's, Carlton for 20 years and Anglican Chaplain to Melbourne University. He became Principal of Ridley Mission and Ministry College, Melbourne in 2002 and has published several books on biblical spirituality and exposition including *Hearing God's Words* and *Written for Us*.

1. Introduction

In William Fuller's 'Booke to the queene,' he complains that Queen Elizabeth 'hath so insufficientlie heard, believed, and taken to heart what God hath commanded you, and so weakly and coldly obeyed,' that 'but halflie by your majesty hath God been honoured, his church reformed and established, his people taught and comforted.'[1] His complaint is of a church 'but halfly reformed,' a church in which the Reformation has proceeded 'but halfly forward and more than halfly backward.'[2] The great Puritan plan to reform the national church was to continue for one hundred years. Some gave up the attempt and started new churches in the American colonies; many resigned in 1662 rather than continue ministry in a church that made unacceptable demands on them, and was so resistant to reform.

The subject of this lecture is the reformation of the church. We will outline the Puritan attempt to reform the church by political action and by the preaching of the word. We will identify with the great dilemma of those who wish to purify the church in any age; how can we best achieve reformation, and what should we do when that reformation limps on 'but halfly forward,' or when it seems to be going backward? This is the problem of living in a mixed church, when those opposed to its reformation by the word of God seem to have power and influence, and when ungodly patterns of life and ministry seem to be increasing. The dilemma of the Puritans from 1559 to 1662 is shared by would-be reformers in every age, not least our own.

For those Puritans who were motivated by godly zeal, the honour of Christ, and obedience to the word of God, were certainly committed to the reformation of the national church. Theirs was not just a quest for personal reformation, nor merely the reformation of local congregations. Their aim was the reformation of the national church in England, the body John Foxe called 'the true members and

---

[1] William Fuller, *Booke to the queen, The Second part of a Register*, ii. 52, quoted in Patrick Collinson, *The Elizabethan Puritan Movement*, (London: Jonathan Cape, 1967), p 29.
[2] Fuller, ii, 60, in Collinson, *The Elizabethan Puritan Movement*, p 36.

faithful Congregation of Christ's Church, wheresoever either congregated together, or dispersed through the whole Realm of England.'[3] In the words of the Admonition to Parliament of 1572, their complaint was that 'we in England are so far off from having a Church rightly reformed, according to the prescript of God's Word, that as yet we are not come to the outward face of the same.' [In this lecture the word 'church' usually means 'denomination.']

By 'Puritans' I mean those whose concerns were primarily religious, who were committed to Reformed theology and the reformation of the church, whether their preferred system of church government was that of reformed Episcopacy, Presbyterianism, or Independency.

I realise that at least two groups of writers on Puritanism prefer the theory that Puritans cannot be Anglicans, nor can Anglicans be Puritans. Some Non-Conformists take this stance because they want to emphasise the gulf between Anglicanism and Puritanism, to show that true Puritanism is found outside Anglicanism.[4] Some Anglican writers take this stance because they want to claim that Puritanism has no place in mainstream Anglicanism.[5]

However Patrick Collinson has shown that Puritanism was part of Anglicanism: 'our modern conception [that] Anglicanism commonly excludes puritanism is ... a distortion of part of our religious history,'[6] and A. G. Dickens claims that 'Puritanism in our sense was never limited to Nonconformists; it was a powerful element in the origins of the Anglican Church and it was through that Church that it won its abiding role in the life and outlook of the nation.'[7]

The leaders of Puritan Anglicans included: Archbishop Grindal of Canterbury, who tried to defend Puritan practice against the attacks

---

[3] John Foxe: *To the True and Faithfull Congregation of Christ's Universal Church*, in T H L Parker, ed., *English Reformers*, Library of Christian Classics, vol. XXVI, (London: SCM, 1966), p 73.

[4] For example David Budgen, ed., *Anglican and Puritan Thinking*, (Huntingdon: The Westminster Conference, 1977), and D M Lloyd-Jones, *The Puritans – Their Origins and Succesors*, (Edinburgh: Banner of Truth, 1987).

[5] For example John F H New, *Anglican and Puritan – The Basis of their Opposition*, (London: A & C Black, 1964).

[6] Collinson, *The Elizabethan Puritan Movement*, p 467.

[7] A G Dickens, *The English Reformation*, (London: Collins, 1967), p 428.

of Queen Elizabeth; Archbishop Williams of York, author of *The Holy Table, Name and Thing*, a sturdy defence of the Reformed theology and practice of the Lord's Supper; and Archbishop Ussher of Armagh, who together with Richard Baxter promoted a Reformed model of Primitive Episcopacy.[8] Nigel Atkinson has shown that Richard Hooker, that great architect of Anglicanism, was clearly in the Reformed tradition, and was closer to Calvin in theology than some of his Puritan critics.[9] Even in the days of the Commonwealth, 300 Episcopal Puritans [called 'Evangelicals' by a contemporary writer] used to meet regularly in Oxford for Anglican worship.[10] We should not underestimate the 'Anglicanism' of some of those who left the Church of England in 1662. Henry Havers, the Rector of Stambourne in Essex was one such; the congregation who left with him were still using the Prayer Book in 1735.[11] Paul Zahl points out that the English Reformation lasted 170 years, from 1520 to 1690, and resulted in 'a Protestant Reformed Church and a Protestant Reformed nation.'[12]

It is important to recognize that the Puritans had two methods of reformation, one that we can describe as reformation 'from above,' and the other as reformation 'from below.' Reformation 'from above' was the attempt to change the church by public authority, by appeal to Queen, King, or Parliament, by political influence and legislation. Reformation 'from below' meant publishing Bibles and other literature, producing able ministers, securing appointments to parishes, establishing reformed congregations and communities, and setting up conferences of ministers to promote the reform movement. One was reform by political influence, in an age when the government of the church was under the control of the state. The other was reform by the word of God, what we would now call 'grass roots' reform, in an age when ordinary people were gaining more influence in society and when

---

[8] Patrick Collinson, *Archbishop Grindal 1519-1583 – The Struggle for a Reformed Church*, (London: Jonathan Cape, 1979), Barrie Williams, *The Work of Archbishop John Williams*, (Abingdon: Sutton Courtenay Press, 1980), p 106ff., and Geoffrey F Nuttall, *Richard Baxter*, (London: Nelson, 1965), p 80.
[9] Nigel Atkinson, *Richard Hooker and the Authority of Scripture, Tradition and Reason*, (Carlisle: Paternoster, 1997).
[10] V H H Green, *Religion at Oxford and Cambridge*, (London:SCM, 1964), p 147.
[11] Charles Haddon Spurgeon, *Memories of Stambourne*, (Pasadena, Tex: Pilgrim Publications, 1975), p 44.
[12] Paul F M Zahl, *The Protestant Face of Anglicanism*, (Grand Rapids: Eerdmans, 1998), p 27.

democratic power was increasing. First we look at a brief survey of reform 'from above.' We will then look at reform 'from below' in more detail.

2. Reform 'From Above'

Patrick Collinson has written that the Elizabethan Puritans 'were organized to secure reform in the whole body of the Church, and by means of public authority ... to complete the English Reformation.'[13] We look first at this attempt to reform 'from above.'

The success of reformation 'from above' depended on the policies of the King or Queen, the possibilities of influencing those policies, the attitudes to reform of the Archbishops and Bishops, and the power and membership of the Parliament.

In the 1560s, the issue was that of clerical dress. Some Puritans opposed the cap and surplice, because they regarded them as reminiscent of popish garments. Queen Elizabeth was determined to retain them, Archbishop Grindal disliked them, but adopted a general policy of insisting on them, because they were things of no importance, and in these matters it was best to obey lawful authority. The cap and surplice remained in common use.

In the 1570s the issue was that of church government. Cartwright promoted the Presbyterian polity of the ruling power of courts set up by local congregations. This policy had no place for the government of the church by bishops or magistrates. These ideas made no progress at the time, though they were to bear fruit in the 1640s. They had the effect of dividing the Puritans into those who were committed to Presbyterian policy, and those who wished to, or were prepared to, retain bishops. Although the Puritans had not won any political victories, they managed to continue and increase their ministries. Some powerful lay leaders and sympathetic bishops protected them, and so managed to dull the effects of Queen Elizabeth's opposition to them. This protection disappeared from the 1580s, with

---

[13] Collinson, *The Elizabethan Puritan Movement*, p 13.

the death of Archbishop Grindal and of lay leaders such as the Earl of Leicester and Sir Walter Mildmay.[14] Even though the Puritans commanded a majority in the House of Commons at the end of Elizabeth's reign, they had not yet gained great political influence.

The Puritans hoped for some improvement in their cause as King James began his reign in 1603, and they made their moderate proposals for reform in their Millenary Petition at the Hampton Court conference. They failed, not because the King opposed Puritan theology but because he was reluctant to allow any dissent. Obedience to church rules was a matter of civil obedience, and no civil disobedience was allowed in any part of national life. The Puritans regarded the content of worship and church government as religious issues. For the King these were matters of political obedience, so he resisted any sign of rebellion.

From now on the Puritans divided into those who believed that these debated matters of liturgy and church government were of essential importance, so that no compromise could be accepted, and those who believed that these matters were not essential, and that some compromise was acceptable and even strategic. Some of those Independents who separated from the Church of England left for America in 1620, unwilling to submit to the pressure of belonging to a church not fully reformed. Those who remained were also divided on whether church government should be Reformed Episcopal, Presbyterian or Independent. They were also under increasing anti-Puritan pressure under Archbishop Laud. The effect of Laud's persecutions on the one hand, and more extreme Puritan claims on the other, made it increasingly difficult for Anglicans like Williams and Ussher to maintain and promote Puritan Anglicanism.

With the execution of King Charles in 1649, those Puritans who gained political power were the Independents, while the Presbyterian and Episcopal Puritans lost any influence. On the surface the Commonwealth seemed to have been the triumph of the Puritan reform movement. If it had succeeded in the long term, the English church would have been a Puritan church. It did not succeed. In terms of politics it could not succeed, because though the monarchy had been removed, no satisfactory replacement was put in place. The Parliament was clearly not representative, and an alternative Cromwell dynasty was

---

[14] Collinson, *The Elizabethan Puritan Movement*, p 387.

not available. It was also a costly success, in that it was victory only for the Independent Puritans, and not Presbyterian and Episcopal Puritans. The success of the Puritan movement also brought with it the seeds of its failure, because it gathered to itself political Puritans, committed to the politics of revolution and democracy, but not committed to Gospel priorities.[15]

Though the Presbyterian Puritans were influential in bringing Charles II to power in 1661, he was unsympathetic to their polity or theology, and in 1662 those Puritan ministers of the Church of England who refused to submit to the new requirements resigned from their ministries. Again the King was determined to win political obedience, and used liturgical submission as the test. The Puritans had been divided, and were now conquered. The Independents had gone to America, or been discredited with the fall of the Commonwealth. The committed Presbyterians resigned in 1662, and those Puritans who remained within the Church of England were discredited by their association with other Puritans, and disheartened by accusations of compromise.

Most viewed the political attempt at Puritan reform as a failure, caused in part by the theological divisions within Puritanism, in part by its political ineptitude, and in part by the historical accidents of the power play between monarchs, parliaments, and people.

So far I have given a summary of the attempt to reform the church 'from above' from 1559 to 1662, in which the Puritans tried to use public authority, monarch and parliament, to achieve their program of reformation. Of course as far back as 1582, Robert Browne had argued for 'reformation without tarrying for any.' He wrote as a Puritan committed to the independence of the church from secular authority, and the Independent model of congregational life. He was arguing for reform 'from below' and against reform 'from above.' As we have seen, reform 'from above' was less than successful: what can we say of reformation 'from below'?

---

[15] Christopher Hill, *Society and Puritanism in Pre-Revolutionary England*, (London: Mercury, 1966), pp 13-29.

3. Reform 'From Below'

This was a program to reform the church by the Word of God. It was not merely an attempt to reorganise church life in a way that satisfied Puritan preferences; religion was a public duty, not a private opinion, and they knew that a reformed church best served the welfare of church, nation and people, and the honour of God.[16]

This reform 'from below' was reformation by the Word of God, by studying, teaching, and applying the Bible. The Bible not only provided the model of a reformed church, but was itself also the means by which it would be reformed. How did the Puritans reform the church 'from below' by the Word? What were the ingredients of their reform program?

3.1 Bibles and Christian books

This was the age of new translations of the Bible into English and of the growth of printing and publishing. In addition to the Bible translations of Tyndale and Coverdale in the 1530s, English refugees in Geneva completed the *Geneva Bible* in 1560, including comments of interpretation throughout. In the five years from 1578, there were no less than 16 editions of the *Geneva Bible* printed in England, some of which included a Puritan revision of the Prayer Book.[17] Even the *Bishops' Bible*, published in 1568, included Protestant comments, though not as strongly worded as in the Geneva Bible. The *Authorised Version* had its origin in the Hampton Court conference of 1604 as a result of a request by the Puritan John Reynolds. As Christopher Hill puts it, England developed a biblical culture: 'The vernacular Bible became an institution in Elizabethan England–the foundation of monarchical authority, of England's Protestant independence, the text book of morality and social subordination.'[18]

In addition to Bibles, most with interpretive comments, Puritan literature also included sermons [such as Richard Sibbes' *The Bruised*

---

[16] Collinson, *The Elizabethan Puritan Movement*, p 25.
[17] Collinson, *The Elizabethan Puritan Movement*, p 165.
[18] Christopher Hill, *The English Bible and the Seventeenth-Century Revolution*, (London: Penguin, 1994), p 4.

Reed and Smoking Flax], biographies [John Foxe's *Book of Martyrs]*, discussions of moral and social issues [Richard Baxter's *The Christian Directory]*, and works of practical and pastoral theology [Baxter's *The Reformed Pastor*, and William Perkins' *The Art of Prophesying]*. In Haller's words: 'By 1640 the number of books circulating among the people had increased and accumulated beyond anything that had ever been known in England before, and a prodigious amount of that material came from the pens and brains of the Puritan preachers.'[19] This represented a massive educational program, in producing the literature, in circulating it, and in ensuring sufficient education so that people could read it. They made good use of the printing press, the new technology of their day, to continue the process of reform.

3.2 Preachers of the Word

One of the great achievements of the Puritans was the number of preachers of the Word they produced. They rightly saw that to reform the church and convert the nation they needed a great company of well-qualified preachers. In Baxter's words: 'All churches rise and fall as the ministry doth rise and fall [not in riches or worldly grandeur] but in knowledge, zeal and ability for their work.'[20] The Puritans knew that they needed good quality ministers to preach the gospel, teach godliness from the Bible, and grow the church.

William Perkins wrote: 'The means God uses to restore a sinner after a fall is to raise him through repentance to a better condition ... the instrument by whom this remarkable work is to be accomplished is ... a minister of God, lawfully called and sent by his church for such a great duty.'[21] Henry Barrow's *'True Description of the Visible Church'* includes this model of ordained ministry: 'Their doctor or teacher must be a man apt to teach, able to divide the word of God aright, and to deliver sound and wholesome doctrine ... he must be mighty in the Scriptures, able to convince the gain-sayers, and carefully to deliver his doctrine pure, sound and plain, not with curiosity or affectation, but so that it may edify the most simple ... to feed the sheep of Christ in green

---

[19] William Haller, *The Rise of Puritanism*, (Philadelphia: University of Pennsylvania Press, 1972), p 82.
[20] Baxter, in J I Packer, *A Quest for Godliness – The Puritan Vision of the Christian Life*, (Wheaton: Crossway, 1990), p 38.
[21] William Perkins, *The Art of Prophesying*, (Edinburgh: Banner of Truth, 1996), p 84.

and wholesome pastures of his word ... he must guide and keep those sheep by that heavenly and pastoral staff of the word ... discerning their diseases, and thereby curing them ... that the church may increase with the increasing of God, and grow up into him which is the head, Jesus Christ.'[22]

The program to reform people, church and nation depended on producing able ministers of the Word. This ministry also called for people who were ready to respond to the Word of God. In the words of Richard Rogers: 'God hath appointed this preaching of his Word to perfect the faith of his elect ... First ... they are cleansed from error and darkness about religion and manners ... and grow more sound in the knowledge of the truth ... and this is the mean whereby they are fast settled into a godly course.'[23] Puritan preachers flourished because Puritan hearers wanted to receive that Word of God.

3.3 Biblical training for ministry

They provided biblical and effective training for ministers. This training had two parts; the training that potential preachers received in their local church, and academic training at University.

The Puritans rightly recognized that a formative influence on preachers is the ministry that has nurtured them in Christ, and has provided them with early ministry opportunities. This happened in the context of family life, with its provision of mutual encouragement in godliness, and discussion of the sermons heard in church. Many Puritan clergy also trained up young preachers in their local churches, and gave them opportunities to preach trial sermons in meetings of local ministers.

The Puritans also used the new forms of education that were part of the Humanist tradition, and adapted them for the training of ministers at Universities. In addition to the training provided in other colleges, Puritans founded two new colleges in Cambridge; Emmanuel in 1584, and Sidney Sussex in 1596. Both were established in order to

---

[22] Henry Barrow, in Iain H Murray, *The Reformation of the Church*, (Edinburgh: Banner of Truth, 1965), pp 198, 199.

[23] Richard Rogers, in Peter Lewis, *The Genius of Puritanism*, (Haywards Heath: Carey Publications, 1975), p 41.

provide preachers. These preachers became the chief force for the spread of Puritanism among all classes of society. When Queen Elizabeth questioned Sir Walter Mildmay about his founding of Emmanuel College, he commented: 'I have set an acorn, which when it becomes an oak, God alone knows what will be the fruit thereof.'[24]

Those who trained in Cambridge could also hear good preachers in local churches, such as Richard Sibbes at Holy Trinity and William Perkins at St. Andrew's.

3.4   A new style of preaching

They created a new style of preaching to bring the Word of God to their generation. They preached in English, and their preaching reflected the more popular and appealing style of Medieval outdoor preaching which Latimer had used so effectively to serve the Reformation. They created a new style of preaching, a new rhetoric that was both *practical* and *affectionate; practical* because they taught what to believe and how to act, and *affectionate* because they appealed to the imagination through the emotions. Their detailed study of scripture was matched by their study of human beings, especially in struggles of faith and unbelief. In their preaching they were 'Physicians of the soul.'[25] Their plain prose style was in contrast both to the ignorance of many preachers, and to the scholarly complexities of Lancelot Andrews and John Donne.[26]

William Perkins has provided an outline of the Puritan sermon:

Preaching involves;

1. Reading the text clearly from the canonical Scriptures.

2. Explaining the meaning of it ... in the light of the Scriptures themselves.

3. Gathering a few profitable points of doctrine from the natural sense of the passage.

4. If the preacher is able, applying the doctrines thus explained to the life and practice of the congregation in straightforward,

---

[24] Haller, *The Rise of Puritanism*, p 20.
[25] Haller, *The Rise of Puritanism*, p 3.
[26] Hill, *Society and Puritanism in Pre-Revolutionary England*, p 508.

plain speech.[27]

Perkins wrote new training manuals for preachers, *The Art of Prophesying* in 1592, and *The Calling of the Ministry* in 1605.

On one occasion, Laurence Chaderton, later Master of Emmanuel College, had been preaching for two hours and announced that he would soon stop. His congregation replied 'for God's Sake Sir, Go on, go on.'[28] Good preaching from the pulpit developed an appetite for good preaching in the congregation. The Word reformed the church.

3.5 In-service training for ministers

The Puritan program of reform depended on a good supply of able and godly preachers, and they provided what we now call 'in-service training' by two structures, *Prophesyings* and *Conferences*.

Prophesyings were meetings of ministers at which a number preached sermons, received comments on their sermons, discussed the interpretation of the text, and discussed matters of ministry. Often several learned ministers chaired the event, and prospective preachers also contributed. They based these Prophesyings on the system employed in Zurich in training ministers in exegesis, and they derived the name from Paul's words: 'Two or three prophets should speak, and the others should weigh carefully what is said.' They held these on market days, and so many people were able to hear the sermons and take part in at least some of the program.

These Prophesyings provided training and mutual encouragement for ministers, the chance for young or potential preachers to test their abilities, and for good quality preaching to be heard by the lay people who attended. Sometimes these events were initiated by the Bishop, but in most instances they were organised by local ministers. In the Diocese of Norwich prophesyings were grafted into the structure of meetings of rural deaneries. Archbishop Grindal was one who recognised the need for these events in order to promote the training of the clergy, and he defended the practice from biblical, patristic, medieval and modern sources. It was his commitment to these

---

[27] Perkins, *The Art of Prophesying*, p 79.
[28] Haller, *The Rise of Puritanism*, p 55.

which led Queen Elizabeth to suspend him from functioning as Archbishop of Canterbury, because she wanted to stop the Prophesyings, and he refused to act on her request. Despite this official opposition, these events provided effective training in ministry, and some of those who led them became leaders of an army, providing leadership in reform for clergy who did not find that in their Bishops.

Conferences were private meetings of clergy in a local area who had covenanted to meet together for mutual encouragement, usually once a month. The meetings included a sermon, a chapter by chapter exegesis of a book of the Bible, prayer, discussion of issues of ministry and Puritan policy, and matters of discipline. Local ministers set up these programs, and they committed themselves to the decisions of the Conference.[29]

The Puritan program of reform depended on a good supply of able ministers on the Word, and we have seen the great energy they expended in achieving this. A. G. Dickens comments on the Puritan preachers: 'their preaching ability and their numbers had no equivalent in pre-Reformation or mid-Tudor England.'[30] They were also better trained: in the Diocese of Worcester the percentage of clergy who were University graduates grew from 19% in 1560, to 84% in 1640.[31]

3.6 New models and opportunities for ministry

While some Puritans were appointed as Rectors or Curates of parishes, others went on itinerant ministry around England, or became chaplains in Puritan households. They were not often offered higher ecclesiastical positions, and when they were offered them, did not always accept. They had to work hard at finding opportunities for ministry in a church that did not always welcome them. Puritan lay people did their best to secure good ministers, and the gentry and nobility used their influence when they could. Laurence Chaderton at Emmanuel College became a mentor to many young preachers, and people often contacted him when looking for a new minister.

---

[29] Collinson, *The Elizabethan Puritan Movement*, pp 222-239.
[30] Dickens, *The English Reformation*, p 428.
[31] Dickens, *The English Reformation*, p 419.

However the great Puritan venture was the creation of a new model of ministry, the appointing of 'Lecturers.' A Lecturer had the task of preaching regularly in a church, in a position funded by Puritan lay people. Lectureships were often founded in parishes where the Rector or Curate had little ability in preaching the Bible, and where the rising educational standards and expectations of the people led to a demand for good preaching. The Lecture was a teaching sermon, and the people expressed their eagerness by paying for and attending the lectures.

One striking example in London was in the London parish of St. Antholin's Budge Row, where Charles Offspring was the Puritan Rector for forty years. Here a team of three preachers gave early morning Lectures six days a week. These lectures were preceded by an hour of psalm singing.[32] In addition to providing edification for the people of St. Antholin's, these Lectures also gave training in preaching to those who would later minister throughout England. London Puritans also founded a society to fund Lectureships across England, 'to plant a powerfull Ministry in Cities and Market-Towns here and there in the Country for the greater propagation of the Gospell.'[33] This society was closely associated with St. Antholin's church, and was known as the Collectors of St. Antholin's, or the Feoffees for Impropriated Tithes. It operated from 1626 until it was suppressed in 1633.[34] Haller comments that if it had not been closed down 'the English church ... would have been reformed by the spiritual brotherhood from within, bishops or no bishops.'[35]

In addition to using recognized models of ministry, the Puritans were creative in developing new models that worked effectively within the church, and worked to reform it.

3.7 Committed and trained lay people

Puritans regarded the godly family as a key unit in God's economy:

---

[32] Collinson, *The Elizabethan Puritan Movement*, p 50, and Hill, *Society and Puritanism in Pre-Revolutionary England*, ch. 3, and Paul S Seaver, *The Puritan Lectureships*, (Stanford: Stanford University Press, 1970).
[33] Haller, *The Rise of Puritanism*, p 81.
[34] Isabel M Calder, *Activities of the Puritan Faction of the Chruch of England 1625-33*, (London: SPCK, 1957).
[35] Haller, *The Rise of Puritanism*, p 81.

husband and wife have the task of 'erecting and establishing Christ's glorious kingdom in their house,' for 'a household is as it were a little commonwealth, by the good government of which God's glory may be advanced,' and 'these families ... are ... little churches, yea even a kind of Paradise on earth.'[36] They published Bibles with notes commenting on the text and other Christian literature to strengthen this ministry within households. In some cases, the godly family provided an alternative source of Christian nurture when the ministry of the local church was weak and unprofitable. This meeting of a family for prayer and instruction could easily be extended to include neighbours and friends.

We should not think that the Puritan movement was predominantly clerical in character. It was a mark of the success of Puritan ministry that it attracted *so* much lay support from every part of society. Magistrates and the nobility were often present at Prophesyings, and those who gave money for the appointment of Lecturers in churches included those who signed with a mark as well as the well educated. When Archbishop Grindal suspended a popular Lecturer at St. Giles' Cripplegate, sixty women came to his house to remonstrate with him; he requested they send instead 'half-a-dozen of their husbands.' Opposition to vestments was expressed by laity as much as clergy. Andrew Marvell objected to 'so many cringes and genuflexions that a man unpractised stood in need to entertain both a dancing-master and a remembrancer,' and complained that 'these things were very uncouth to English Protestants, who naturally affect a plainness of fashion, especially in sacred things.'[37]

It was when the Puritan movement was losing political power after 1590 that the attempt to reform the nation turned to an attempt to reform families, towns, parishes, and individuals, in what has been called 'the birth of the great age of puritan religious experience.'[38] This saw the production of literature that dealt with religious experience, Christian biography, journals of daily piety, issues of social and personal morality, and Christian life. The relative lack of success in reforming

---

[36] From Leland Ryken, *Worldly Saints*, (Grand Rapids: Academie, 1986), pp 47, 75, 85. See also *The Spiritualization of the Household*, ch. 13, in Hill, *Society and Puritanism in Pre-Revolutionary England*.

[37] Andrew Marvell, *Selected Poetry and Prose*, edited by Robert Wilcher, (London: Methuen, 1986), p 147 (from *The Rehearsal Transposed*).

[38] Collinson, *The Elizabethan Puritan Movement*, p 433.

church and nation led to a concentration on personal and community reform. Puritanism had a program for personal and community change, as well as for the reformation of the church.

There was generous support both in London and in the country for Puritan ministry, and of course the final demonstration of this was found in the increasing Protestantism of the Parliament, leading to what used to be known as 'the Puritan Revolution' of the Commonwealth. Lay Puritanism opposed the anti-Puritan policies of monarchs and bishops, and the political revolution was the sign both of the strength of the Puritan movement and of the effectiveness of their reform program.

3.8 Godliness in daily lives

The renewed study of the Bible led to the development of reformed patterns of church life and godliness. The Puritans needed to do this to find patterns that were biblical, and to develop models of godliness for ordinary lay people in the world.

John Dod published his *A Plaine and Familiar Exposition of the Ten Commandments* in 1603. Richard Baxter wrote the most complete example in his *Christian Directory,* with its four parts: Christian Ethics [or Private Duties], Christian Economics [or Family Duties], Christian Ecclesiastics [or Church Duties], Christian Politics [or Duties to our Rulers and Neighbours]. In this work Baxter carries on the medieval tradition of systematic ethics found for example in Aquinas' *Summa Theologica,* and tackles the subject in cases, that is specific examples. So he takes cases like these: 'Whether a vow of chastity or celibate may be broken, and in what cases,' 'Doth adultery dissolve marriage?,' 'May a man be oft or twice ordained?,' 'Is it lawful to stand up at the Gospel as we are appointed?,' 'The duty of physicians,' 'May I take that which another is bound to give, and will not?,' 'When is it lawful to go to law?,' 'What must be the qualifications for a bosom friend?,' 'Is it better to give in life-time or in death?'[39] Here is healthy 'casuistry,' in which he deals with 'cases' with biblical wisdom and integrity, and with relevance to the daily issues of ordinary Christians. These new patterns of

---

[39] Richard Baxter, *A Christian Directory,* (Ligonier: Soli Deo Gloria Publications, 1990), pp iii-xix.

godliness were an important aspect of the reformation of church and nation.

The Puritans also objected that in the Elizabethan church the power of excommunication was mostly used for trivial offences against Ecclesiastical courts. They wanted an effective power of discipline in local churches, and tried to set this up in a variety of informal ways in conferences or 'classes' of clergy and local elderships.

3.9 Gospel and Church

They knew that the gospel would produce the church, and also reform it. The early Puritans were not influenced by the individualism of later Protestantism, and knew that the full earthly effect of the gospel was not the conversion of individuals but the forming of the church. As Baxter wrote: 'It is the *Church of* GOD which we must oversee–that Church for which the word is chiefly upheld, which is sanctified by the Holy Ghost, which is the mystical body of Christ.'[40]

They also developed a clear model of the church that they expected. Though they disagreed among themselves about the biblical requirements for church government, whether Episcopal, Presbyterian, or Independent, they still agreed on the shape of a reformed church. Henry Barrow outlined this shape in his *'A True Description of the Visible Church'* of 1589. He has what we might call a 'high' view of the church: not a merely human institution, nor only a useful provision for individual Christians.

> As there is but one God and Father of all, one Lord over all, and one spirit: so there is but one truth, one faith, one salvation, one church, called in one hope, joined in one profession, guided by one rule, even the word of the most high ... it consisteth of a company of faithful and holy people gathered together in the name of Jesus Christ their only king, priest, and prophet, worshipping him aright ... keeping the unity of faith in the bond of peace and love unfeigned ... it is called the city, house, temple, and mountain of the eternal God ... it shall appear most beautiful, yea most wonderful, and even ravishing the senses to conceive, much more to behold, what then to enjoy so blessed a

---

[40] Richard Baxter, *The Reformed Pastor*, (Edinburgh: Banner of Truth, 1974), p 130.

communion ... In this church is the truth purely taught, and surely kept: here is the covenant, the sacraments, and promises, the graces, the glory, the presence, the worship of God.[41]

However the church was always in need of reformation. The options were to leave the Church of England or to stay in and reform it. The call to leave was most often expressed by the Independents or Congregationalists: Presbyterian and Episcopal Puritans were committed to staying and reforming it.

So for example Thomas Cartwright answered those who claimed that the church was so corrupt that true believers should leave it. Peter Lake has summarised his arguments:

1. The church must be mixed, as it is made up of people who are a mixture of grace and sin. The search for a pure church is doomed to failure.

2. The church is like a disobedient wife: still a wife 'not having abandoned her husband by atheism nor by idolatry.'

3. It is wrong to judge before the time. The time for the separation of sheep and goats is at the return of Christ, and not before.

4. Christ did not separate himself from the church of his time, even though the people of God had allowed corruptions to enter into holy things, and despite the enmity of the leaders of God's people against him.

5. Peter and the other apostles still treated the Jews as the people of God, despite their sins.

6. The Church of England still retained the preaching of the Word, ministry and sacraments, and so continued to be the church of God.

7. As in the church the godly were 'the leaven that leavened the whole lump,' so in the church's ministry it is the activity of Puritan ministers that helps the church remain the church of God.[42]

---

[41] Barrow, in Murray, *The Reformation of the Church*, pp 196-197, 202.
[42] Peter Lake, *Moderate Puritans and the Elizabethan Church*, (Cambridge: Cambridge University Press, 1982), pp 80-86.

Puritans also worked for the reform of their local churches by forming 'covenant communities' within those churches for mutual edification, rebuke and exhortation. These were led by ministers, but they also provided opportunities for lay people to engage in this ministry especially within households.

3.10 Prayer and suffering

They knew that they had to pray and to suffer for the gospel to produce the church. They encouraged their followers to pray for the church. Jeremiah Burrows, preaching on Gospel Worship, says: 'The church is, as it were, in the midst of the sea, tossed up and down in a great storm. Now why do you not pray as earnestly for the kingdom of Christ among His churches as for yourselves when you are in a storm at sea?'[43]

They also knew that they were called to suffer for the gospel. John Calvin's sermons on Timothy and Titus were translated into English and published in London in 1579. He comments on 2 Timothy 3:11: '[St Paul] was faithful in preaching the word of God where it was received, so when there were any persecutions, they never saw him any changling, in so much that he spared not his own life' and he adds 'we must dispose ourselves, if it please God, to venture our lives for the witness of the Gospel.'[44] The Puritans knew from their experience that the reformation of the church was always achieved through suffering, including persecution from those both outside and inside the church.

They were most effective in bringing about change when they implemented the changes they wanted, and suffered the consequences until the church as a whole caught up with them. This was a far more effective method of making changes than that of thinking and writing about possibilities. It provided a visible model of biblical ministry, and encouraged commitment from young adherents. While it was not always successful, it was then as always the best way to achieve change; the same method was used so effectively by the Oxford Movement in the 19th century.

---

[43] Jeremiah Burrows, *Gospel Worship*, (Ligonier: Soli Deo Gloria Publications, 1990), p 365.

[44] John Calvin, *Sermons on the Epistles to Timothy and Titus*, (Edinburgh: Banner of Truth, 1983, Reprint of 1579 London Edition), p 912, with modern spelling.

3.11 Gospel outreach

As we have seen, they reformed the church because this would serve the nation, and they trained more ministers so that the Word of God would be preached. One of the reasons for endowing Lectureships was so that the gospel would be preached in new places in England. They also made sure that able gospel preachers went to the new colonies in America.

This gospel outreach was not in a religious vacuum. Indeed Richard Baxter encouraged the training of many ministers with these words:

> Papists are up, and Atheists and Infidels and Jews are up, and abundance of secret Apostates are up openly reproaching the Ministry, that privately deride Christ and the Scripture, and the life to come ... Quakers are up, and all the prophane as farre as they dare: And shall we not be up to further that Gospel and Ministry and Church of Christ, which so many bands of the Prince of darknesse are armed to assault?

and he hoped that these ministers would be raised for Wales as well as England.[45] They recognized a universal, urgent and continuing need for able preachers of God's Word.

3.12 Planning for the future

The Puritan program of reform also included preparing preachers for the next generation. It is obvious that any plan to reform a national church must have a long term view; and equally obvious that training up the next generation of minsters is the most effective way to achieve that reform.

Many preachers recognized their responsibility to train up the next generation. At Reading for example, Thomas Taylor maintained 'a little nursery of young Preachers, who under his faithful Ministry flourished in knowledge and piety.' Richard Greenham did the same at Dry Drayton, as did Richard Rogers at Wethersfield.[46] John Preston declined to become a university lecturer, choosing rather to continue local church preaching, because 'preaching was like to work more and

---

[45] Baxter, in Nuttall, *Richard Baxter*, pp 79, 80.
[46] Haller, *The Rise of Puritanism*, pp 148, 28, 35.

win more souls to God,' yet he was also aware the advantage of preaching at Cambridge, because he was then likely to 'beget begetters,' to produce preachers.[47] That is, he saw the strategic value of converting people who would then be able to become preachers themselves, and so increase the ministry.

Robert Stock, Rector of All Hallows was commended because: 'Many famous lights in God's Church and faithfull Ministers of the Word do profess to have lighted their candles at his Lampe.'[48] So young preachers learnt their model of ministry before they went for academic training, and they were likely to reproduce that ministry by which they had themselves been formed. The Puritans wanted to convert and train up the next generation of preachers.

4. Evaluation

This program of reform 'from below' was successful to a remarkable degree. We can demonstrate this in four ways.

First, when the moment came for decisive political action in reform 'from above' in the setting up of the Commonwealth and Puritan church structures in the 1640s, such an achievement was only possible because of the reformation 'from below.' Without the grass roots movement of reform, there would not have been enough political strength to achieve the reform 'from above.' For political power without the support of the people cannot succeed in the long term. Puritanism's best chance lay in its reform 'from below.'

Second, although it is commonly held that the Puritan movement failed in its attempts to reform the national church, we should not ignore its very considerable achievements in changing English national church life. The fact that England became so resolutely Protestant in the Glorious Revolution of 1689, was due to the work of the Puritans over the previous 130 years. It is also the case that Anglican preaching after 1662 followed the plain style of the Puritans rather than the

---

[47] Haller, *The Rise of Puritanism*, p 73.
[48] Haller, *The Rise of Puritanism*, pp 148, 73, 291.

intellectual style of some pre-1662 Anglicans.[49] Christopher Wren's intention to design and build church buildings as 'auditories for the Word of God' after the fire of London of 1666 similarly indicates the triumph of Puritan principles. Many features of the post-1662 Church of England reflect Puritan priorities, even if they lacked the spiritual fervour of the constructive days of Puritanism.

Third, the Puritans left behind a positive model of ministry that would last for at least three centuries. So, for example, C. H. Spurgeon, the great and effective preacher of the 19th Century [1834-1892], was trained up in his early years by his grandfather, James Spurgeon. James Spurgeon was minister of the Congregational Church at Stambourne for fifty years, and had a deep knowledge of Puritan writings as well as of the Bible. Charles began reading those Puritans at an early age, and was also instructed in those doctrines by Mary King, his housekeeper when he was a schoolboy at Newmarket. He later wrote: 'Out of the present contempt into which Puritanism has fallen, many brave hearts and true will fetch it, by the help of God, ere many years have passed.'[50] Of his own ministry he said: 'Believing that the Puritanic school embodied more of gospel truth in it than any other since the days of the apostles, we continue in the same line of things, and, by God's help, hope to have a share in that revival of Evangelical doctrine which is as sure to come as the Lord himself.'[51] He also wrote: 'The doctrine that I preach to you is that of the Puritans: it is the doctrine of Calvin, the doctrine of Augustine, the doctrine of Paul, the doctrine of the Holy Ghost.'[52]

The 20th century has also seen successful ministries in Britain that have reflected Puritan priorities and methods, not least in preachers such as Martyn Lloyd-Jones, J. I. Packer, John Stott, R. C. Lucas, and Willie Still. The Puritan model of ministry is still productive.[53]

Fourth, the social effects of Puritanism were evident for nearly 300 years. The social reform movements of the 19th century were a

---

[49] Hill, *Society and Puritanism in Pre-Revolutionary England*, p 508.
[50] Arnold Dallimore, *Spurgeon – The Early Years*, (London: Banner of Truth, 1962), p 11.
[51] Dallimore, *Spurgeon – The Early Years*, pp 387, 8.
[52] Spurgeon, *Memories of Stambourne*, p 127.
[53] See also Wallace Benn, *The Baxter Model* (Hartford: Fellowship of Word and Spirit, 1993).

result of the expression of Puritan democratic principles, and England's residual 'no Popery' sentiment, still effective in Parliament in 1929, was also a long term result of Puritan teaching. It is not too much to claim that the comparative vigour of evangelical faith in England today as compared with the rest of Europe is due in part to the Puritan reform program of 1559-1662.

At the same time they failed to achieve that measure of reform for which they struggled for so long. This was because they could not agree on what a reformed church would look like (Episcopal, Presbyterian, or Independent). They were internally divided, and often at odds with each other. They were also defeated by their political weakness, and by the accidents of England's political development, especially in the various policies of the monarchs of their age.

They also suffered from unrealistic expectations of the extent of reform that would be possible. Henry Barrow's *'A True Description out of the Word of God, of the Visible Church*[54] is moving to read not only because of the beauty of church life that it describes, but also because it describes a church that has never existed, and will never exist on earth. It pictures the ideal church, which did not exist in New Testament times, and which is an unrealistic model for any age. It was bound to bring disappointment. In Calvin's words: 'Saint Paul meant to meet with such stumbling blocks as trouble us and torment us very much: when we do not see the church of God so well reformed as we would desire, we think all is lost ... men must not discomfort themselves too much, but wait patiently ... for the end shall always be good, so that we be constant, and not shaken.'[55]

Another reason for the lack of effectiveness was that some Puritans began to change their theology in the 1620s towards 'Cambridge Platonism,' a kind of moral Rationalism. They wanted to leave behind controversy in religion, and the result was that they ignored the traditional heart of Puritan theology, the person and atoning work of Christ. Instead they pointed to Christ as a moral teacher of laws that would bring about moral purity.[56]

---

[54] Murray, *The Reformation of the Church*, pp 196-202.
[55] Calvin, *Sermons on the Epistles to Timothy and Titus*, p 834, with modern spelling.
[56] Basil Willey, *The Seventeenth-Century Background*, (London: Penguin, 1962), p 139.

Some of those who were disappointed went to the colonies in America for a new start. In the words of one of them '[in New England] the Lord will create a New Heaven and New Earth, new Churches and new Commonwealth together.'[57] Others who were still ministering in 1662 resigned rather than continue in a church that placed so many restrictions on them.

What should reformers do when their long term program of reform has not succeeded as they have hoped and prayed?

It would be presumptuous to say what others should have done in another age. However here are four comments on the Puritans we have been studying:

1. Their sense of failure should not lead us to undervalue what they achieved. If they did not succeed in reforming the church as they wished, they still preserved and preached the gospel in England in their own generations, worked to support gospel outreach in America and elsewhere, and provided as much as they could for the future. They did what each generation of God's people is called to do, in proclaiming the word of God. The fact that nearly 2000 minsters resigned in 1662 [about 20% of the clergy] is a reflection of the success of the Puritan reform program, especially if we remember that in addition many godly ministers decided to continue in Church of England ministry. Also around 120,000 lay people suffered for being Non-Conformists after 1662, and there were many who stayed in the Church of England as well.

2. In their desire to reform the church, they had unrealistic expectations. The church is made up of new generations of sinners, and so will always need to be reformed. And if the sinner is saved by grace, so is the church. If the sinner is justified by grace, so is the church. The church on earth will always be sinful, and any attempt at reformation must accept this reality. There are many warnings that the last days will be days of confusion and error in the church of God, and those last days include the time of the New Testament, the time of the Puritans, as well as our own days. They should not have been surprised that their efforts did not achieve what they had hoped for.

---

[57] Capt. E. Johnson, in Avihu Zakai, *The Gospel of Reformation – the Origins of the Great Puritan Migration*, Journal of Ecclesiastical History, vol. 37: 4, 1986, p 600.

3. A strong theme in the last sermons of those who resigned in 1662 was the reality of God's judgment coming on the church. So Edmund Calamy preached: 'Did the church at Ephesus lose the candlestick, because they had lost their first love? And have not we lost our first love to the gospel and its ordinances?' He quotes the martyr Bradford, 'Lord, it was my unthankfulness for the gospel that brought in popery in Queen Mary's day; and my unfruitfulness under the gospel that was the cause of the untimely death of King Edward the Sixth.'[58]

John Whitlock taught his hearers: 'The silencing of ministers calls aloud on us all to humble ourselves under the mighty hand of God. It bids us repent of our sins, the causes of God's judgments.'[59]

Any reformers have to leave room for the judgments of God on a church, see them as part of God's good gospel plan, and not give up because of them. For God may judge a church by silencing true preachers and sending false ones. In Calvin's words: 'it is certain that if matters go on, God must send worse confusions by a thousand parties than ever were in Papistry. For those blind creatures did never so extremely offend against God as we do nowadays.'[60] We must leave room for the judging and correcting hand of God.

4. Some Puritans were committed to the Bible as the 'regulative principle,' to the idea that godly practices are restricted to those actions ordained in the Bible. It is hard to think of a biblical precedent for resignation from the ministry. In Elijah's time of despair, God refused him permission to give up his task of reforming God's people, and instead recommissioned him for further service that would achieve both the judgment and saving plan of God. Paul warned Timothy of the difficulties of gospel ministry, of opposition from the majority of teachers in the church at Ephesus, of the prevalence of false doctrine, and of growing impatience with sound doctrine among his hearers. Yet there was no suggestion that he should give up; rather a

---

[58] Iain H Murray, *Sermons of the Great Ejection*, (London: Banner of Truth, 1962), p 27.
[59] Murray, *Sermons of the Great Ejection*, p 197.
[60] Calvin, *Sermons on the Epistles to Timothy and Titus*, p 969, with modern spelling.

challenge to persist in his ministry. As John Flavel wrote: 'O be not too quick to bury the Church before she is dead.'[61]

There is now more scope for us to help to reform the church 'from above,' as decision-making power is now spread more widely through Synods, and that work is worth doing. However reform 'from below' is more lasting, and without it reform 'from above' will not be effective.

5. Conclusion

God's call to the Puritans in 1559-1662 was to preach the gospel, to convert unbelievers, to reform the church, and to shape their lives by the Bible. His call to us is the same. We can learn much that is useful and positive from them, especially in their work in reforming the church 'from below,' by the preaching of the Word. We might remember that all effective reforms come 'from below,' as they have again and again over the last four hundred years of the church. We should also note that although change always appears to happen slowly, a great deal of change can occur in 100 years, as is evident from the history of the Church of England from 1559 to 1662, and again from 1890 to 1990.

In this lecture I have concentrated on reform in the Church of England, but my comments apply as well to the reformation of any denomination, even those founded by Non-Conformist Puritans

What I have given so far is in the form of a Lecture as we understand it in the 20th century. However as we have seen, when this Lectureship was endowed, a Lecture was not an academic exercise, but a challenge to biblical godliness. Let me demonstrate that I have been true to the original intention of this Lectureship by showing that the Puritan program to reform the church was nothing other than an application of biblical principles to the church of their day.

---

[61] Flavel in I D E Thomas, *A Puritan Golden Treasury*, (Edinburgh: Banner of Truth, 1977), p 58.

The Puritans rightly saw that their context was that of the church in the last days, a post-apostolic church, with all the pressures of ungodly religion, declension from the gospel, and corrupt behaviour. As Paul encouraged Timothy and Titus in their ministries, God provides sufficient instructions for the Puritans and ourselves to know how to live and minister in our different times. The Puritan program of reform 'from below' reflected the instructions that Paul gave to Timothy and Titus.

1. The Puritans printed **Bibles and Christian books:** Timothy was told that the Scriptures make us wise for salvation through faith in Jesus Christ, and that he is to use these Scriptures in his preaching and teaching [2 Timothy 3: 15-4: 2, 1 Timothy 4: 13].

2. The Puritans recognized the key role of **Preachers of the Word:** Titus was told to make up what is lacking and appoint elders for the churches who are of sound moral character, and who are able to teach the truth and correct error [Titus 1: 5-9].

3. The Puritans provided **Biblical Training of Ministers:** Timothy was urged to pass on apostolic words in which the gospel is preserved by training faithful people who will be able to teach others, and Paul trains by example as well as by instruction [2 Timothy 1:13,14 and 2:2].

4. The Puritans created **a new style of Preaching,** and worked hard at finding an effective method of communication: Paul urged Timothy to teach with great patience and careful instruction, and to pay attention to his teaching [1 Timothy 4:13, and 2 Timothy 4:2].

5. The Puritans provided support and **in-service training for Ministers:** Paul provided this in 1 and 2 Timothy and Titus, and also appealed for support in his own ministry [2 Timothy 4:9-22].

6. The Puritans created **new models and opportunities for ministry:** Paul encouraged Timothy to look for new opportunities and to fulfil his ministry [2 Timothy 4:5,9].

7. The Puritans had **committed and trained lay people:** Titus was told to encourage members of the church to teach each other [Titus 2].

8. The Puritans promoted **godliness in daily living:** Titus was to

teach different groups how to lead godly lives, how to adorn the teaching of Christ [Titus 2,3].

9. The Puritans recognized the centrality of **gospel and Church** in God's saving plan: Paul taught how believers are to live in the church [1 Timothy 3:15].

10. The Puritans were committed to **prayer and suffering** for the sake of the church: Paul instructed Timothy and Titus on how to reform the churches of their day, and called on them to join with him in suffering for the gospel [2 Timothy 1, 2].

11. The Puritans promoted **gospel outreach:** Paul tells Timothy to do the work of an evangelist, and his aim was that the gospel might be fully proclaimed, that all the nations might hear it [2 Timothy 4:5,17].

12. The Puritans had a strategy of **planning for the future:** Paul encouraged Timothy and Titus to plan for future ministry in subsequent generations [2 Timothy 2:2, Titus 1:5-9].

I am not suggesting that we should adopt an archaic style of ministry in imitation of the Puritans. They were the biblical radicals of their day, and we should be the biblical radicals of our day. Nor have I fallen into the 20th century trap of trusting in methodology, of claiming that what the Puritans did was successful, and if we do the same, we will be successful too. What we should gain from the Puritan attempt to reform the church is an encouragement to follow their example in so far as it reflects the instructions of the Word of God, and the encouragement of seeing our place and role in God's great gospel plan for the world for the 21st century, that at the name of Jesus every knee will bow, and every tongue confess that Jesus Christ is Lord, to the glory of God the Father.

Let me urge you to find your place in this gospel plan, to do the work of an evangelist, to build up and reform the church, and to preach Christ in all his glory as God's Son, the Head of his church, and our Saviour.

Bibliography

Nigel Atkinson, *Richard Hooker and the Authority of Scripture, Tradition and Reason*, Carlisle, Paternoster, 1997.
Richard Baxter, *A Christian Directory*, Ligonier, Soli Deo Gloria Publications, 1990.
Richard Baxter, *The Reformed Pastor*, Edinburgh, Banner of Truth, 1974.
Wallace Benn, *The Baxter Model*, Hartford, Fellowship of Word and Spirit, 1993.
R. S. Bezzant, *Elizabethan Puritans 1572-1587*, unpublished essay, 1983
David Bugden, ed., *Anglican and Puritan Thinking*, Huntingdon, The Westminster Conference, 1977.
Jeremiah Burrows, *Gospel Worship*, Ligonier, Soli Deo Gloria Publications, 1990.
Isabel M. Calder, *Activities of the Puritan Faction of the Church of England 1625-33*, London, S. P. C. K., 1957.
John Calvin, *Sermons on the Epistles to Timothy and Titus*, Edinburgh, Banner of Truth, 1983, Reprint of 1579 London Edition.
Patrick Collinson, *Archbishop Grindal 1519-1583 — The Struggle for a Reformed Church*, London, Jonathan Cape, 1979.
Patrick Collinson, *The Elizabethan Puritan Movement*, London, Jonathan Cape, 1967.
Arnold Dallimore, *Spurgeon — the Early Years*, London, Banner of Truth, 1962.
Gerald R. Cragg, *Puritans in the Period of the Great Persecution 1660-88*, Cambridge, Cambridge University Press, 1957.
A. G. Dickens, *The English Reformation*, London, Collins, 1967.
V. H. H. Green, *Religion at Oxford and Cambridge*, London, S. C. M., 1964.
William Haller, *The Rise of Puritanism*, Philadelphia, University of Pennsylvania Press, 1972.
Christopher Hill, *The English Bible and the Seventeenth-Century Revolution*, London, Penguin, 1994.
Christopher Hill, *Society and Puritanism in Pre-Revolutionary England*, London, Mercury, 1966.
Peter Lake, *Moderate Puritans and the Elizabethan Church*, Cambridge, Cambridge University Press, 1982.
Peter Lewis, *The Genius of Puritanism*, Haywards Heath, Carey Publications, 1975.
D. M. Lloyd-Jones, *The Puritans — Their Origins and Successors*, Edinburgh, Banner of Truth, 1987.
Andrew Marvell, *Selected Poetry and Prose*, edited by Robert Wilcher, London, Methuen, 1986.
Iain H. Murray, *The Reformation of the Church*, Edinburgh, Banner of Truth, 1965.
Iain H. Murray, *Sermons of the Great Ejection*, London, Banner of Truth, 1962.
John F. H. New, *Anglican and Puritan — The Basis of their Opposition*, London, A. & C. Black, 1964.
Geoffrey F. Nuttall, *Richard Baxter*, London, Nelson, 1965.
J. I. Packer, *A Quest For Godliness — The Puritan Vision of the Christian Life*, Wheaton, Crossway, 1990.

T H. L. Parker, ed., *English Reformers,* Library of Christian Classics, vol. XXVI, London, S. C. M., 1966.
William Perkins, *The Art of Prophesying,* Edinburgh, Banner of Truth, 1996.
Leland Ryken, *Worldly Saints,* Grand Rapids, Academie, 1990.
David Samuel, *The Evangelical Succession,* Cambridge, James Clarke, 1979.
Paul S. Seaver, *The Puritan Lectureships,* Stanford, Stanford University Press, 1970.
Charles Haddon Spurgeon, *Memories of Stambourne,* Pasadena, Texas, 1975.
I. D. E. Thomas, *A Puritan Golden Treasury,* Banner of Truth, 1977.
Basil Willey, *The Seventeenth-Century Background,* London, Penguin, 1962.
Barrie Williams, *The Work of Archbishop John Williams,* Abingdon, Sutton Courtenay Press, 1980.
Paul F. M. Zahl, *The Protestant Face of Anglicanism,* Grand Rapids, Eerdmans, 1998.
Avihu Zakai, *The Gospel of Reformation — the Origins of the Great Puritan Migration,* Journal of Ecclesiastical History, Vol. 37: 4, 1986, pp 584-602.

The Pilgrim's Principles: John Bunyan Revisited

J.I. Packer

1. A Puritan Pastor 219
2. A Puritan Pilgrim 221
3. The Puritan Pilgrimage 229
   - 3.1 *The conversion of sinners.* 231
   - 3.2 *The conflicts of Christians.* 234
   - 3.3 *The communion of saints.* 236
   - 3.4 *The calling of pastors.* 237
   - 3.5 *The closure of life.* 238
4. A Puritan Heritage 241

JAMES I. PACKER began his ministry as Curate of St. John the Baptist, Harborne Heath in Birmingham. After several years in England as Principal of Tyndale Hall, Bristol and Warden of Latimer House, Oxford he moved in 1979 to Regent College, Vancouver (Canada). He is arguably the most significant and influential Reformed Evangelical Anglican writer of the last 100 years, and has played a key role in the revival of interest in Reformed and Puritan theology over the last six decades. His 1955 DPhil from Oxford was on redemption in the thought of Richard Baxter. He has since published a large number of books including the classic *Knowing God* and *Among God's Giants: The Puritan Vision of the Christian Life*. He is also General Editor of the English Standard Version.

1. A Puritan Pastor

During his years in the forces in England's first Civil War, which ended in 1646, he was not a believer; but he came to faith soon after. The story of how he changed, says Michael Mullett, 'made up an edifying narration of debauchery giving way to holiness."[1] Before long he was the pastor of a small separatist congregation in Bedford. *Separatist* here should be understood as a scholars' code word, meaning more than separated from all thought of being part of a parish-based national church, episcopal or presbyterian, controlled by Parliament or Synod. The seventeenth-century word for that side of separatism was *independent,* and under the Commonwealth independent churches mushroomed. But the heart of what we now call separatism was the positive purpose of being separated from the world to live together as a band of 'visible saints,'[2] practising personal holiness, biblical worship, pastoral care in the form of mutual watchfulness, encouragement, and admonition, and communal decision-making on all matters affecting the life of the group. The seventeenth-century word for this side of separatism was *congregational.* In terms of this vision of church life, the pastor's role was to teach people how to understand and apply the word of God, and to lead them in obeying it. The modern parallel is the house-church, as developed among the Christian Brethren and more recently among the charismatics. Back, now, to our story.

As a separatist pastor within this frame, he did the work of an evangelist with force and skill. Here is a first-hand description of his ministry. 'This man made it much his business to deliver the people of God from all those faults and unsound rests that, by nature, we are prone to take and make to our souls. He pressed us to take special heed that we took not up any truth upon trust–as from this, or that, or any other man or men – but to cry mightily to God that he would convince us of the reality thereof, and set us down therein, by his own Spirit, in

---

[1] Michael Mullett, *John Bunyan in Context* (Pittsburgh: Duquesne University Press, 1997), p 43.
[2] Title of a book by G.F.Nuttall: *Visible Saints: the Congregational Way, 1640-1660* (Oxford: Blackwell, 1957).

the holy Word.'³ Though he was a convinced Baptist, he would not let membership of the congregation depend on whether one had been baptized as a believer, or indeed whether one had been baptized at all. That was because biblically he could only see baptism as an 'external' of Christian faith, instituted to help in one's personal discipleship rather than to be a rite of entry into the church community and of admission to the Lord's Table. This view of baptism is pictured in *Pilgrim's Progress,* part two, where Christiana and company are required to wash in what Bunyan's margin calls *'the Bath Sanctification,'* and (so we read) 'they came out of that *Bath* not only sweet and clean: but also much enlivened and strengthened in their Joints.'⁴ In his last letter to the congregation, written on his deathbed, came the sentence: 'Concerning separation from the church about baptism, laying on of hands, anointing with oil, psalms, or any *externals,* I charge every one of you . . . that none of you be found guilty of this great evil.'⁵ Apart from his limited view of baptism, however, he was an evangelical whom we should much admire, and in whom Anglican evangelicals in particular should take an interest, if only because for the last two years of his life, under the Cromwellian system of established independency, he was rector of St John's Church, Bedford.

'Wait a minute,' says someone; 'that does not sound right; is it John Bunyan that you are talking about?' No, not yet; the man I have been profiling is John Gifford, who discipled Bunyan and under God shaped his mind on all main points of faith and life. Gifford, who had been a major in the Royalist army, came to Bedford after the war, set up as a physician, and was converted there. He was one of the twelve founder-members of the church whose pastor he later became. Like Bunyan, he had no formal theological education, and was never ordained in any formal sense; but he had a heart for God, he loved the Bible, he had come to faith dramatically out of personal despair (triggered, in his case, by gambling debts), and he was a clear, shrewd

---

³ John Bunyan, *Grace Abounding to the Chief of Sinners,* 1666, sec. 117 (cited from *Grace Abounding and The Life and Death of Mr Badman* [London: J.M.Dent, Everyman's Library, 1928], p 37f.). Additions to the original text that appear in later printings are noted by G.B.Harrison, *Ibid.,* p x.
⁴ John Bunyan, *The Pilgrim's Progress* (Oxford: Oxford University Press, Oxford Standard Authors, 1945), p 246f. In this and all other quotations from the allegory I reproduce Bunyan's italics, which he uses both for contrasts and as attention-getters.
⁵ Cited from Henri Talon, *John Bunyan* (London: Rockliff, 1951), p 269, n.60.

guide on matters of inward spiritual self-knowledge and experience. In the providence of God he was thus ideally fitted to be Bunyan's mentor, and such he became. When Bunyan identified himself to the godly Bedford women with whom he had made friends as being still an unconverted seeker, they 'told Mr Gifford of me, who himself also took occasion to talk with me, and . . . invited me to his house, where I should hear him confer with others, about the dealings of God with the soul; from all which I received more conviction . . .' Thereafter Bunyan 'sat under the ministry of holy Mr Gifford, whose doctrine, by God's grace, was much for my stability;'[6] and when, two or three years later, he had become sure of his faith, it was Gifford who baptized him, in the river Ouse. (The church had no building of its own till it acquired a barn in 1672, and baptistries in any case did not exist till long after.)

'Holy Mr Gifford' was evidently the model for at least three of the characters in *Pilgrim's Progress*. The first is Evangelist, who directed Christian to the wicket-gate at the start of his journey and reappeared shortly after to tell him why it would be suicidal for him to follow the advice of Mr Worldly-Wiseman and put his spiritual future into the hands of Mr Legality. The second is the 'very grave Person' with 'the best of Books in his hand' and the world 'behind his back' whose portrait Christian saw in the house of the Interpreter: 'one of a thousand' who 'can beget Children, travail in birth with Children, and nurse them himself when they are born.' The third is Mr Great-heart, the Interpreter's heroic servant, who is appointed as guide to Christiana and her family and who couriers them with others safely to the river of death, explaining dangers, teaching faith and killing giants all along the way. Gifford influenced Bunyan decisively, and after his death in 1655 it was Gifford's torch, doctrinal, ecclesiastical and experiential, that Bunyan carried to the end of his days.

2. A Puritan Pilgrim

Now let us look at Bunyan himself. Three things need to be said here about him.

---

[6] *Grace Abounding*, secs. 77, 117; Everyman ed., pp 26, 37.

First, he was a Puritan, in the basic sense in terms of which all the various faces and facets of historical Puritanism link up. This needs saying, for the authoritative scholar Richard Greaves, who on Bunyan's beliefs is clear and exact, tells us baldly that Bunyan was 'a sectary and not a Puritan.'[7] That is very misleading.

For in the first place *sectary* (that is, member of a sect) was in Bunyan's day a term of abuse, as imprecise and prejudicial as the word *Puritan* itself had been in actual use for the previous sixty years. It was not a word that Bunyan would, or should, have owned. On the lips of those whom Greaves describes as Puritans, namely Protestants who held to the ideal of a purified national church (Presbyterians, as they were mostly called in the 1640s and 1650s), sectary implied not only membership of some gathered congregation or other, but some oddity, unorthodoxy, and fanaticism as well. But Bunyan's ecumenical evangelicalism, unoriginal, uneccentric and undeviating, was as far from that kind of sectarianism as one can well imagine, and it is unwarrantable to imply otherwise.

And in the second place, as scholars nowadays rightly see, Puritanism was at heart a commitment to a broadly Reformed theology expressed in a piety and a worldview that required all life to be made 'holy to the Lord' through a Bible-based, Christ-exalting, Holy Spirit-oriented devotional discipline of considerable rigour. Political, ecclesiastical and sociological differences between one Puritan and another were there, but they were secondary, and belonged within the frame of revamped Augustinian godliness that bound all Puritans together. In this sense Bunyan was as Puritan as anyone you can think of.

It is true that up to 1640 Puritanism as a movement had been led by Oxford and Cambridge clergy, men of learning and social status, whereas Bunyan, like George Fox, was an instance of what in my youth would have been called 'blue-collar' lay leadership, emerging from the world of artisans, who in Bunyan's day were called 'mechanicks.'[8] Lay spiritual leadership of this kind was born in England among the Bible-

---

[7] Richard L. Greaves, *John Bunyan* (Appleford UK: Sutton Courtenay Press, 1969), p 23.
[8] Hence the title of W.Y. Tindall's ground-breaking if dismissive book, *John Bunyan, Mechanick Preacher* (New York: Columbia University Press, 1934).

searchers of the Parliamentary army, into which Bunyan was drafted at age sixteen and in which he served for two and a half years, from 1644 to 1647. Perhaps it was in the army that his idea of preaching as the spontaneous outpouring of 'what I felt, what I smartingly did feel'[9] was first formed. It is also true, as historians like Christopher Hill underline, that Bunyan's mindset had something in it of the poor man's perkiness in challenging the privileged and well-heeled,[10] as well as of the pastor's perception that pride of place and possessions keep sinners from self-knowledge and so from true faith in Christ. Yet Bunyan's mature understanding of personal religion and pastoral ministry, as expressed in thirty years of writing, is as authentically Puritan as can be, as will shortly appear.

Second, Bunyan was a very able Puritan. This too needs saying, for once we note that he was a tinker of limited education it is all too easy to write him off as a simple soul of limited ability, who despite his vividness of imagination and language need not be taken seriously as a thinker and teacher. But this also is wrong. Certainly, he was a tinker by trade, just because he was his father's son: he was sent to school to learn to read and write, but at an early age he was apprenticed to his father, a brazier, evidently with the intention that he should work permanently in the family shop. It does not look as if he and his father were ever close (he was sixteen when his mother and sister died, and within three months his father remarried, and he himself joined the army, so a sense of distance thereafter is fully understandable): at all events, he chose to ply his trade as an itinerant, and it was a happy providence that he did, otherwise he would never have met the Bedford Christians who set his feet on the path of life. Certainly, too, he lacked the breadth of mind and knowledge that higher education would have given him, and sometimes this shows. Then, again, the church he joined and subsequently pastored seems to have had between thirty and fifty members, not more, and that sounds less than impressive.

But consider: in thirty years Bunyan wrote no less than sixty theological books, doctrinal, devotional, allegorical and controversial, filling the three volumes of George Offor's large-page, small-print edition (over two thousand pages and two million words all told), which

---

[9] *Grace Abounding*, sec. 276; Everyman ed., p 85.
[10] Christopher Hill, *A Tinker and a Poor Man* (New York: Norton, 1990), pp 16-25 and *passim*.

Banner of Truth keeps in print for us, and the seventeen volumes in which Oxford University Press now makes Bunyan available for scholars.[11] When he preached in Bedford he drew hundreds, and in London he drew up to three thousand at one time. He was a valued friend of the great John Owen, who arranged for his own regular publisher to print the first edition of *Pilgrim's Progress,* and who told Charles II that he would gladly trade all his learning for Bunyan's power to preach. Think too of the sustained imaginative power that produced *Pilgrim's Progress,* and the *Holy War,* of which it has been said that it would be the greatest religious allegory in English were not *Pilgrim's Progress* greater; and think of Bunyan's capacity for producing edifying rhymes at the drop of a hat (granted, most were doggerel, but some of Bunyan's verse is true poetry); dwell also on his effortless flow of the most forceful, racy, down-to-earth, dignified colloquial Anglo-Saxon that England had known since William Tyndale; and it becomes obvious that Bunyan's natural ability, needing to be sanctified, certainly, but there from the start, was simply enormous.

Third, Bunyan was a Puritan who suffered. That in itself was hardly remarkable; all Puritans in the turbulent seventeenth century expected to suffer, and most did. Suffering, which the world would inflict out of malice and God would send and sanctify as a nurturing discipline, was to them par for the Christian course. In *The Character of an Old English Puritane, or Nonconformist,* a booklet written in 1646, John Geree said that the Puritan saw all life as warfare—meaning what we would call spiritual warfare—and his motto as he squared up to it was *Vincit qui patitur* (he who suffers wins).[12] Among the Puritans, however, Bunyan stands out for the magnitude both of his inward suffering (five years of mostly agony as he sought an assured faith) and of his outward suffering (twelve years in gaol between 1660 and 1672, with six months more in 1676-77). Something must be said about each of these spectacular hardships.

The inward suffering is narrated in stunning detail in *Grace Abounding to the Chief of Sinners,* a personal testimony that Bunyan first printed in 1666 and dedicated to 'those whom God hath counted

---

[11] For detailed contents of ed. George Offor, *The Works of John Bunyan* (Edinburgh: Banner of Truth, 1991) and general ed. Roger Sharrock, *The Miscellaneous Works of John Bunyan* (Oxford: Clarendon Press, 1976-94), see Mullett, pp 291-295.

[12] Cited from Gordon Wakefield, *Puritan Devotion* (London: Epworth Press, 1957), p x.

him worthy to beget to faith, by his ministry in the word.' This dedication reveals Bunyan's pastoral purpose, namely encouragement to younger believers, and explains the half-homiletical style of his writing: like the apostle Paul, he sees his own story as in some ways exemplary, and shares it with others to help them forward. The book probably expands the testimony he gave when he sought formal admission to Gifford's church; certainly, his detailed recording of what happened from fifteen to twenty years earlier is a notable feat of memory. The story has seven stages. First, Bunyan marries a godly girl and develops an ignorant religiosity (secs. 1-19). Second, Bunyan practises outward reformation (secs. 20-36). Third, Bunyan meets women from Gifford's church who shared their Christian experience 'as if joy did make them speak' (sec. 38), and seeks heart-conversion without finding it (secs. 37-88). Fourth, Bunyan gains assurance of Christ's love to him and of his present salvation from biblical texts and Luther's commentary on Galatians, but is then tempted to believe he has committed the unpardonable sin (secs. 89-199). Fifth, Bunyan regains his assurance and realises that his two years and more of despair had done him good (secs. 200-264). Sixth, Bunyan moves into a preaching ministry that God blesses (secs. 265-317). Seventh, Bunyan finds his faith, hope, and confidence strengthened during his time in prison (secs. 318-339). The story ends with three paragraphs embodying the very quintessence of John Bunyan, which I now quote in full.

> Of all tears, they are the best that are made by the blood of Christ; and of all joy, that is the sweetest mixed with mourning over Christ. Oh! It is a goodly thing to be on our knees, with Christ in our arms, before God. I hope I know something of these things.
>
> I find to this day seven abominations in my heart: (1) Inclinings to unbelief. (2) Suddenly to forget the love and mercy that Christ manifesteth. (3) A leaning to the works of the law. (4) Wanderings and coldness in prayer. (5) To forget to watch for that I pray for. (6) Apt to murmur because I have no more, and yet ready to abuse what I have. (7) I can do none of those things which God commands me, but my corruptions will thrust in themselves; 'When I would do good, evil is present with me.'
>
> These things I continually see and feel, and am afflicted and oppressed with; yet the wisdom of God doth order them for my good. (1) They make me abhor myself. (2) They keep me from

trusting my heart. (3) They convince me of the insufficiency of all inherent righteousness. (4) They show me the necessity of flying to Jesus. (5) They press me to pray unto God. (6) They show me the need I have to watch and be sober. (7) And provoke me to look to God, through Christ, to help me, and carry me through this world. Amen.[13]

Grace Abounding has always been acknowledged as a classic witness to the ups and downs, anxieties and agonies, trials and triumphs, of a sensitive soul seeking God in Christ through recurring temptations to doubt and despair, such as most serious Christians encounter at some point. More recently, however, Bunyan's book has been recognized as an equally classic clinical description of a distinct though related source of suffering, namely one mode of that form of melancholia which pastors once called scruples and psychiatrists nowadays call obsessive-compulsive disorder. Discussing Bunyan, psychiatrist Gaius Davies speaks of the obsessions that operate in this condition as 'home-made but disowned.' In an obsessional disorder' (he writes) 'a person's thoughts, ideas or images start in his or her own mind, and yet are resisted as if they were alien intruders.'[14] But one cannot get rid of them; instead, one is constantly 'compelled to think, feel, say or do something which seems silly or bad,' and the attempt to avoid yielding to this pressure produces inhibitions about doing ordinary things for fear that doing them would be somehow wrong. Though the condition is agonizingly fear-ridden, there is in it 'no real derangement of mind: there is only profound pain of mind'[15] –and even though the afflicted

---

[13] *Grace Abounding*, Everyman ed., p 102. Bunyan's words to his converts in the Preface (clearly, like most prefaces, written last) further confirm that Bunyan is lifting the veil on his inward experience for pastoral purposes: 'If you have sinned against light; if you are tempted to blaspheme; if you are down in despair; if you think God fights against you; or if heaven is hid from your eyes, remember it was thus with your father, but out of them all the Lord delivered me ... I could ... have stepped into a style much higher than this in which I have here discoursed, and could have adorned all things more than here I have seemed to do, but I dare not. God did not play in convincing of me, the devil did not play in tempting of me, neither did I play when I sunk as into a bottomless pit, when the pangs of hell caught hold upon me; wherefore I may not play in my relating of them, but be plain and simple, and lay down the thing as it was.'

[14] Gaius Davies, *Genius and Grace* (London: Hodder & Stoughton, 1992), p 65. 'Home-made but disowned' is a phrase taken from Professor Sir Aubrey Lewis.

[15] *Ibid.* p 66, citing Henry Maudsley.

person feels that he or she is going mad, the waking nightmare is compatible with continued public activity. Now a pattern of distress and desperation due to obsessive-compulsive negations of God's grace runs right through Bunyan's account of his spiritual struggles; he thought it was all Satanic,[16] and we need not dispute that, noting only that it was this pathological mental mechanism that Satan exploited as he strove to ruin Bunyan's soul. Bunyan was highly strung and intensely imaginative; in his youth something frantic and insecure inside him led him, as he puts it, to play the madman, swaggering, swearing, showing off, lying, blaspheming, and generally going wild; as a man in his early twenties anxiously seeking God he saw visions, dreamed dreams, heard voices, and felt texts come at him like thunderbolts; and it was in this temperamental soil that his obsessive-compulsive states of doubt, denial, and despair had their roots, as one element in the inward suffering that he endured.

It looks as if preaching and then prison, which between them established Bunyan's public identity as Christ's servant and martyr, had a therapeutic spinoff for him; certainly, we hear no more of his obsessive-compulsive symptoms after he was gaoled in 1660. During the five years of his preaching ministry prior to 1660, they had sometimes recurred, as witnesses the following:

> Sometimes ..., when I have been preaching, I have been violently assaulted with thoughts of blasphemy, and strongly tempted to speak the words with my mouth before the congregation. I have also at some times, even when I have begun to speak the Word with much clearness, evidence, and liberty of speech, yet been before the ending of that opportunity so blinded, and so estranged from the things I have been speaking, and have also been so straitened in my speech, as to utterance before the people, that I have been as if I had not known or

---

[16] Compare this, from *The Pilgrim's Progress*, p 81, describing Christian's journey through the Valley of Humiliation: 'One thing I would not let slip, I took notice that now poor *Christian* was so confounded, that he did not know his own voice . . . one of the wicked ones got behind him, and stept up softly to him, and whisperingly suggested many grievous blasphemies to him, which he verily thought had proceeded from his own mind [margin: *twas Satan that suggested them into his mind*]. This put Christian more to it than any thing that he met with before . . . could he have helped it, he would not have done it; but he had not the discretion neither [sic] to stop his ears, nor to know from whence those blasphemies came.'

> remembered what I have been about, or as if my head had been in a bag all the time of the exercise.[17]

But that is Bunyan in 1666 looking back on how things had been between six and eleven years earlier. It really does seem that, by an intriguing irony, the stepping up of his outward suffering had helped to reduce its inward counterpart.

About Bunyan's imprisonment itself little need be said. He was sent to Bedford county gaol, and kept there, because he would not undertake not to preach at the unauthorised, un-Anglican gatherings that in those days were called conventicles. Though, in the ecclesiastical sense, a layman, Bunyan had become Bedfordshire's most popular and influential preacher; the magistrates, as servants of the restored Crown, Charles II, saw him as a subversive and one of whom they should make an example.[18] In prison he had no heating and slept on straw, but he enjoyed fair health, kept cheerful, made himself a flute, and wrote books. For the rest, I quote Talon:

> At the beginning, between the Autumn Assizes of 1661 and the Spring Assizes of 1662, a friendly gaoler granted Bunyan certain liberties. But his enemies raised a protest, the gaoler was given a warning, and Bunyan knew imprisonment at its strictest up to 1668. This period was followed by a less rigorous regime up to 1672.
>
> In order to support his dependants, Bunyan spent his time making 'many hundred grosse of long-tagged thread laces.' During his leisure hours he instructed his fellow-prisoners, gave counsel to people who came to him for advice, and managed, though far from the faithful of his church, to maintain a spiritual authority over them. And he was sometimes able to preach long sermons ...[19]

In January 1672, shortly before his release, the church formally chose him as their pastor, and that was his role for the rest of his life.

---

[17] *Grace Abounding*, sec. 293; Everyman ed., p 89.
[18] The best reconstruction of this politicking is in Christopher Hill, *op. cit.*, pp 103-110.
[19] Henri Talon, *op. cit.*, p 9f.

3. The Puritan Pilgrimage

My purpose now, against the background filled in so far, is to focus on the two parts of *Pilgrim's Progress* as a narrative index to the mainstream Puritan understanding of the Christian life.[20] Thus to limit my focus is in no way unfair to Bunyan, for Pilgrim's Progress is far and away the best of him, and it touches, at least, on everything that he wrote about elsewhere. This work, which has been continuously in print for over three hundred years and has been translated into over two hundred languages, is a pioneering masterpiece that is studied today from many academic angles: as an echo of the Middle Ages, as an apotheosis of the folk tale, as a forerunner of the novel, and so on. But I aim to review it as what Bunyan himself, the evangelist and pastor, meant it to be and thought it actually was–namely, a teaching tool, a didactic parable with all sorts of imaginative overtones explaining the Christian life to ordinary people, a sequence of enlightening and edifying similitudes (Bunyan's word), a biblical dream tale with characters drawn from waking life, a story that by God's grace might begin to become the reader's own story before he or she was through. In his 236-line Apology, in rhyming couplets, that introduces what became part one, Bunyan tells us how it all started.[21] His account is worth quoting at length.

> When at the first I took my Pen in hand,
> Thus for to write; I did not understand
> That I at all should make a little Book
> In such a mode; Nay, I had undertook
> To make another, which when almost done,
> Before I was aware, I this begun.
> And thus it was: I writing of the Way
> And Race of Saints, in this our Gospel-Day,
> Fell suddenly into an Allegory
> About their Journey, and the way to Glory,
> In more than twenty things, which I set down;

---

[20] Part one, 1678; part two, 1684. Some additions, e.g. Mr Worldy-Wiseman, Mrs Diffidence, most of the By-ends episode, the pillar of Lot's wife at the Hill Lucre, and the trumpeting and bell-ringing at the Celestial City, were made in the second and third editions of part one (1678, 1679).

[21] *The Pilgrim's Progress*, pp 3-10.

> This done, I twenty more had in my Crown,
> And they again began to multiply,
> Like sparks that from the coals of fire do fly.
> So he began to write out what had come to him.
> Neither did I but vacant seasons spend
> In this my Scribble; nor did I intend
> But to divert myself in doing this,
> From worser thoughts, which make me do amiss.
> Thus I set Pen to Paper with delight,
> And quickly had my thoughts in black and white,
> For having now my Method by the end,
> Still as I pull'd, it came; and so I penn'd
> It down; until at last it came to be
> For length and breadth the bigness which you see.

Then he asked his friends what he should do with it. To the fantasy element in the story-telling, the humour that breaks surface in the dialogue and character descriptions, and the sheer entertainment value of the swiftly-moving sequence of adventures, there were different reactions.

> Some said, John, print it;
> others said, Not so:
> Some said, It might do good;
> others said, No.

After proceeding to speak to the fears of those who thought his book would confuse its readers and cheapen holy things, Bunyan concludes his Apology as follows:

> This Book it chalketh out before thine eyes
> The man that seeks the everlasting Prize:
> It shows you whence he comes, whither he goes,
> What he leaves undone; also what he does:
> It also shows you how he runs and runs
> Till he unto the Gate of Glory comes ...
> This Book will make a Traveller of thee,
> If by its Counsel thou wilt ruled be;
> It will direct thee to the Holy Land,
> If thou wilt its Directions understand:
> Yea, it will make the slothful, active be;
> The Blind also, delightful things to see ...
> Would'st read thyself, and read thou know'st not what

> And yet know whether thou art blest or not,
> By reading the same lines? O then come hither,
> And lay my Book, thy Head, and Heart together.

The 240-line poem prefixed to part two (titled 'The Author's Way Sending Forth His Second Part of the Pilgrim') ends similarly:

> Now may this little Book a blessing be,
> To those that love this little Book and me;
> And may its buyer have no cause to say,
> His money is but lost or thrown away:
> Yea may this Second *Pilgrim* yield that Fruit
> As may with each good *Pilgrim's* fancie suit;
> And may it perswade some that go astray
> To turn their Foot and Heart to the right way.[22]

So the stories of first Christian and then Christiana taking their journey to the Celestial City are offered as pastoral instruction, and are to be appreciated as such.

Accordingly, I propose now to comment briefly on what this two-part work has to say about the following basic Christian and Puritan concerns: the conversion of sinners; the conflicts of Christians; the communion of saints; the calling of pastors; and the closure of life. Both parts illustrate these themes, and include didactic discussion of them; what is said and shown with regard to each theme is typically Puritan, though Bunyan imparts his own flavouring to each out of his personal and pastoral experience and his distinctive typologico-analogical way (such we may call it) of bringing biblical passages to bear on matters of spiritual life; and what Bunyan affirms in every case is, if I am any judge, timely truth for us today. This, I think, will become plain as we proceed.

3.1   *The conversion of sinners.*

On this theme, Bunyan's narratives labour three points.

Point one is that conversion is the start of a lifelong journey that has as its destination the promised Celestial City. This truth is taught by the very shape of the story. What Bunyan gives us, twice over, is a

---

[22] *Ibid.*, p 206.

biblically-informed quest narrative—one of the world's oldest story forms, here used to delineate the profoundest way in which one can ever visualize one's own Christian life. Conversion appears as the quest story's opening chapter.

Point two is that conversion is a complex, often long-drawn-out process that advances by stages from conviction of sin and need as its beginning to assurance of salvation as its climax. It involves learning the key gospel truths, internalizing them in a life-shaping way, and being so changed at heart that revulsion at sin, desire for God, love for Christ and eager hope of being with him in heaven become basic to one's being. This truth about the great change is taught by the story's initial sequences: first from the City of Destruction through the Slough of Dispond[23] to the wicket-gate, where the keeper, a Christ-figure, called Good Will in part one, encourages travellers to move forward along the narrow way; then from the wicket-gate via the House of the Interpreter, where lessons about Christian life are learned, to the cross and tomb, where Christian's burden fell off, and where Christiana, who had found the reality of pardon and peace already in the House of the Interpreter, learned from Mr Great-heart the truth of justification by faith through Christ's substitutionary death and gift of righteousness. (We may note in passing that Great-heart's way of explaining this, in terms of Christ's four righteousnesses,[24] is the only instance of doctrinal idiosyncrasy anywhere in *Pilgrim's Progress;* apart from this, all that is taught is conventionally Puritan in Westminster, Savoy, and London confessional terms.)

---

[23] 'This *Miry Slough* is such a place as cannot be mended. It is the descent whither the scum and filth that attends conviction for sin doth continually run, and therefore it is called the *Slough of Dispond:* for still as the sinner is awakened about his lost condition, there ariseth in his soul many fears and doubts and discouraging apprehensions, which all of them get together, and settle in this place: And this is the reason of the badness of the ground' (*Ibid.,* p 19).

[24] Righteousness as God, as man, and as divine-human mediator, are Christ's own inalienably, but the righteousness of his obedience he parts with. 'Here then is a Righteousness that Christ as God, as Man, as God-man has no need of ... and therefore he can spare it, a justifying Righteousness that he for himself wanteth not, and therefore he giveth it away' (*Ibid.* p 250). This is an odd way to express imputed righteousness; it is unique to Bunyan so far as I know.

At the cross Christian receives remission of sins, new raiment replacing his rags, and the sealed roll certifying to him his title to glory, and he sings for joy:

> Blest Cross! Blest sepulchre! Blest rather be The Man that there was put to shame for me.

And Bunyan adds a doggerel verse, to make quite sure readers understand the significance of the episode.

> Who's this; the Pilgrim. How! 'tis very true,
> Old things are past away, all's become new.
> Strange! He's another man upon my word,
> They be fine Feathers that make a fine bird.[25]

So, too, when Great-heart has explained justification by faith to Christiana, so that she understands pardon by word (promise) and deed (payment), she rhapsodizes:

> It makes my Heart bleed to think that he should bleed for me. Oh! Thou loving one, Oh! Thou blessed one. Thou deservest to have me, thou hast bought me: Thou deservest to have me all, thou hast paid for me ten thousand times more than I am worth. No marvel this made the water stand in my Husband's Eyes ...[26]

The Puritan way was to extend the term *conversion* to cover the whole process of being effectually called,[27] and Bunyan is a typical Puritan at this point. Where some evangelists today lay all their emphasis on the moment and mechanism of a human decision, this Puritan evangelist

---

[25] *Ibid.*, p 46.
[26] *Ibid.*, p 252.
[27] 'All those whom God hath predestinated unto life, and those only, he is pleased, in his appointed and accepted time, effectually to call, by his Word and Spirit, out of that state of sin and death, in which they are by nature to grace and salvation, by Jesus Christ; enlightening their minds spiritually and savingly to understand the things of God, taking away their hearts of stone, and giving unto them a heart of flesh; renewing their wills, and, by his almighty power, determining them to that which is good, and effectually drawing them to Jesus Christ; yet so, as they come most freely, being made willing by his grace' (*Westminster Confession*, x.i).

(for such Bunyan pre-eminently was)[28] stressed the need to realise that one is in God's hand for the entire process, and humbly to seek continuance of the process till God gives assurance that it is done.[29] The difference is something we need to think about.

Point three is that Satan will manipulate every resource he can muster to prevent individuals from setting out on the pilgrim path that leads to conversion, Christian life and final glory. This is pictured by Beelzebub's castle, from which are launched arrows and a dog against those who approach the wicket-gate. (The ongoing Satanic opposition to Christians belongs under the next heading.)

3.2 The conflicts of Christians.

Bunyan pictures contending against the world, the flesh and the devil as the constant discipline of those on the pilgrim path: they advance against a steady flow of obstructions and opponents, with which they have to deal, though there are spells of refreshment and encouragement for them between battles. Christian successfully fights Apollyon, who is out to destroy him, and Great-heart, on behalf of the women under his care, fights giants Grim, Despair, Maul and Slay-good (giants are enemies with more than human strength). He also fights the Monster. The battles are won through divine strength every time. These clashes represent conflict with the devil, a very real personage as far as Bunyan is concerned. Then, again, Christian and Faithful face the anti-pilgrim pressures of Vanity Fair, where Beelzebub is in charge, and hostility reaches the point of executing Faithful; and Mr Stand-fast has to resist Madam Bubble, who said: 'I am the Mistress of the World, and men are made happy by me.'[30] These represent the spirit of worldliness, as do most of the minor characters and phony pilgrims whom Christian and

---

[28] 'When I have been preaching, I thank God, my heart hath often all the time ... with great earnestness, cried to God that he would make the Word effectual to the salvation of the soul ...' 'In my preaching I have really been in pain, and have, as it were, travailed to bring forth children to God' (*Grace Abounding*, secs. 280, 290; Everyman ed., pp 86, 89).

[29] So Good Will at the wicket gate, when asked if he could help Christian get rid of his burden, replied: 'As to thy burden, be content to bear it, until thou comest to the place of Deliverance; for there it will fall from thy back itself -which it duly did (*The Pilgrim's Progress*, p 35, cf. p 46).

[30] *The Pilgrim's Progress*, p 359.

Christiana have one way or another to circumvent. On top of all this, we watch Christian and Hopeful paying the price of leaving the rough road for the soft green of By-path Meadow and then finding themselves unable to resist Giant Despair, or to keep out of Doubting Castle. Bunyan inserts a versified comment on their captivity to make sure we see that their fault was self-indulgence, failing to fight the flesh when they should have done.

> The Pilgrims now, to gratify the Flesh,
> Will seek its ease; but Oh! How they afresh
> Do thereby plunge themselves new griefs into:
> Who seek to please the Flesh, themselves undo.[31]

Bunyan's positive point in all this is that believers have to become battlers, facing and fighting everything and everyone that would divert them from following the path of life. The enemies and enmities are there, and Christians must not crumple before them, but take them on. Christian is taught this in the House of the Interpreter, where he sees *'the Valiant Man'* (Bunyan's margin) armed with a sword, protected by his helmet, 'cutting and hacking most fiercely' as he engages with the armed warriors who would stop him entering the palace for which he put his name down. As he fights, voices from the palace itself cry to him

> Come in, come in,
> Eternal glory thou shalt win.

Christian, we are told, 'smiled, and said, I think verily I know the meaning of this.'[32] As Alexander Whyte once put it, 'it's a sair fecht [Scots: meaning a demanding and draining conflict, a sore fight] all the way.' Are we as clear on this, I wonder, as Bunyan was?

To reinforce this message, Bunyan introduces as one of the pilgrims in part two Mr Valiant-for-Truth, whom Great-heart's pilgrim party meets just after he has beaten off three thugs who threatened his life if he would not abandon his pilgrimage. His sword–'a right

---

[31] *Ibid.*, p 140.
[32] *Ibid.*, p 41f.

Jerusalem blade,' Great-heart calls it–is an emblem of the Word of God.[33] The dialogue proceeds as follows:

> **V.** It is so. Let a man have one of *these Blades,* with a Hand to wield it, and skill to use it, and he may venture upon an Angel with it... Its Edges will never blunt. It will cut *Flesh,* and *Bones,* and *Soul,* and *Spirit,* and all.
>
> **G.** *But you fought a great while, I wonder you was not weary?*
>
> **V.** I fought till my sword did cleave to my Hand; and when they were joined together, as if a Sword grew out of my Arm, and when the Blood ran thorow my Fingers, then I fought with most Courage. (Bunyan's margin here reads: *'The Word. The Faith. Blood.'*)
>
> **G.** *Thou hast done well. Thou hast resisted unto Blood, striving against Sin.*[34]

Here, surely, we are coming up to the true biblical notion of spiritual warfare, on which it would be good to dwell; but I have to move on.

3.3 The communion of saints.

Communion means sharing, and Bunyan's message here is a simple one: the saints should travel in company, sharing their insights and experiences as they go, and so helping each other along. Part one of the allegory is sometimes critiqued as the saga of an improperly isolated individual, and Puritanism itself is critiqued for encouraging isolation and individualism in the Christian's discipleship. But mainstream

---

[33] *Ibid.,* p 347. Two other images for the Word of God also appear in part two: (1) The *mirror* (looking-glass) that Mercy desires. 'The Glass was one of a thousand. It would present a man, one way, with his own Feature exactly, and turn it but another way, and it would show one the very Face and Similitude of the Prince of Pilgrims himself. Yea I have talked with them that can tell, and they have said that they have seen the very Crown of Thorns upon his Head, by looking in that Glass, they have therein also seen the holes in his Hands, in his Feet, and his Side' (p 343f.). (2) The *map* that Great-heart consults. 'He had in his pocket a Map of all ways leading to or from the Celestial City; wherefore he . . . takes a view of his Book or Map, which bids him be careful in that place to turn to the right-hand-way And had he not been careful to look in his Map, they had all, in probability, been smothered in the Mud' (p 354f.).

[34] *Ibid.,* p 347f.

Puritanism never was in that sense an individualistic movement, and Bunyan's pilgrim, though very much an individual, like Bunyan himself, is neither individualistic nor isolated. He has first Faithful and then Hopeful to travel with; he has Evangelist and the Interpreter and the Shepherds to teach him where and how to go; and he is in conversation with his companion all the time. Then in part two, Christiana travels in company with her children and Mercy, and has Great-heart as guide, instructor and courier, and several more join their party before they reach the river. It would be a mistake to dismiss their flow of talk and sharing of lives that Bunyan records in both parts as a mere didactic device, although it certainly is that; but Bunyan's evident message is that this is how it ought to be, on a regular basis. Christians should share themselves spiritually so as to build each other up in Christ. This is fellowship, and fellowship is the oxygen of the Christian life. We do well to ask ourselves whether we are taking account of this in our own walk of faith in our Lord.

3.4   The calling of pastors.

In part two pastor Bunyan projects his understanding of the pastor's role most fully and memorably in the person of Mr Great-heart. Christopher Hill is surely right when he describes part two as 'an allegory about the congregation, as part 1 had been an allegory about the individual saint.'[35] Great-heart, whose very name speaks of boundless courage and patient sympathy, walks and talks continually with those he leads and serves, while at the same time being alert to foresee dangers and protect his charges from them. (This is how he understands his appointed task,[36] and this is what his aggressive practice of giant-killing is all about.) Insofar as part two has a hero, Great-heart is he, and it is hardly too much to say that the unifying theme of part two is pastoral ministry.

At various points in the story Great-heart receives into the pilgrim party three strong saints, whose presence fortifies everyone, namely Mr Honest, Mr Stand-fast, and Mr Valiant-for-Truth, and four weak Christians, whose presence slows them all down, namely Mr

---

[35] A Tinker and a Poor Man, p 180.
[36] 'My name is *Great-heart*, I am the guide of these Pilgrims which are going to the Celestial Country' (*The Pilgrim's Progress*, p 294).

Feeble-mind, saved from the hands of Giant Slay-good, Mr Dispondency and his daughter Much-afraid, both rescued from the dungeons of Giant Despair, and Mr Ready-to-halt, who hobbles along slowly on crutches; though, be it said, in his one moment of joy, celebrating the end of Doubting Castle and the death of Giant Despair, he takes Much-afraid's hand 'and to dancing they went in the Road. True he could not dance without one Crutch in his hand, but I promise you, he footed it well.'[37] Special care is now shown toward the weak ones. The Shepherds (pastoral persons themselves) invite all four, by name, into their palace before admitting anyone else. They let the four choose the dinner menu–'a Feast of things easy of Digestion'–'for, they said, all things must be managed here for the supporting of the Weak.'[38] Great-heart ensures their safety as they cross the enchanted ground: *'Feeble-mind,* Mr *Great-heart* commanded should come up after him, and Mr *Dispondency* was under the eye of Mr *Valiant.*[39] Bunyan is here picturing the patient attention pastors must give to the good-hearted but time-consuming spiritual cripples and mentally handicapped saints who are found in just about every congregation in the world.

Finally, Mr Great-heart as Christiana's pastor prepares her for dying;[40] which brings us to our final topic.

3.5 The closure of life.

So far from being, as it is today in the West, the great unmentionable, death was to the Puritans in a real sense life's climax, for which every saint must prepare. God fixes the time, and it may be later, just as it may be sooner, than was expected; but believers ought always to be ready for it. Making a good end was seen as an integral part of godliness. Seventeenth-century Christians would die, not in a sedated coma in a care centre, as is usual in our world, but at home, conscious, more or less, to the last, with the family and others present, and they must honour God then no less than at other times; while deathbed words, spoken from the border of eternity, were expected to have special

---

[37] *Ibid.*, p 336.
[38] *Ibid.*, p 341.
[39] *Ibid.*, p 353.
[40] 'She bid that he should give Advice how all things should be prepared for her Journey. So he told her, saying, Thus and thus it must be, and we that survive will accompany you to the River-side' (*Ibid.,* p 363).

weight, whether as a backward look, a forward look, a final message, a last farewell, or all those four together. In both parts of *Pilgrim's Progress* Bunyan's sense of the significance of dying, as well as of the poignancy of the event for family and friends, pulls out of him some of his finest and most evocative writing. This is particularly so in the set-piece that ends part two, where the last words of each pilgrim who walks down into the river are recorded. No doubt memories of actual deathbeds helped pastor Bunyan here. Says Christiana, who goes first: *'I come Lord, to be with thee and bless thee.'* Says Mr Ready-to-halt: *'Welcome Life.'* Says Mr Feeble-mind: *'Hold out Faith and Patience.'* Mr Dispondency, whose daughter Much-afraid elects to go into the river with him, makes a speech that is worth remembering, as follows:

> Myself and my daughter, you know what we have been, and how troublesomely we have behaved ourselves in every Company. My will and my Daughter's is, That our *Disponds* and slavish Fears, be by no man ever received, from the day of our *Departure,* for ever ... For, to be plain with you, they are Ghosts, the which we entertained when we first began to be Pilgrims, and could never shake them off after. And they will walk about and seek Entertainment of the Pilgrims; but for our sakes shut ye the Doors upon them.[41]

Being despondent, Bunyan is telling us, is not the Christian way. Dispondency's last words, following his speech, were Farewell Night, Welcome Day; and his daughter went through the river singing, though, we are told, 'none could understand what she said.'

These were followed by Mr Honest, whose last words were Grace Reigns, and by Mr Valiant-for-Truth, who said: Death, where is thy sting? Grave, where is thy Victory? It was for him that 'all the Trumpets sounded ... on the other side.' (That was how the triumph of Cromwell's New Model army was proclaimed on the battlefield of

---

[41] *Ibid.,* p 367. Bunyan lays emphasis on both the wrongness of Christians indulging fear and gloom and the fact that some cannot help being fear-ridden; note Mr Great-heart's account of Mr Fearing, who 'had, I think, a *Slough of Dispond* in his mind, a Slough that he carried every where with him, or else he could never have been as he was' (p 297-303). Great-heart observes: *'Men of my Calling, are oftentimes intrusted with the Conduct of such as he was'* (p 296).

Naseby in 1645, and on battlefields thereafter: this, we may guess, was the source of Bunyan's idea.)[42]

Last of all, rounding off Bunyan's story, Mr Stand-fast made his crossing. He uttered a speech 'when he was about half way in' the river–that is, when the process of his dying was well under way. This also was a speech to remember, so here is an extended extract from it.

> This River has been a terror to many, yea the thoughts of it also have often frightened me. But now methinks I stand easy . . . The Waters indeed are to the Palate bitter, and to the Stomach cold, yet the thoughts of what I am going to, and of the Conduct that waits for me on the other side, doth lie as a glowing Coal at my Heart.
>
> I see myself now at the end of my Journey, my toilsome Days are ended. I am going now to see that Head that was crowned with Thorns, and that Face that was spit upon, for me.
>
> I have formerly lived by Hear-say, and Faith, but now I go where I shall live by sight, and shall be with him, in whose Company I delight myself.
>
> I have loved to hear my Lord spoken of, and wherever I have seen the print of his Shoe in the Earth, there I have coveted to set my Foot too.
>
> His Name has been to me . . . sweeter than all Perfumes. His Voice to me has been most sweet, and his Countenance I have more desired than they that have most desired the Light of the Sun. His Word I did use to gather for my Food, and for Antidotes against my Faintings. He has held me ... Yea, my Steps hath he strengthened in his Way.[43]

Then came the last words, as death tightened its grip: *Take me, for I come unto thee.* And Mr Stand-fast, with the others, was gone. There the book ends.

---

[42] 'Bunyan must have been present when orders were given 'that all the trumpets in the camp should sound . . . and that the soldiers should shout for joy' to celebrate a victory' (Christopher Hill, *op. cit.*, p 242).

[43] *The Pilgrim's Progress*, p 370.

Was there wisdom in the Puritan concern about dying well, in the sustained *memento mori* of Puritan preaching, and in Bunyan's presentation of the death whereby Christians go to glory as the true climax of their lives? Was this sick morbidity, or healthy realism? Does the question need discussion? Does it not answer itself? I think so.

4. A Puritan Heritage

As you can see, my interest in Bunyan, as in all the Puritans, is primarily theological and pastoral. My aim in this all-too-sketchy survey of Bunyan and his best book has been to spread that interest; there is no secret about that. What *Pilgrim's Progress* in particular shows us about the Christian life always was, and is still, profoundly true, and we miss much deep biblical wisdom and help if Bunyan's masterpiece has not become part of our regular reading. I predict that once you get into Bunyan you will not let him go, or rather he will not let you go, and you will thank God that ever you made his acquaintance. I urge, then, that the next move should be yours; and with that I close.

Conversion to Communion: Thomas Cranmer on a Favourite Puritan Theme

Ashley Null

Introduction 245
1. Cranmer's Evangelism 247
2. Cranmer on Scripture 249
3. Cranmer on Justification 252
4. Cranmer on Predestination 253
5. Cranmer on Conversion 256
6. Cranmer on Communion 259
7. Concluding Thoughts on Thomas Cranmer 262

J. ASHLEY NULL is Canon Theologian of the Diocese of Western Kansas in the United States, Fellow of the London Society of Antiquaries and the Royal Historical Society, Adjunct Lecturer in Anglican Studies for the Theology Faculty of Humboldt University of Berlin as well as Moore Theological College, Sydney, and Visiting Fellow of the Faculty of Divinity, Cambridge University. He did his initial theological work in Yale Divinity School before working on the theology of Thomas Cranmer for a PhD at Cambridge which was subsequently published as *Thomas Cranmer's Doctrine of Repentance: Renewing the Power to Love* (OUP, 2000). He is a frequent contributor to scholarship on the English Reformation and is currently working on a critical edition of Cranmer's theological notebooks or 'Great Commonplaces' for Oxford University Press.

Introduction

> I beseech God bless my good Uncle Brent and make him now to know [that] which in his tender years he could not see ... And the Lord open His gracious countenance ... unto my aunt, that she may also make a blessed change.[1]

So prayed an Elizabethan preacher for his relatives forty years after Henry VIII broke relations with the Roman Pontiff. No doubt, however, our cleric's desire for blessed change was not confined only to his relatives. Indeed, above all else, Puritans longed for a general reformation in religion of the Church of England – a change which would be a real blessing because it was based on nothing but the pure Word of God. In the eyes of the godly, the Elizabethan church was only half-way reformed, but the queen was determined to live by her motto, *'semper eadem'* – 'Always the same.' Little wonder, then, that blessed change was the heart cry of the Puritan movement.

Elizabeth had founded her church on two legacies of England's earlier experiment with Protestantism – Erastian polity and Edwardian liturgy – and both were increasingly anathema to the godly as her reign progressed. Using her prerogative as supreme governor, Elizabeth willed the public face of English religion to be an essentially eclectic adaptation of the more Protestant 1552 prayer book with small, but significant holdovers from the more Catholic 1549. These included the words of administration suggestive of Christ's real presence in the sacrament and the rubric about using vestments for services, both seriously irksome stumbling blocks for many Puritan preachers. Such concessions to Catholicism, and perhaps to the Queen's own conscience, were frustrating signs of regression at a time when they looked for further advancement. That Elizabeth also used her royal prerogative to force the bishops to impose compliance on recalcitrant clergy only inflamed their longing for blessed change, especially when she made matters worse by preventing Edmund Grindal, Archbishop of Canterbury, from exercising his office, precisely because he refused to suppress the Puritan practice of community preaching conferences. Her

---

[1] As quoted by Patrick Collinson, *The Elizabethan Puritan Movement* (London: Jonathan Cape, 1967), p 23.

Tudor blood was not amused by Grindal's suggestion that she should submit to her clergy in matters of religion rather than the other way around.

So the godly prayed, preached and plotted for change. They also founded numerous divinity lectureships, not only to promote pure biblical teaching but also to provide posts for those Puritan ministers who would not scruple to wear the surplice or officiate by the prayer book.[2] Arguably, the most famous was our own St Antholin's, in whose name we gather today, and indeed the oldest, if those who suggest that the series began under Edward VI are correct. The lectureship in Puritan divinity at St Antholin's, Budge Row, has been graced by such influential Christian leaders as John and Charles Wesley in the eighteenth century and the three leaders of the first Puritan controversy under Elizabeth – Robert Crowley, John Philpott, and John Gough.[3]

In such a venerable lecture series as this, founded, as it were, to be the wellspring of non-conformity in England, what could possibly be a more unexpected topic than the man about whom I wish to speak today – Thomas Cranmer? After all, who, more than he, was the public face of both Edwardian Erastianism and Edwardian Liturgy? Is not Cranmer reported to have said at the coronation of the boy-king Edward, 'Your majesty is God's vice-gerent and Christ's vicar within your own dominions, and to see, with your predecessor Josiah, God truly worshipped'?[4] Has not liturgical scholarship proved right that memorable jibe of John Field, the London field marshall of Elizabethan Puritan agitation, that Cranmer's prayer books were 'culled and picked out of that popish dunghill, the mass book'?[5] Although Foxe did his best to enlist Cranmer as the true 'St Thomas of Canterbury' because of his

---

[2] For the history of Puritan lectureships, see Paul S. Seaver, *The Puritan Lectureships: The Politics of Religious Dissent, 1560-1662* (Stanford, California: Stanford University Press, 1970).

[3] St Antholin's lectures began no later than 1559. For its history from Elizabethan times to the Twentieth Century, see Isabel M. Calder, 'The St Antholin Lectures,' *Church Quarterly Review* 160 (1959), 49-70. For the possible Edwardian origins of the lectureship, see H. Gareth Owen, 'The London Parish Clergy in the Reign of Elizabeth I' (PhD thesis, London University, 1957), p 370.

[4] John Edmund Cox, *Miscellaneous Writings and Letters of Thomas Cranmer* (Cambridge: Cambridge University Press, 1846) [Henceforth Cox II], p 127.

[5] This bitter assessment was part of Field's caustic contribution to the *Admonition to the Parliament*; Collinson, *Elizabethan Puritan Movement*, p 120.

death under Mary,⁶ the polity and liturgy he bequeathed represented to Puritans all that was not blessed in the Church of England, all that still needed changing. What do he and the founders of our lectureship have to do with one another?

Much, for they were all adherents of Reformed theology. While this has not been the conventional portrait of Cranmer for over a century, recent studies have confirmed Cranmer's basic agreement with that Southern strain of continental Protestantism that became known as Reformed, at least as it was emerging during his lifetime.⁷ The theological stream which ran so fast through St Antholin's did not spring up in England only upon the return of the Marian exiles, but in Cranmer's day and by Cranmer's encouragement. The blessed personal change sought by Puritans for their family, friends and flock Cranmer also desired for the elect of England of his era. Conversion from sin to communion with God was a favourite Puritan theme, and nothing was closer to Cranmer's own heart; consequently, he enshrined his Reformed understanding of the process in the formularies he bequeathed to the Church of England. Those wishing to find Anglican legitimacy for the Puritan approach to the cure of the English soul need look no further than the pioneering work of Thomas Cranmer himself.

1. Cranmer's Evangelism

Like his first royal master, Cranmer did not make himself easy to love.⁸ In an era noted for the fervent courage of many martyrs for faith, Cranmer's very survival under a king as unprincipled, or at least unpredictable, as Henry VIII has made him suspect. His late vacillation under Mary has only seemed to confirm the image of a man ruled more by the grip of fear than the assurance of the faith. Yet fearful men do

---

⁶ John Foxe, *Acts and Monuments* (London: John Day, 1570), p 2066.
⁷ See Diarmaid MacCulloch, *Thomas Cranmer: A Life* (London: Yale University Press, 1996) and Ashley Null, *Thomas Cranmer's Doctrine of Repentance: Renewing the Power to Love* (Oxford University Press, 2000).
⁸ For a review of Cranmer historiography, see Jasper Ridley, *Thomas Cranmer* (Oxford: Claredon Press, 1962), pp 1-12; Peter Newman Brooks, *Cranmer in Context: Documents from the English Reformation* (Minneapolis, Minn.: Fortress Press, 1989), pp 117-127.

not often pass off lightly the criticism of their inferiors; nor do theologically unprincipled prisoners defiantly urge a Spanish Catholic like Mary to repudiate the pope as Antichrist. Fundamentally, Cranmer was a man of faith, and his fundamental principle was that God's love for his enemies worked everything to good.

Indeed, despite the pressures of his office and his era, Cranmer's most striking characteristic was to forgive his enemies. To be sure, Cranmer could act sternly toward evangelicals who, in his view, endangered the whole reforming enterprise by contravening authority with their 'outrageous doings.'[9] He could also be equally harsh with religious conservatives he considered repeat offenders. Nevertheless, his customary response to personal wrongs was unmerited forgiveness, often to the irritation of his friends and the delight as well as abuse of his foes. According to Ralph Morice, his principal secretary,

> [a] notable quality or virtue he had: to be beneficial unto his enemies, so that in that respect he would not be known to have any enemy at all. For whosoever he had been that had reported evil of him, or otherwise wrought or done to him displeasure, were the reconciliation never so mean or simple on the behalf of his adversary, if he had any thing at all relented, the matter was both pardoned and clearly forgotten ... So that on a time I do remember that Dr Heath, late archbishop of York, partly disliking this his overmuch leniency by him used, said unto him, "My Lord, I now know how to win all things at your hands well enough." "How so?" (quoth my Lord.) "Marry, (said Dr Heath,) I perceive that I must first attempt to do unto you some notable displeasure, and then by a little relenting obtain of you what I can desire."[10]

Such habitual benevolence was not merely the naivety of an innocent in high office. Rather, Cranmer's demonstrated love for those who opposed him was the conscious decision of a dedicated evangelist. When queried why he was so lenient with 'papists,' he replied:

---

[9] For Cranmer's attitude toward disobedient evangelicals, see John Gough Nichols, *Narratives of the Days of the Reformation* (Westminster: Camden Society, 1859), p 247.

[10] Nichols, *Narratives,* pp 245-6. For examples of this leniency, see *Ibid.* pp 157, 251-252, 269-272 and MacCulloch, *Cranmer,* pp 318, 321.

> What will ye have a man do to him that is not yet come to the knowledge of the truth of the gospel ... if it be a true rule of our Saviour Christ to do good for evil, then let such as are not yet come to favour our religion learn to follow the doctrine of the gospel by our example in using them friendly and charitably.[11]

Clearly, Cranmer intended his well-known reputation for giving grace to the unworthy to be a cardinal signal, a scarlet cord hung openly from the window of Canterbury, that those with eyes to see would perceive the truth of the gospel which he wished to impart to the Church of England.

For Cranmer's commitment to love his enemies was more than just another example of traditional medieval piety. It was the very foundation of his living Protestant faith. The logic is breath-takingly simple. Christ commands us to love our enemies so that we show ourselves sons of our Father in Heaven. If the highest expression of divine love is to love one's enemies, that must be the very same kind of love by which God saves sinners. And that, in fact, is what the Apostle Paul himself wrote in Romans 5:10 – 'when we were enemies, we were reconciled to God through the death of His Son.' Since God loved those who had not a right to be loved, Cranmer reached out to his opponents with unmerited forgiveness and favour in hope that they would realise that God did likewise when he brought salvation. This emphasis on God's love for the unworthy is the common thread that runs throughout Cranmer's theological writings.

2. Cranmer on Scripture

The radical simplicity of this principle cut through key tenets of medieval teaching. In keeping with the root meaning of the Latin word *justificare*, 'to make righteous,' the Catholic understanding of *justification* was as a process of transformation to personal holiness. Hence, the primary interest of much of late scholastic penitential instruction lay in encouraging sinners to demonstrate through genuine sorrow and good works that they no longer wanted to be God's enemy.

---

[11] Nichols, *Narratives,* pp 246-247.

Penitents who did their best to show an increasing love for God gradually acquired an acceptable degree of worthiness that was the necessary preparation for divine forgiveness. Influenced by the Augustinian revival, Cambridge theologian John Fisher insisted that human actions needed the supernatural assistance of God's grace to be effective towards justification, and Gardiner, Cranmer's chief opponent, agreed.[12] Once sinners had first co-operated with divine grace toward their justification, they would then receive a supernatural infusion of divine goodness that finished the process of making them fully worthy to be accepted by God.

By his forties, however, Cranmer had concluded that giving human worthiness any role in justification was clean contrary to God's Word. He equated personal merit in any form with the 'works-righteousness' condemned by Paul; consequently, he argued that justification was either totally by the worthiness of our efforts or completely by undeserved divine grace – Scripture gave no other option:

> But certain it is, that our election cometh only and wholly of the benefit and grace of God, for the merits of Christ's passion, and for no part of our merits and good works: as St Paul disputeth and proveth at length in the epistle to the Romans and Galatians, and divers other places, saying, 'if from works, then not from grace; if from grace, then not from works.'[13]

Any attempt to make ourselves acceptable to God as the basis for forgiveness was an insult to the depth of the divine love shown for an unworthy humanity by Christ's death on the cross.[14] In short, it was 'the work and glory of God alone to justify the ungodly, to forgive sins, to give life freely out of his goodness, not from any merits of our own.'[15]

For the mature Cranmer, the medieval church failed to understand the mutual incompatibility of grace and human worth

---

[12] Stephen Gardiner, *A declaration of such true articles as George Ioye hath gone about to confute as false* (London: John Herford, 1546), fols 94v-95r.
[13] Cox II, p 95.
[14] '*Sanguis Christi, multis modis contumelia afficitur. Primum, ab iis qui praeter Christi sanguinem, alia excogitant aut supponu[n]t remedia, satisfactiones, aut pretia pro abluendis peccatis,*' British Library Royal MS 7B.XII [Henceforth 'Cranmer's Great Commonplaces' (CGC) II], 226r.
[15] '*Solius dei opus est et gloria, iustificare impium, remittere peccata, donare vitam ex sua bonitate gratis, non ex ullis nostris meritis,*' CGC II, 226v.

because they had hidden the light of God's Word under the bushel-basket of human tradition. Good intentions, holy visions, academic reasoning, venerable teachings, even Church councils – none of these had authority to supersede the plain sense of the Bible, for all of these were subject to the deceitful deceptions of human sinfulness. Pride might lead people to think they could eventually merit God's approval, but that was not the true gospel. God's Word clearly proclaimed free salvation of the unworthy in Jesus Christ.

Therefore, the blessed change of conversion began with looking to Scripture alone. Cranmer bequeathed this principle to the Church of England in 'A Fruitful Exhortation to the Reading and Knowledge of Holy Scripture,' the opening sermon of the 1547 *Book of Homilies* and widely accepted as his own.[16] According to this homily, God gave human beings the Bible as 'a sure, a constant and a perpetual instrument of salvation.' On the one hand, Scripture was God's chosen medium **to tell** human beings the truth about the world around them and the struggles within them: 'In these books we may learn to know ourselves, how vile and miserable we be, and also to know God, how good he is of himself and how he communicateth his goodness unto us and to all creatures.' On the other hand, the Bible was also the means through which God worked supernaturally **to turn** people's hearts to himself and the doing of his will: '[The words of Holy Scripture] have power to convert [our souls] through God's promise, and they be effectual through God's assistance;' 'the hearing and keeping of [Scripture] maketh us blessed, sanctifieth us and maketh us holy.' As sinners read of the eternal punishments justly prepared for them and then realised the unconditional mercy of his pardon that God offered in Christ, a new loving faith in God would arise from the bottom of their heart. Hence, Cranmer urged the people of England to 'diligently search for the well of life in the books of the New and Old Testament, and not run to the stinking puddles of men's traditions, devised by man's imagination for our justification and salvation.'[17]

---

[16] Ronald B. Bond, *Certain Sermons or Homilies (1547) and A Homily against Disobedience and Wilful Rebellion (1570): A Critical Edition* (Toronto: University of Toronto Press, 1987), p 28.

[17] *Ibid.*, pp 61-62; cf. Cox II, pp 113-114.

3. Cranmer on Justification

Because of Scripture, Cranmer decided to part company with Fisher and Gardiner. He denied the possibility of any middle transitional stage between the children of God and of the Devil,[18] and he also rejected their traditional factitive understanding of justification where God first made sinners inherently righteous so that he could then accept them. Protestants had noted that the Greek New Testament word for *justificare* was δικαιουν [*dikaioun*], a legal term meaning to pronounce a defendant 'not guilty'; consequently, they taught that justification came in a moment of belief that changed a sinner's status before God without changing his personal worthiness for acceptance. Cranmer came to agree. Believing God justified people 'although they were sinners,'[19] he embraced the forensic understanding that God imputed Christ's righteousness to the ungodly who turned to him in faith.[20] Those who heard God's Word and trusted in his promise of free salvation in Jesus were credited with Christ's worthiness.

Although some scholars have argued otherwise, Cranmer's 'Homily of Salvation' (1547) made this standard Protestant teaching normative for the Church of England.[21] Cranmer opened the sermon by describing justification in terms of forensic imputation, albeit in non-theological terms: (i) justifying righteousness was an alien righteousness: 'Because all men be sinners and offenders against God

---

[18] '*Nec medium est ullum inter filios dei et diaboli*,' CGC II, 213r.
[19] Marginalium: '*Iustificavit nos deus cum peccatores essemus*,' CGC II, 104v.
[20] '*Iustificare subinde significat, iustum pronuntiare, declarare, aut ostendere*,' CGC II, 84r.
[21] Ridley considered them to fall 'a good way short' of Protestantism; *Cranmer*, p 266; Cf. David Loades, 'Thomas Cranmer: A Biographical Introduction,' *Thomas Cranmer: Essays in Commemoration of the 500th Anniversary of his Birth*, ed. Margot Johnson (Durham: Turnstone Ventures, 1990), pp 1-24 (16). According to John T. Wall, Jr the homily reflects Cranmer's Erasmian Humanism; 'Godly and Fruitful Lessons: The English Bible, Erasmus' Paraphrases, and the Book of Homilies,' *The Godly Kingdom of Tudor England: Great Books of the English Reformation*, ed. John E. Booty (Wilton, Conn.: Morehouse-Barlow Company, 1981), pp 85-125. Alister McGrath, however, has interpreted the 'Homily of Salvation' as a mixture of both Protestant and patristic doctrine, the fiduciary basis of justification being strongly Melanchthonian but its nature conforming to Augustine's factitive approach; *Iustitia Dei: A History of the Christian Doctrine of Justification*, 2nd ed. (Cambridge: Cambridge University Press, 1998), p 288.

... every man of necessity is constrained to seek another righteousness, or justification to be received at God's own hands;'[22] (ii) the righteousness given to the believer through faith because of Christ was not true inherent righteousness but merely reckoned as such by God: 'this justification ... is taken, accepted, and allowed of God for our perfect and full justification;'[23] (iii) the only possible source for justification was the imputation of an alien righteousness: 'Christ is now the righteousness of all them that truly do believe in him ... forasmuch as that which their infirmity lacketh, Christ's justice hath supplied.'[24] Significantly, at no point in this description of justification did Cranmer make any reference to the infusion of a personal righteousness as the basis for the believer's pardoning by God.

In this homily Cranmer also carefully defined the nature of the faith that brought about imputed righteousness. Firstly, saving faith came 'by God's working in us' through the hearing of the Word.[25] Secondly, this 'act to believe in Christ' was not the basis for justification, but only what sent the sinner to Christ for pardon. Indeed, faith was 'far too weak and insufficient and imperfect' to merit remission of sins in its own right.[26] Thirdly, justifying faith was more than just intellectual assent to dogmatic statements. Since demons also believed the principal truths of Christianity, 'right and true Christian faith' was not only agreement with Scripture but also 'a sure trust and confidence in God's merciful promises, to be saved from everlasting damnation.'[27] According to Cranmer, saving faith always included assurance of a believer's own salvation.

4. Cranmer on Predestination

Although modern scholarship has rarely acknowledged it, Cranmer's language of assurance was rooted in a commitment to predestination,

---

[22] Cox II, p 128.
[23] *Ibid.*
[24] *Ibid.*, p 130.
[25] *Ibid.*, p 129.
[26] *Ibid.*, pp 131-132.
[27] *Ibid.*, p 133.

for his insistence on the personal unworthiness of the justified inevitably led him to hold to unconditional election and effectual grace. Since divine love loves those who have no right to be loved, God saved sinners unconditionally, without any regard for personal merit, whether acquired or infused. Yet if divine love requires that salvation come as an unconditional gift, then God's love must also be able to ensure the full acceptance of that gift. Otherwise human response to divine love would become a necessary condition, and people would be forced ultimately to rely on their own efforts to co-operate with God, something Cranmer considered 'the ready way unto desperation.'[28] Therefore, God's love must have the power both to awaken love for God among God-haters and to ensure the perseverance of that love for eternity. With his fellow Protestants, Cranmer concluded that the justified were also the elect, so that God gave saving faith only to those whom he had chosen to deliver from eternal damnation before the foundation of the world.[29] Because of their prior election, the justified could be certain of their perseverance: 'the elect shall not wilfully and obstinately withstand God's calling'; they 'will follow Christ's precepts, and rise again when they fall'; and 'they shall perpetually continue and endure.'[30]

In 'Cranmer's Great Commonplaces,' the personal manuscript record of his theological research, Cranmer gathered evidence primarily from Augustine to prove that salvation *sola gratia* meant by predestination without any foresight of an individual's merits. Accordingly, justifying grace was not made available to all.[31] Rather, before the foundation of the world, God chose a set number of people, his elect, to spend eternity with him.[32] He first gave them the grace of conversion to bring about their justification, and then he gave them the

---

[28] *Ibid.*, p 94.
[29] Commenting on a correction to the Bishops' Book suggested by Henry VIII, Cranmer wrote: 'These two words ... signify that our election and justification cometh partly of our merits, though chiefly it cometh of the goodness of God;' Cox II, p 95. Note that he rendered the phrase 'election and justification' as singular, using it as the subject of the third-person singular verb 'cometh' and as the antecedent of the singular neuter pronoun 'it.' That one so sensitive to language as Cranmer should write in such a manner can only mean that he considered election and justification to be part of a unitary process, each equally rooted in divine action and both always occurring in the same human lives.
[30] *Ibid.*, pp 91-92.
[31] CGC II, 270r.
[32] *Ibid.*, 121v, 279v.

grace of perseverance so that they would continue in their justification until they entered the age to come.[33] God gave his justifying grace freely to the elect before considering any future merits and based solely on the hidden judgement of his will.[34] Like a potter who made from the same lump of clay one vessel for honour and another for disrepute, God simply decided to separate out from the mass of damned humanity some which he chose to save according to his own inscrutable counsel.[35] While none of those predestined would be lost, none of those passed over could ever be saved.[36]

A Christian believed in the Lord by his own will and free choice.[37] Nevertheless, salvation was not determined by human consent because the gift of grace imparted the Holy Spirit which brought about whatever good pertained to salvation, including consent.[38] Like the conversion of Paul on the road to Damascus or Xerxes in the presence of Esther, by his omnipotent power God drew the unwilling to himself, took away their heart of stone, gave them his Spirit and made them willing.[39] Although some might want faith to begin as a human initiative to which God then granted saving grace, in fact, without God's calling, no one was able to believe.[40] This inability of the non-elect to believe explained why some hearing the gospel came to faith and others did not.[41] While it was understandable that such a teaching might be difficult to accept, who was man to question his maker, the depths of whose wisdom was beyond the capacity of the human mind? A beast might as well have questioned why it was not made human, as a man to question why God prepared one person for eternal blessedness and another for eternal damnation.[42]

The full doctrine of predestination found in Cranmer's private papers was not discussed in his homilies. Its only public expression was in the doctrinal formula of the Edwardian era, the Forty-Two Articles.

---

[33] *Ibid.*, 105v; cf. *ibid.*, 282v.
[34] *Ibid.*, 230r, 273r, 280r.
[35] *Ibid.*, 291r.
[36] *Ibid.*, 279v-280r.
[37] *Ibid.*, 104v, 270.
[38] *Ibid.*, 277r.
[39] *Ibid.*, 118r, 227v, 271r-272r.
[40] *Ibid.*, 272v, 249v.
[41] *Ibid.*, 279v, 285v.
[42] *Ibid.*, 120r, 291v-292r.

On the one hand, Article X described its basis. Using scriptural language, the article suggested that grace was effectual, bringing about regeneration by redirecting the will itself, not simply by offering to the will the choice for regeneration:

> The grace of Christ or the holy Ghost by him given doth take away the stony heart, and giveth an heart of flesh. And although, those that have no will to good things, he maketh them to will and those that would evil things, he maketh them not to will the same: Yet nevertheless he enforceth not the will.[43]

Unfortunately for the Puritans, Article X was one of those deleted to make the Thirty-Nine Articles. On the other hand, Article XVII described the benefits of predestination and was retained by the Elizabethan Church. Like the earlier homilies, this article concentrated on how election provided 'sweet, pleasant, and unspeakable comfort to godly persons.' Those who felt the Spirit of God at work in them could rest assured that any lapse from grace in their lives was only temporary. Significantly, this saving work was defined as repentance, ie, 'mortifying the works of the flesh, and their earthly members, and drawing up their mind to high and heavenly things.'[44] Clearly, then, in Cranmer's understanding of predestination God determined in his hidden counsel to whom he would give saving grace, and this grace would effectually bring about a redirection of the will, namely, its conversion from sin towards communion with God.

5. Cranmer on Conversion

Naturally, Cranmer considered this blessed change in the will to be the *decisive moment* for justification. According to his great notebooks,

> He who now has turned to God, grieves from his heart to have sinned, and he has in his heart a firm amendment of a better life – he has rejected all will to sin. Why is he not already just? For whatever of fault still remains, he has from infirmity, not

---

[43] Charles Hardwick, *A History of the Articles of Religion* (London: George Bell & Sons, 1904), p 302.
[44] *Ibid.*, p 312.

from the wickedness of his heart.[45]

Plainly, Cranmer did not believe that justification based on the external merits of Christ had no internal effect in the justified. Quite to the contrary. For if the glory of divine love was to love the unworthy, the duty and joy of the justified was to return that love to God and to others. Consequently, in the moment of justification Cranmer held that God imparted both faith and love. The believer's faith laid hold of the extrinsic righteousness of Christ on which basis alone his sins were pardoned. At the same time, however, the Holy Spirit indwelt the believer, stirring in him a love for God and his commandments. This renewal of a person's will would naturally issue forth in a godly life marked by obedience to divine precepts and repentance for on-going shortcomings caused by the infirmities of human nature. In short, Cranmer believed that justification was being made 'right-willed' by faith, not being made inherently righteous, and its evidence was love and repentance toward God and neighbour.

This narrowing of justification to the moment when God renewed the will enabled Cranmer to counter two arguments put forward by the religious conservatives of his day. On the one hand, Fisher and Gardiner had argued for the necessity of good works before justification. Claiming support from Augustine, Cranmer could argue that no work was good before a man had a renewed will, but once he had a good will, he was already pleasing to God before he performed any subsequent works.[46] Therefore, works had no part in the act of justification. On the other hand, his critics accused justification by faith of encouraging moral laxity. Why should people strive to fight against sin, if their eternal future was already secure? Cranmer's emphasis on the conversion of the will meant that a believer's renewed affections would naturally manifest in a life of right actions. Although good works did not justify, the truly justified were never without good works:

For although God forgives sins because of faith in the blood of

---

[45] '*Qui iam conversus ad deum, peccavisse ex animo dolet, et correctionem vitae melioris firmam in animo habet, omnem peccandi voluntatem abiecit, cur non iam iustus sit? Cum quicquid vitii adhuc supersit, ex infirmitate habeat, non ex animi malitia?* CGC II, 225v.

[46] '*Bona opera non habet, cui deest voluntas bona. Quisquis autem bonam habet voluntatem, iam vir bonus est, et deo gratus, ac iustificatus. Ergo qui iustificatus non est, bona opera non habet,*' CGC II, 225v.

Christ, none the less he only forgives those who repent, who forgive sins, who give alms, who are clean in heart, who chastise their body and redirect it into service, who love God and neighbour, who extend themselves in good works, who are earnest to show themselves approved through their good works, not only to God but also to all men, who take off the old man with his works and put on the new man who is created by God, who drive out of their heart the love of sin and bring in the love of God and neighbour, who crucify their flesh with [its] affections and lusts.[47]

Thus, only if believers led a life of on-going repentance could they certify their consciences that their election was sure and stable.[48]

With assurance we come back to the heart of Cranmer's theology. Faith had to include assurance. Grace had to ensure assurance. Life had to be lived to support assurance. Why was assurance so important to Cranmer? Because it provided the *determining motive* for the believer's new life in Christ. Article X made clear that God did not force the will when he redirected it. How, then, did saving grace effectually draw the human will to love God and to obey his commandments? Gratitude – the gratitude that only came from the assurance of salvation.

In Catholic teaching, Christians were to face the future with a sober uncertainty about their eternal fate, striving to lead a godly life in a constant state of both hope and fear. Cranmer, however, concluded the medieval teaching of conditional salvation based on human performance actually promoted self-righteous pride or self-damning despair, and neither inspired true love for God. Only the promise of free salvation made possible by God's utterly gracious love inspired a lasting

---

[47] '*Licet enim propter fidem in sanguinem Christi condonet deus peccata, tamen non nisi resipiscentibus, nisi dimittentibus peccata, nisi eleemosynam facientibus, nisi mundis corde, nisi castigantibus corpus suum et in servitutem redigentibus, nisi deum et proximum diligentibus, nisi in bona opera se extendentibus, nisi intentibus ut per bona opera se probatos exhibeant, non solum deo sed etiam omnibus hominibus, nisi exuentibus veterem hominem cum operibus suis, et induentibus novum hominem qui secundum deum creatur, nisi animo suo expellentibus dilectionem peccati, et admittentibus dilectionem dei et proximi, nisi carnem suam crucifigentibus cum affectibus et concupiscentiis,*' CGC II, 226r.
[48] Cox II, pp 138-141.

grateful human love:

> But, if the profession of our faith of the remission of our own sins enter within us into the deepness of our hearts, then it must needs kindle a warm fire of love in our hearts towards God, and towards all other for the love of God, – a fervent mind to seek and procure God's honour, will, and pleasure in all things, – a good will and mind to help every man and to do good unto them, so far as our might, wisdom, learning, counsel, health, strength, and all other gifts which we have received of God, will extend, – and, *in summa*, a firm intent and purpose to do all that is good, and leave all that is evil.[49]

Only the certainty of being eternally knit to God by his love could empower human beings to love him and one another in return: 'For the right and true Christian faith is ... to have sure trust and confidence in God's merciful promises to be saved from everlasting damnation by Christ: whereof doth follow a loving heart to obey his commandments.'[50] When the benefits of God's merciful grace were considered, unless they were 'desperate persons' with 'hearts harder than stones,' people would be moved to give themselves wholly unto God and the service of their neighbours.[51] Naturally, Cranmer intended this Christian love to be extended to foes as well as friends, for 'they be his creation and image, and redeemed by Christ as ye are.'[52] Thus, assurance made possible the blessed inner change in the justified – a loving, living faith that purified the heart from sin's poison and made 'the sinner clean a new man.'[53] This gospel of transforming gratitude was what Cranmer tried to spread with his evangelism of 'overmuch leniency.'

6. Cranmer on Communion

So at last we have come to the heart of Cranmer's theology. God's gracious love inspires a grateful love in his children, turning their wills

---

[49] *Ibid.*, p 86.
[50] *Ibid.*, p 133.
[51] *Ibid.*, p 134.
[52] *Ibid.*, p 149.
[53] *Ibid.*, p 86.

from wrong to right and binding them to their Heavenly Father as well as to one another forever. Now if loving gratitude is the means for true communion with God, there can be only one instrument which inspires it – God's Word. For only in the Bible do we learn of our need and God's promises. And if true communion with God is a joining of our wills to his, there can be only one instrument which informs it – God's Word. For only in the Bible do we learn what to seek and how far we fall short. According to Cranmer, the key to godly communion is to 'read, mark, learn and inwardly digest'[54] God's Word.

> This Word whosoever is diligent to read and in his heart to print that he readeth, the great affection to the transitory things of this world shall be diminished in him, and the great desire of heavenly things that be therein promised of God shall increase in him. And there is nothing that so much establisheth our faith and trust in God, that so much converteth innocence and pureness of the heart, and also of outward godly life and conversation, as continual reading and meditation of God's Word. For that thing which by perpetual use of reading of Holy Scripture and diligent searching of the same is deeply printed and graven in the heart at length turneth almost into nature. And moreover, the effect and virtue of God's Word is to illuminate the ignorant and to give more light unto them that faithfully and diligently read it, to comfort their hearts, and to encourage them to perform that which of God is commanded.[55]

We have now come full-circle. Conversion to God is birthed by his working through Scripture to tell us and turn us to himself. Communion with God is sustained and strengthened by his working through the same Scripture, continually telling and turning, that he might tether us to ever-increasing conformity to Christ. Little wonder, then, Cranmer urged that 'these books, therefore, ought to be much in our hands, in our eyes, in our ears, in our mouths, but most of all in our heart.'[56]

Such, of course, ironically, was the goal for his prayer books,

---

[54] Joseph Ketley, ed., *The Two Liturgies ... in the Reign of King Edward VI* (Cambridge: Cambridge University Press, 1844), p 439.
[55] Bond, *Homilies*, p 63.
[56] *Ibid.*, p 62.

especially the sacraments. Undoubtedly, Scripture was 'the heavenly meat of our souls,'[57] but Baptism and Holy Communion were its sensible enactment. The use of water, bread and wine, when joined to God's Word, enabled believers to 'see Christ with our eyes, smell him at our nose, taste him with our mouths, grope him with our hands, and perceive him with all our senses.'[58] Sacraments did indeed confer grace, but not as a separate, second, parallel channel in addition to Scripture. They were means of grace precisely because their use of elements made the promises of Scripture sink more easily into the depths of human hearts, since people's senses were more fully engaged by the presentation.

Thus, the ultimate expression of Cranmer's vision of God's gracious love inspiring grateful human love was the 1552 Holy Communion service. In what he intended to be the central act of English worship, Cranmer wove together his great themes of free justification, on-going repentance, communal fellowship, and godly living and placed them in a sacramental setting which clarified God's incomprehensible sacrificial love for the unworthy as their sole source. Cranmer dropped the explicit invocation of the Holy Spirit over the elements and made their reception the immediate response to the words of Institution. As a result, receiving the sacramental bread and wine, not their prior consecration, became the liturgy's climax. Now the sacramental miracle was not changing material elements but reuniting human wills with the divine. And since he repositioned the prayer of oblation as a post-communion prayer, the community's sacrifice of praise and thanksgiving was their newly-empowered *response* to God's grace at work in them, not its grounds as previously. Now grateful service was the necessary effect of that gracious reunion and godly love the natural response to remembering God's love.[59] Lastly, he inserted the recital of the Ten Commandments near the beginning of the service and moved the preparation for communion prior to the Great Thanksgiving. Now the new order took participants through the steps which Cranmer believed led to conversion of the will and new life in

---

[57] *Ibid.*
[58] John Edmund Cox, ed., *Writings and Disputations of Thomas Cranmer ... relative to the Sacrament of the Lord's Supper* (Cambridge: Cambridge University Press, 1844) [Henceforth Cox I], p 41.
[59] For these and similar changes, see Colin Buchanan, *What did Cranmer think he was doing?*, 2nd edn. (Bramcote: Grove Books, 1982), pp 21-29.

Christ: Fear inspired by the Law, Faith springing forth from the Gospel, God's gift of Repentance, Re-entry into God's presence, and the Reception of power for a renewed holiness. In short, just as in his doctrine of justification, the supernatural action in Cranmer's Communion service was the renewal of the communicants' will to love Christ and one another, and all because they had first been loved by him.[60]

7. Concluding Thoughts on Thomas Cranmer

In the end, repentance, not love, has come to symbolise Cranmer himself, his life's work being interpreted by his last days. In the eyes of his critics, Cranmer's recantations prove that at best he was weak and vacillating. In the hearts of his admirers, however, Cranmer's last-minute renunciation of his recantations proved his true commitment to the Protestant faith. But what of Cranmer himself, how did he interpret his last days and the meaning they gave to his life? According to a contemporary account, having previously been distraught, Cranmer came to the stake with 'a cheerful countenance and willing mind.'

> Fire being now put to him, he stretched out his right Hand, and thrust it into the Flame, and held it there a good space, before the Fire came to any other Part of his Body; where his Hand was seen of every Man sensibly burning, crying with a loud Voice, *This Hand hath offended.* As soon as the Fire got up, he was very soon Dead, never stirring or crying all the while.[61]

His Catholic executioners surely thought Cranmer was making satisfaction to his Protestant God. Yet his doctrine of salvation would have taught him otherwise, for the God he served saved the unworthy. Having believed in his own justification by faith, Cranmer would have

---

[60] '[I]n the Lord's supper neither the substance nor accidences of bread and wine be changed ... but the alteration is inwardly in the souls of them that spiritually be refreshed and nourished with Christ's flesh and blood,' Cox I, p 254.

[61] From the description of Cranmer's death by 'J. A.,' BL Harley MS 422, fols 48-52; reprinted in John Strype, *Memorials of ... Thomas Cranmer, sometime Lord Archbishop of Canterbury,* 2 vols in 1 (London: Richard Chiswell, 1694), Book 3, chap. 21, i. p 389.

thought he could fall totally, but not finally. As God's child, the burden of all the multitude of his sins was no cause for him to distrust or despair of help at his Father's hand. For the incredible richness of God's merciful love for him would never have shone brighter than on that cloudy day, precisely because he, the chief promoter of the new faith, had fallen so far as to become a declared enemy of the gospel. To Cranmer, his hand in the fire would have been an act of loving service from a grateful heart turned back to God by the power and promise of his immeasurably loving grace. His final resolve would have been a joyous confirmation that he was indeed one of the elect in whom there would be no fault found in the end. His firmness of purpose would have been sustained by the hope he expressed in the Burial Office that was never read for him: 'the souls of them that be elected, after they be delivered from the burden of the flesh, be in joy and felicity.'[62]

What, then, can be said of Cranmer's reformed theology? Ultimately, Cranmer conceived of God's work in the world as changing human wills, not human worthiness, and he believed God did so by loving the unworthy elect so unconditionally as to inspire in them a reciprocal love for him and others. Such was his gospel. Such was the blessed change he bequeathed to the Puritans. Such is his legacy for Anglicans today, if they so wish.

---

[62] Ketley, *Two Liturgies*, p 319.

Index

Adiaphora, 57, 59

Adoption, 125, 133

Anglican, 3-5, 24-27, 29, 40, 49, 75, 96, 141, 142, 150, 162, 167, 186, 188, 189, 206, 214, 218, 220, 228, 247

Antinomianism, 12, 28, 101, 105-107

Anxiety, 69, 149

Application, 6, 9, 22, 49, 56, 57, 60, 121, 211

Arminianism, 102, 103, 105-107, 109, 116, 121

Assurance, 26, 95, 106, 109, 115, **120-122**, 136, 143, 152, 155, 159, 162, 163, 164, 225, 232, 234, 247, 253, 258, 259

Atonement, 99, 102, 106, 112, 114, 117, 120

Authorities, 15, 21, 34, 53, 56, 57, 101, 128

Baptism, 54, 58, 220

Baxter, Richard, 1, 3, **22-43**, 47-50, 80, 96, 142, 143, 146, 189, 194, 201, 202, 205, 207, 214, 218

Beza, Theodore, 54, 55, 58, 60, 143, 150, 155, 163, 165

Bunyan, John, 3, 22, 56, 146, 154, **171-183, 217-241**

Calvin, John, 16, 25, 52, 54, 55, 58, 60, 83-85, 88, 91, 100, 143, 150, 153, 155, 162, 163, 172, 173, 189, 204, 207, 208, 210, 214

Calvinism, 18, 50, 62, 105, 106, 162, 165

Cartwright, Thomas, 19, 54, 151, 190, 203

Catechism, 13, 31, 36, 37, 47, 48, 62, 151

Catholicism, 28, 39, 172, 245, 278

Chaderton, Laurence, 61, 144, 197, 198

Communion, 3, 29, 39, 47-49, 54, 58, 82, 87-89, 163, 203, 217, 231, **236**, 243, 247, 256, **259-261**

Comprehension, 29, 30, 99

Conform, 34, 50, 54, 88

Conscience, 6, 31, 39, 42, 54, 100, 115, 121, 136, 143, 150, 152, 154, 157-160, 162-164, 166, 180, 245

Conversion, 3, 15, 22, 32, 36-38, 42, 56, 66, 69, 76, 77, 80, 146, 150, 152, 153, 155, 156, 162, 202, 217, 225, **231-234**, 243, 247, 251, **254-257**, 260, 261

Cranmer, Thomas, 3, 50-2, 58, **243-263**

Creed, 29, 31, 151

Cross of Christ, 3, 12, 22, 36, 54, 57, 76, 79, 86, **95-123**, 134, 135, 138, 140, 178, 180, 182, 183, 232, 233, 238, 250

Crowley, Robert, 14, 15, 246

Culture, 65, 76, 97, 123, 178, 193

Index

Death, 28, 33, 37, 38, 40, 47, 88, 89, 98, 130, 143, 145, **148, 149, 152, 154, 157, 159-161**, 178, 182, 191, 201, 210, 220, 221, 233, **238-241**, 247, 262

Death of Christ, 66, 76, 88, 89, 98, 105, 107, **109-123**, 129, 133, 178, 182, 232, 249, 250

Demonic, 127-129, 132, 139, 140

Denominationalism, 39

Depression, 149, 155

Discipline, 20, 34, 36, 38, 71, 78, 86, 143, 146, 153-155, 198, 202, 222, 224, 234

Dod, John, 146, 201

Doubt, 1, 7, 33, 36, 70, 130, 131, 135, 143, 162, 226, 239, 245

Duty, 2, 79, 81, 133, 143, 154, 155, 193, 194, 201, 257

Edwards, Jonathan, 65, 146

Ejection, 32, 175

Election, 110, 111, 159, 162, 163, 183, 250, 254, 256, 258

Eternal life, 9, 89, 105, 155

Eternity, 17, 41, 108, 110, 150, 161, 238, 254

Evangelical, 2-4, 24, **63-93**, 94, 142, 169, 176, 182, 183, 207, 215, 218

Evangelism, 26, 27, 35, 37, 48, 65-67, 69, 77, 88, 108, 110, 113, 115, 139, 143, 144, 146, 151, 165, **205**, 243, **247**, 259

Faith, 3, 5, 6, 21, 26, 27, 36, 37, 39, 47, 52, 56, 61, 63-65, **67-73**, 77, 80-89, 101, 105-119, **120-122, 125**, 126, **127-140**, 143, 150-155, 157, 158, **163, 164**, 195, ˜196, 202, 208, 212, 219-221, 223-225, 232, 233, 237, 239, 240, 247, 249, **251-262**

family, 35, 37, 55, 56, 155, 158, 162, 172, 195, 199, 201, 221, 223, 238, 247

Future, 67, 70, 71, 80, 82, 87, 93, 109, 123, 149, 183, 185, **205**, 209, 213, 221, 255, 257, 258

Geneva Bible, 7, 62, 129, 130, 131, 132, 193

Gifford, George, 129, 132, 133, 135, 136, 220, 221, 225

Glory, 5, 30, 34, 47, 49, 62, 99, 109, 112, 115, 120, 122, 140, 143, 161, 200, 203, 213, 233, 234, 235, 241, 250, 257

Godliness, 1, 35, 53, 54, 56, 61, 146, 154-156, 160, 185, 194, 195, **201**, 202, 211, 212, 214, 222, 238

Gospel, 4, 5, 17, 25, 30, 36, 54, 60, 61, 65-67, 69, 83, 88, 98, 105, 110, 115, 116, 120-123, 132, 135, 139, 144, 147, 150, 151, 154, 166, 167, 179, 180, 185, 192. 194, 199, 201, **202**, 204, **205**, 207, 209-215, 229, 232, 249, 251, 255, 259, 261, 263

Government, 11, 17, 53, 54, 56, 59, 61, 100, 131, 177, 188, 189, 190, 191, 200, 202

Grace, 1, 6, 7, 26, 28, 30, 38, 88, 89, 101, 106, 109, 111, 117, 120, 121, 136, 143, 148, 152, 156, 157, 158, 160, 161, 163, 164, 173, 181, 203, 209, 221, 227, 229, 233, 249, 250, 254-258, 259, 261, 263

Grindal, Edmund, 5, 6, 10, 16, 56, 188-191, 197, 200, 214, 245

Heaven, 9, 27, 31, 37, 41, 101, 116, 121, 131-133, 136, 149, 151, 154, 172, 173, 175, 183, 209, 226, 232, 249

Hell, 36, 37, 149-151, 226

Holiness, 10, 15, 26, 48, 49, 55, 56, 87, 95, **116-120**, 122, 143, 174, 219, 249, 262

Holland, Henry, 134, 135, 137, 155

Holy Spirit, 6, 26, 31, 49, 57, 61, 110, 117, 118, 119, 150, 152, 156, 163, 222, 255, 257, 261

Homilies, 13, 19, 150, 251, 252, 255, 256, 260

Honesty, 41, 160

Hooker, Richard, 53, 57, 59, 146, 189, 214

Horton, Thomas, 8, 9, 10, 85

Humility, 7, 10, 41, 160

Independent, 29, 132, 191, 192, 202, 208, 219

Judgment, 29, 31, 33, 37, 110, **111-115**, 143, 164, 166, 180, 210

Justice, 32, 33, 40, 112-114, 155, 180, 253

Justification, 47, 107, 110, 125, 133, 174, 176, 232, 233, 243, 249, **252-257**, 261, 262

Latimer, Hugh, 11, 52, 61, 196

Latimer Trust, 1, 2, 9, 18, 24, 142, 218

Law, 13, 26, 39, 54, 59, 103, 106, 107, 113, 114, 121, 147, 159, 166, 201, 225, 261

Lay, 13, 60, 72, 152, 185, 190, **197-201**, 204, 206, 209, 212, 222, 226, 228, 231, 233, 249

Lecturer, 13, 16, **18-21**, 27, 50, 54, 144, 205

Love, for humans, 29, 37, 40, 41, 43, 158, 202, 248-250, 257-259, 261-263

Love, of or for God, 26, 31, 33, 37, 56, 60, 90, 98, 110, 112, 113, 115, 121, 133, 143, 159, 161, 165, 210, 225, 232, 240, 248-250, 254, 257-259, 261-263

Love, of preaching, 3, 5, 7, 22, 48, 73, 88, 231

Luther, Martin, 11, 47, 52, 54, 58, 60, 73, 88, 89, 100, 225, 277

Marriage, 40, 57, 92, 201

Meditation, 31, 70, 72, 90, 91, 143, 161, 260

Meetings, 1, 35, 55, 56, 103, 195, 197, 198

Mere Christianity, 26, 29

Ministry, 4-6, 9, 13, 16, 17, 19, 21, **23-25**, 27, 30, **35-41**, 55, 64, 66, 70, 96, 99, 102-104, 106, 111, 123, **141**, 142, 144, **146-148**, **150**, **155**, 159, 162, 170, 185-187, 194, 195, **197-201**, 203-207, 209-213, **218-221**, 223, 225, 227, **237**

Miracles, 129, 131, 132, 135

Moralism, 117, 139, 208

Mortification, 119, 133, 153, 173, 178, 181

Non-conformist, 28, 29, 50, 58, 100, 102, 146, 171, 224, 246

Obedience, 36, 37, 59, 90, 91, 94, 111, 116, 117, 122, 153, 155, 157, 187, 191, 192, 232, 257

Index

Order (in Church or State), 8, 10, 19, 21, 35, 48, 52, 53, 58, 146, 150, 162

Owen, John, 3, 6, 7, 8, 10, 12, 15, 16, 17, 21, 47, 62, 72, 93, **95-123**, 146, 171, 173, 181, 224, 246

Perkins, Williams, 3, 6, 10, 22, 55, 58, 129, 133, 134, 136, 137, 138, **141-167**, 194, 196, 197, 215

Piety, 7, 38, 73, 143, 144, 152, 156, 172, 176, 178, 182, 183, 200, 205, 222, 249

Pilgrim, 1-3, 22, 27, 49, **169-183**, 189, **217-241**

Politics, 12, 28, 71, 147, 191, 201, 246, 277

Power, 17, 26, 40, 65, 70, 72, 75, 83, 85, 97, 98, 104, 106, 109, 112, 118-120, 125, **128-136**, 138, 139, 144, 150, 160, 187, 190-192, 200, 202, 206, 211, 224, 233, 247, 251, 254, 255, 262, 263

Prayer, 13, 14, 25, 27, 29, 31-34, 53, 55, 57, 70, 71, 80, 82, 91, 128, 129, 133, 143, 146, 148, 151, 157, 159, 160, 162, 166, 185, 189, 193, 198, 200, **204**, 213, 225, 245, 246, 260, 261

Preaching, **3**, **5-11**, 13, 14, 17-22, 26, 28, 33, 35, 38, 39, 42, 48, 50, 54, 66, 98, 101, 103, 104, 108-111, 122, 123, 144, 146, 148-150, 152, 171, 179, 181, 185, 187, **195-199**, 203-206, 211, 212, 223, 225, 227, 234, 241, 245

Precise, 7, 59, 78, 100, 138, 143

Predestination, 60, 101, 105, 149, 162, 165, 243, 253, 254, 255, 256

Presbyterian, 15, 18, 19, 29, 40, 49, 54, 146, 190-192, 202, 203, 208

Providence, 122, 131, 143, 147, 159, 160, 221, 223

Public worship, 53, 58

Redemption, 24, 36, 76, 89, 109, 112, 139, 142, 218

Reform, 15, 54, 56, 180, **187-213**

Regeneration, 26, 36, 107, 118, 121, 143, 153, 155, 164, 256

Regulative principle, 210

Renewal, 3, 45, 62, 117, 127, 143, 257, 262

Repentance, 6, 26, 36, 107, 108, 143, 150, 153, 154, 155, 157, 166, 174, 181, 194, 244, 247, 256, 257, 258, 261, 262

Sacraments, 19, 20, 28, 63, **87**, 88, 94, 151, 157, 203, 261

St Antholin's, 1-3, **10-19**, 22, 23, 49, 80, 183, 246, 247

Sanctification, 26, 30, 116, 117, 121, 136, 174, 220

Satan, 3, 37, 56, 115, 121, **125-140**, 227, 234, 276

Scripture, 5, 12, 19, 31, 37, 39, 49, 51, 53, 54, 57-60, 66, 73, 75-77, 79, 82, 83, 88, 90, 101, 110, 125, 129, 130, 133-135, **137-138**, 164, 178, 179, 189, 196, 205, 214, 243, **249-253**, 260, 261

Self-knowledge, 26, 221, 223

Separation, 61, 84, 162, 166, 191, 203, 219, 220

Servants, 1, 2, 22, 27, 49, 228

267

Sin, 31, 36-38, 104, 110-115, 117, 119, 121, 122, 147, 150, 151, 157-160, 166, 181, 182, 203, 225, 232, 233, 236, 247, 256-259

Sovereignty, 95, **108**, 129, 133, 143, 165

Sovereignty, 95, 108

Spiritual warfare, 22, 224, 236

Spirituality, 3, **63-94**, 99-101, 107, 123, 138, 139, 144, 156, 172, 173, 176, 178, 183, 186

Suffering, 133, 178, 185, 204, 213, 224, 226, 228

Surplice, 52, 53, 57, 190, 246

Teaching, 8, 13, 16, 17, 26, 27, 56, 57, 60, 61, 98, 101, 110, 111, 126, 129, 131, 136, 146, 150, 154, 163, 164, 175, 178, 179, 182, 193, 199, 208, 212, 213, 221, 229, 246, 249, 252, 255, 258

Temptation, 32, 104, 119, 130, 133, 134, 137, 138, 160

Training, 4, 8, 16, 56, 63, 87, 170, 185, 195, 197, 199, 205, 206, 212

Trent, 174

Trial, 10, 11, 33, 34, 166, 195

Truth, 6, 31, 43, 50, 57, 92, 97, 98, 101, 113, 123, 125, 130, 134, 146, 154, 163, 175, 179, 188, 194, 195, 202, 204, 207, 210-212, 214, 215, 219, 224, 231, 232, 235, 237, 239, 249, 251

Unity, 28, 29, 30, 37, 58, 112, 202

Victory, 131, 132, 133, 135, 138, 140, 192, 239, 240

Virtues, 155, 181

Walker, George, 16, 19, 127, 128, 129, 139

Warriors, 1, 2, 22, 27, 49, 235

Word, 3, 5-8, 10, 12, 13, 17-21, 25-27, 35, 38, 48, 49, 52, 55-58, 61, 72, 75, 84, 85, 99, 101, 110, 130, 131, 134, 136, 137, 145, 147, 148, 151, 152, 157, 158, 159, 160, 173, 177, 179, 185, 187-189, 193-198, 202-215, 219, 220, 222, 225, 227, 229, 233, 234, 236, 240, 245, 249-253, 260, 261

Writing, 19, 28, 39, 40, 68, 98, 101, 104, 117, 147, 151, 204, 223, 225, 229, 239

St. Antholin's Lectureship Charity Lectures

1991	J.I.Packer, *A Man for All Ministries: Richard Baxter 1651-1691.*
1992	Geoffrey Cox, *The Recovery and Renewal of the Local Church – the Puritan Vision.*
1993	Alister E. McGrath, *Evangelical Spirituality – Past Glories – Present Hopes – Future Possibilities.*
1994	Gavin J. McGrath, *"But We Preach Christ Crucified": The Cross of Christ in the Pastoral Theology of John Owen.*
1995	Peter Jensen, *Using the Shield of Faith – Puritan Attitudes to Combat with Satan.*
1996	J.I.Packer, *An Anglican to Remember – William Perkins: Puritan Popularizer.*
1997	Bruce Winter, *Pilgrim's Progress and Contemporary Evangelical Piety.*
1998	Peter Adam *A Church 'Halfly Reformed' – the Puritan Dilemma.*
1999	J.I.Packer, *The Pilgrim's Principles: John Bunyan Revisited.*
2000	Ashley Null, *Conversion to Communion: Thomas Cranmer on a Favourite Puritan Theme.*
2001	Peter Adam, *Word and Spirit: The Puritan-Quaker Debate.*
2002	Wallace Benn, *Usher on Bishops: A Reforming Ecclesiology.*
2003	Peter Ackroyd, *Strangers to Correction: Christian Discipline and the English Reformation.*
2004	David Field, *"Decalogue" Dod and his Seventeenth Century Bestseller: A Four Hundredth Anniversary Appreciation.*
2005	Chad B. Van Dixhoorn, *A Puritan Theology of Preaching.*
2006	Peter Adam, *"To Bring Men to Heaven by Preaching" – John Donne's Evangelistic Sermons.*
2007	Tony Baker, *1807 – 2007: John Newton and the Twenty-first Century.*
2008	Lee Gatiss, *From Life's First Cry: John Owen on Infant Baptism and Infant Salvation.*
2009	Andrew Atherstone, *Evangelical Mission and Anglican Church Order: Charles Simeon Reconsidered.*
2010	David Holloway, *Re-establishing the Christian Faith – and the Public Theology Deficit.*

LS 01	The Evangelical Anglican Identity Problem – Jim Packer	LS 17	Christianity and Judaism: New Understanding, New Relationship – James Atkinson
LS 02	The ASB Rite A Communion: A Way Forward – Roger Beckwith	LS 18	Sacraments and Ministry in Ecumenical Perspective – Gerald Bray
LS 03	The Doctrine of Justification in the Church of England – Robin Leaver	LS 19	The Functions of a National Church – Max Warren
LS 04	Justification Today: The Roman Catholic and Anglican Debate – R. G. England	LS 20/21	The Thirty-Nine Articles: Their Place and Use Today – Jim Packer, Roger Beckwith
LS 05/06	Homosexuals in the Christian Fellowship – David Atkinson	LS 22	How We Got Our Prayer Book – T. W. Drury, Roger Beckwith
LS 07	Nationhood: A Christian Perspective – O. R. Johnston	LS 23/24	Creation or Evolution: a False Antithesis? – Mike Poole, Gordon Wenham
LS 08	Evangelical Anglican Identity: Problems and Prospects – Tom Wright	LS 25	Christianity and the Craft – Gerard Moate
LS 09	Confessing the Faith in the Church of England Today – Roger Beckwith	LS 26	ARCIC II and Justification – Alister McGrath
LS 10	A Kind of Noah's Ark? The Anglican Commitment to Comprehensiveness – Jim Packer	LS 27	The Challenge of the Housechurches – Tony Higton, Gilbert Kirby
		LS 28	Communion for Children? The Current Debate – A. A. Langdon
LS 11	Sickness and Healing in the Church – Donald Allister	LS 29/30	Theological Politics – Nigel Biggar
LS 12	Rome and Reformation Today: How Luther Speaks to the New Situation – James Atkinson	LS 31	Eucharistic Consecration in the First Four Centuries and its Implications for Liturgical Reform – Nigel Scotland
LS 13	Music as Preaching: Bach, Passions and Music in Worship – Robin Leaver	LS 32	A Christian Theological Language – Gerald Bray
LS 14	Jesus Through Other Eyes: Christology in a Multi-faith Context – Christopher Lamb	LS 33	Mission in Unity: The Bible and Missionary Structures – Duncan McMann
LS 15	Church and State Under God – James Atkinson	LS 34	Stewards of Creation: Environmentalism in the Light of Biblical Teaching – Lawrence Osborn
LS 16	Language and Liturgy – Gerald Bray, Steve Wilcockson, Robin Leaver	LS 35/36	Mission and Evangelism in Recent Thinking: 1974–1986 – Robert Bashford

Latimer Publications

LS 37 — Future Patterns of Episcopacy: Reflections in Retirement – Stuart Blanch

LS 38 — Christian Character: Jeremy Taylor and Christian Ethics Today – David Scott

LS 39 — Islam: Towards a Christian Assessment – Hugh Goddard

LS 40 — Liberal Catholicism: Charles Gore and the Question of Authority – G. F. Grimes

LS 41/42 — The Christian Message in a Multi-faith Society – Colin Chapman

LS 43 — The Way of Holiness 1: Principles – D. A. Ousley

LS 44/45 — The Lambeth Articles – V. C. Miller

LS 46 — The Way of Holiness 2: Issues – D. A. Ousley

LS 47 — Building Multi-Racial Churches – John Root

LS 48 — Episcopal Oversight: A Case for Reform – David Holloway

LS 49 — Euthanasia: A Christian Evaluation – Henk Jochemsen

LS 50/51 — The Rough Places Plain: AEA 1995

LS 52 — A Critique of Spirituality – John Pearce

LS 53/54 — The Toronto Blessing – Martyn Percy

LS 55 — The Theology of Rowan Williams – Garry Williams

LS 56/57 — Reforming Forwards? The Process of Reception and the Consecration of Women as Bishops – Peter Toon

LS 58 — The Oath of Canonical Obedience – Gerald Bray

LS 59 — The Parish System: The Same Yesterday, Today And For Ever? – Mark Burkill

LS 60 — 'I Absolve You': Private Confession and the Church of England – Andrew Atherstone

LS 61 — The Water and the Wine: A Contribution to the Debate on Children and Holy Communion – Roger Beckwith, Andrew Daunton-Fear

LS 62 — Must God Punish Sin? – Ben Cooper

LS 63 — Too Big For Words?: The Transcendence of God and Finite Human Speech – Mark D. Thompson

LS 64 — A Step Too Far: An Evangelical Critique of Christian Mysticism – Marian Raikes

LS 65 — The New Testament and Slavery: Approaches and Implications – Mark Meynell

LS 66 — The Tragedy of 1662: The Ejection and Persecution of the Puritans – Lee Gatiss

LS 67 — Heresy, Schism & Apostasy – Gerald Bray

LS 68 — Paul in 3D: Preaching Paul as Pastor, Story-teller and Sage – Ben Cooper

LS69 — Christianity and the Tolerance of Liberalism: J. Gresham Machen and the Presbyterian Controversy of 1922 – 1937 – Lee Gatiss

LS70 — An Anglican Evangelical Identity Crisis: The Churchman – Anvil Affair of 1981–1984 – Andrew Atherstone

LS71 — Empty and Evil: The worship of other faiths in 1 Corinthians 8-10 and today – Rohintan Mody

LS72 — To Plough or to Preach: Mission Strategies in New Zealand during the 1820s – Malcolm Falloon

LS73	Plastic People: How Queer Theory is Changing Us – Peter Sanlon	GGC	God, Gays and the Church: Human Sexuality and Experience in Christian Thinking – eds. Lisa Nolland, Chris Sugden, Sarah Finch
LB01	The Church of England: What it is, and what it stands for – R. T. Beckwith		
LB02	Praying with Understanding: Explanations of Words and Passages in the Book of Common Prayer – R. T. Beckwith	WTL	The Way, the Truth and the Life: Theological Resources for a Pilgrimage to a Global Anglican Future – eds. Vinay Samuel, Chris Sugden, Sarah Finch
LB03	The Failure of the Church of England? The Church, the Nation and the Anglican Communion – A. Pollard	AEID	Anglican Evangelical Identity – Yesterday and Today – J.I.Packer and N.T.Wright
		IB	The Anglican Evangelical Doctrine of Infant Baptism – John Stott and J.Alec Motyer
LB04	Towards a Heritage Renewed – H.R.M. Craig		
LB05	Christ's Gospel to the Nations: The Heart & Mind of Evangelicalism Past, Present & Future – Peter Jensen	BF	Being Faithful: The Shape of Historic Anglicanism Today – Theological Resource Group of GAFCON
LB06	Passion for the Gospel: Hugh Latimer (1485–1555) Then and Now. A commemorative lecture to mark the 450ᵗʰ anniversary of his martyrdom in Oxford – A. McGrath	FWC	The Faith we confess: An exposition of the 39 Articles – Gerald Bray
		TPG	The True Profession of the Gospel: Augustus Toplady and Reclaiming our Reformed foundations – Lee Gatiss
LB07	Truth and Unity in Christian Fellowship – Michael Nazir-Ali	SG	Shadow Gospel: Rowan Williams and the Anglican Communion Crisis – Charles Raven
LB08	Unworthy Ministers: Donatism and Discipline Today – Mark Burkill		

Lightning Source UK Ltd.
Milton Keynes UK
UKHW01f0634111018
330371UK00001B/298/P